Golf University

Become a Better Putter, Driver, and More—the Smart Way

Scott Weems

Skyhorse Publishing

Skyhorse Publishing books may be purchased in bulk at special discounts for sales promotion, corporate gifts, fund-raising, or educational purposes. Special editions can also be created to specifications. For details, contact the Special Sales Department, Skyhorse Publishing, 307 West 36th Street, 11th Floor, New York, NY 10018 or info@skyhorsepublishing.com.

Skyhorse® and Skyhorse Publishing® are registered trademarks of Skyhorse Publishing, Inc.®, a Delaware corporation.

Visit our website at www.skyhorsepublishing.com.

10 9 8 7 6 5 4 3 2 1

Library of Congress Cataloging-in-Publication Data is available on file.

Cover design by Qualcom Designs
Cover photo credit iStock

ISBN: 978-1-51074-305-2
Ebook ISBN: 978-1-51074-306-9

Printed in the United States of America

Contents

Freshman Orientation

Some people say that a book can't teach you how to play golf. I agree and would add that books can't teach you how to be a doctor either, because advanced skills take practice. Yet I would never trust a surgeon who hasn't opened an anatomy textbook, and I would certainly not step on a plane with a pilot who can't explain the concept of lift.

Learning a sport as complex as golf can be intimidating. One problem is that instruction books can make swinging clubs at little white balls sound like neurosurgery. Always keep your right elbow tucked. Keep knees aligned, ensure left wrist is flat at takeback, and never . . . *I mean never* . . . lift your head before entering your follow-through. The sheer number of instructions can be overwhelming, which is why sport can only be mastered through practice. But knowing why golf is so challenging, and also so rewarding, is as important to your swing as anatomy textbooks are to avoiding costly malpractice suits.

Golf is about more than intense practice. If that were all there was to the sport, you wouldn't play. Golf also involves psychology and the thrill of competition. It's played outdoors, so there's also the joy of different weather conditions and course designs. And since it takes both strength and coordination, you're not breaking par without at least some understanding of what your body can do and how a small twist of the wrist can determine the future path of a tiny white ball.

Still, this is just a start. If the game depended only on a mix of psychology and physics, you'd stick with billiards instead.

Golf is also about self-discipline. Easy tasks are seldom rewarding, and golf is the perfect example—I still have the scorecard from my first game, and it wasn't pretty. Twice, I took ten swings to reach the hole . . . and one was a par three! I lost five balls over nine holes, and though in my defense it was a rural, hilly course with lots of leaves on the fairways, my problem wasn't the fairways. I doubt I saw a fairway all day. And this isn't unusual for a beginner.

Golf is difficult, but that's why we love it. It's also old, and that age has given it a rich history and tradition. When Bobby Jones beat Walter Hagen in golf's "Match of the Century," our country still had no Empire State Building. When players teed off at America's first golf club, not far from Savannah, Georgia, George Washington was still our president. And by the time Christopher Columbus discovered the New World, two continental kings had already declared golf illegal, worried that it was distracting soldiers from archery practice.

In short, golf is hard . . . and it's old . . . and it can't be mastered from a book alone. But you can still learn a lot more about how we play.

That's what this book is for. It's for those who love the sport and want to learn more. For those who recognize it for what it really is—a learning process.

And not just about a 1.2-second swing.

I love golf, and I have ever since I first swung a club. My relationship with the sport started at the University of Maryland, which has a course located just off the main campus. As a faculty member, I was able to play and take lessons there relatively cheaply, and it was a great way to learn. I visited the driving range whenever I could, and I spent many hours watching both students and professors struggle with their swings. It was empowering and frustrating at the same time, because I quickly saw that golf doesn't discriminate. Patience is rewarded, but rank and seniority are not. No matter your age, or athletic ability, or even your disposable income, it's easy to play badly. Playing well is also possible—it just takes practice.

I also discovered something else—no matter how hard you practice, there's always more to learn. Even the best players aren't perfect.

For some people, that could be discouraging, but for me, it's the sport's charm. Golf isn't about mastering a set of skills, because mastery is a fool's goal. Even golf's greats—Rory McIlroy, Tiger Woods, Dustin Johnson, to name just a few—still make mistakes. Often. They also practice every day and hire swing coaches because they know that the sport will never be "mastered." It's about the journey, not the destination.

The same applies for our education, which is why school and golf go so well together. Even when I was a graduate student, I knew that the education I was receiving was just a beginning. We go to school because we want to learn, and that doesn't stop when we graduate. We learn new things every day, and if we're lucky, we develop a curiosity that remains a central part of our future lives.

I'm fortunate that as a cognitive neuroscientist, and also an avid golfer, I have a lot to be curious about. This book is written for players and students like me who want to keep learning about the sport we all love.

Take Harvey Penick as an example. Hopefully, you have heard of him, because he's as inspirational a figure as you'll find. Granted, Jack Nicklaus won eighteen majors, and Ben Hogan practically invented the modern golf swing despite being nearly paralyzed in a car wreck, but Penick did something even more remarkable—he made millions of people love the game.

I feel particularly drawn to Penick because, like me, he wasn't an exceptional player. He was good, a lot better than I'll ever be, but he wasn't like Nicklaus or Hogan. He never won a tournament, and he spent almost no time on the professional tour. Instead, he was a world-class instructor, learning something new about golf every day and sharing that knowledge with whomever he could find. For over 60 years, he taught players of all ages and abilities, earning his team at the University of Texas 21 titles and his individual students wins in more than three hundred professional tournaments.

Three hundred! That's more than Jack Nicklaus, Tiger Woods, and Ben Hogan combined . . . with almost a hundred to spare. Not bad for a player who never even placed in a professional competition.

Clearly, you don't have to be as dedicated as Penick to enjoy the game, but we could all benefit from sharing his enthusiasm. Penick loved the sport, and not just playing it. He loved learning about it, talking about it, and exploring it from all angles. Hopefully, by the end of this book, you'll see why.

I believe that sport, like any advanced skill, takes study. In this book, we'll explore the parts of your game that don't ordinarily get your attention, like how golf is driven by physics (it doesn't just have to do with the arc of the swing). Have you ever wondered what's the benefit of a three-layer ball? Or why a lofted pitch shot sticks next to the pin on your home course but rolls off the green everywhere else?

Or why companies constantly advertise revolutions in shaft or clubface designs, even though golf equipment looks basically the same year after year? Some of those designs help your game, but most just take money from your bank account.

You'll also see how economics influences both club management and course design, and how environmental factors make a smart play one day a tragic one the next. You'll even see how the human body has limits for how far it can send a 1.68-inch-diameter ball, depending on fitness, age, and playing style.

In short, you'll learn that the sport is as complex as any topic taught in college, with one key difference. Golf is fun. I enjoyed my psychology classes, and history, and even physics, but not nearly as much as I enjoy hitting little white balls with sticks. It can be an obsession.

Like school, *Golf University* is divided into semesters, starting with introductory classes and moving on to more complex topics. There's even reading lists, though you should feel free to skip any topics that don't interest you (just like real college). But I doubt you'll skip much, because I only included the most interesting topics, ones that will help you improve your enjoyment of the game. Though not a how-to book in the traditional sense, I still expect *Golf University* to make you a better player. Why? For the same reason doctors read anatomy books. Practice isn't everything.

Think of it as going back to school again, except now there are no tests, and you're only attending the classes you love.

And if you're like me, you love golf a lot.

Psychology 101:
The Angel of the Odd and
the Imp of the Perverse

Prerequisites: None

Sergio Garcia has always had a love/hate relationship with golfing crowds. When he won the Masters Tournament in 2017, having forced a playoff with Justin Rose despite falling behind two strokes on the final day, the love couldn't have been stronger. Fifteen years earlier, however, things weren't so positive.

The 2002 U.S. Open, played at Bethpage Black on Long Island, New York, included more than a little bad weather. Rain hampered much of the second day, filling the sky with dark clouds and raising scores for players with later tee times. Garcia, being one of those late starters, wasn't immune, shooting two over par for the day. Afterward, he complained that a delay should have been called and would have, had Tiger Woods been playing. Not generally a forgiving sort, the New York fans took notice. Many made crying sounds when he approached the tee the following morning, yelling "waaaah" and erupting in annoying baby noises. Others called him names. But that was just the start.

The worst part was still ahead. Specifically, somewhere in the middle of his third round, the comments started to get personal. That's when Garcia became struck by a case of the waggles.

Most players know of the waggles. These are the short "preswings" we take to release tension and work on our rhythm. The great Ben Hogan considered the waggle an essential part of the swing, a chance to establish a preshot routine. But for Sergio, that routine got out of hand. Before every shot he took one waggle . . . then two . . . then three or more. Often it took him close to a full minute at address before actually making contact with the ball.

As crowds complained, Garcia started falling apart. More crying noises followed, and more frustration from Garcia. Then one of the spectators remarked, quite loudly, that Garcia's girlfriend had more majors than he did. Which was true, since Martina Hingis, Garcia's then-girlfriend, had five Grand Slam wins under her belt—not counting doubles play. Garcia had none. For the underperforming Garcia, it wasn't easy to hear.

Then he learned the most valuable lesson of his career: never piss off a group of angry New Yorkers, especially using a one-finger salute. Under different circumstances, the gallery might have been more sympathetic, but not this day. The more Garcia waggled, and the more he regripped his club, the worse the ridicule grew. In just a short time, he fell from serious contender to fourth place, and he wouldn't win a tournament again for two years.

More than any other sport, golf is psychological. Not only do we need to manage distractions and emotions, we must control all the intrusive doubts in our heads. Conscious awareness and self-reflection may have helped our ancestors invent democracy and write self-help books, but they do little for directing tiny white balls into round cups.

Garcia learned this the hard way. You don't have to.

Golf is about a lot more than the swing itself. Equipment, playing conditions, and fairway design can all make a big difference on the course. Physical skill and fitness matter too, along with environmental factors like weather and crowds, but more important than all these things is mental outlook. Without a firm control of the mental game, physical performance is meaningless.

The most important thing to recognize about golf is that misses are inevitable. Take putting, one of the most variable aspects of the sport, as an example. Studies show that even professionals miss eight-foot putts half the time. Amateurs do about twice as badly. This means that unpredictability is part of the game, no matter what we do. How we deal with that randomness, and how we let it influence our play, is another matter.

Psychology shows that there are two ways our minds are tripped up by randomness, and to introduce them, I'd like to present a man who I'm pretty sure never even played the game. His name was Edgar Allen Poe, and his imagination gave form to two characters who personify these threats to our mental game. Let's start this psychology class by introducing these characters and explaining why they have such an impact on our lives.

The first creature is the Angel of the Odd, and it hates to be ignored. In Poe's story, this Angel introduces itself to a man and claims to be responsible for all that is strange in the world. When the man expresses skepticism, the Angel burns down his house, breaks his arm, then ruins a relationship with a potential lover. As if that weren't enough, the Angel then prompts the man to fall off a cliff and nearly drowns him in a river. Needless to say, it's not the kind of creature you want to mess with, though when the man does finally admit that the Angel is real, it leaves him alone to recover.

By comparison, the Imp of the Perverse is more subtle. In Poe's story, the Imp meets a man who has just gotten away with murder. There's no way the man can be implicated except if he confesses, yet the Imp needles him and fills him with self-doubt. Through constant pestering, the Imp causes him to do the only thing that could ruin him—admit to the crime. Due to a simple self-destructive impulse, the Imp sends the man to jail forever.

These two creatures have everything to do with our focus on the course, so let's take a look at something that psychologists call "paradoxical behavior" to understand why.

Imagine that the next time you're at the tee box and ready to swing, your partner gives a recommendation—avoid a nearby bunker. That's it. No bets, and no reason for the warning, just a simple recommendation to avoid this potential danger.

How would you respond? One possibility, of course, is that you'd take the advice and lay up far away from the hazard. But this would ignore the Imp of the Perverse, that little devil in our brain that hates to be ignored.

The problem is that brains are very bad at directing attention *away* from things. If you don't believe me, try this simple experiment—don't think of a three-legged elephant. Put any thoughts of elephants, handicapped or otherwise, out of your mind. Don't imagine its rolling belly or probing nose, and definitely don't think of oversize eyes peeking from under rolls of wrinkled, gray skin. If an image of a lopsided elephant accidentally pops into your head, push it out immediately.

If you're like most people, you can't do it, and even by the end of this sentence you've allowed one wayward pachyderm to crash through your consciousness. That's because our brains rely on two competing processes. The first is conscious intent, which we are fully aware of and can change whenever we want. The second is influenced by the Imp, an unconscious monitoring process that runs in the background of our minds.

In Poe's story, the Imp wreaks havoc by constantly reminding the murderer of his crime. This fills him with worry about being caught, and the harder he tries to avoid these intrusions, the stronger they grow. What does this have to do with golf? Nagging doubt is rife on the course too, which is why that earlier recommendation about avoiding the bunker was so dangerous. In fact, thanks to the Imp, there's no surer way of hitting a bunker than allowing yourself to think about that very danger.

Of course, our brains struggle with warnings like this because instructions don't run in the background of our minds. Computers may allow for commands to be held in temporary storage for later, but brains don't work that way. Instead, those instructions stay active in our heads whether we want them there or not. Poe knew about this and gave it a name—the Imp of the Perverse. Call it a three-legged elephant if you want; it won't go away.

The Imp shows up even in controlled laboratory settings, and we know because the psychologist David Wegner has seen it for himself. Let's imagine you've just volunteered for an experiment at his lab at the University of Virginia so we can see it, too.[1]

Dr. Wegner's task is quite simple, actually; your job is to putt a golf ball and have it stop on a glowing blue dot roughly seven feet away. Dr. Wegner hands you a club, then also asks you to keep a six-digit number in your head. That extra task is important, because it keeps your conscious mind from dwelling on anything else. He wants your performance to be unconscious and natural.

Let's say you attempt the shot and land the ball an inch short of the dot. You're happy, because it was a good shot. You'd have liked to be closer, but let's not get greedy.

Simple, huh? Not quite, because this was not the actual task in Wegner's experiment. He also gave some special instructions I didn't mention, and they weren't helpful. Before handing you the club and asking you to remember your special number, he says, "Land the ball on the glow spot, but be careful not to hit the ball past the glow spot. Don't overshoot the glow spot."

You're surprised by the instructions, wondering for a moment if there's a reason for the warning. But you do your best to push such questions from your mind as you step up to the ball.

Do you think you'd do better or worse with these special instructions? If you're like most subjects in the experiment, you overhit the putt, and not by a little bit. In fact, the average miss when Wegner ran the experiment was over twelve inches. If this surprises you, it shouldn't, because we've already introduced the Imp and shown what it can do. Nothing changed with the experiment following the instructions, except for one thing—with those extra words, the Imp was allowed to grab control of your unconscious monitoring, and all chances of leaving your putt short were gone.

The amazing thing is that the Imp doesn't just influence our golf game. Trying to improve our mood, sleep schedule, and even memory for past events can all have negative effects when we try to avoid the opposite behavior.[2]

Things can even get weird. Do you want to know the best way to start a budding romance? The trick is to make that romance secret or forbidden. Parents know this already—tell a son or daughter to avoid a romantic partner, and the opposite is sure to happen. But now scientists know this too, and the evidence comes from a series of experiments concerning the game "footsie." When people play "footsie" with a stranger under a table, then are told to keep it a secret, something unusual happens.[3] We tend to report our partners as more attractive, even when we're told to hold back any feelings. In fact, being told to contain those feelings is enough to make them thrive, and it doesn't matter that the flirting is only part of an awkward experiment. Simply being told to hold back any feelings is enough to make them real.

The effect can even be frightening. In my favorite scientific study of all time,[4] one scientist showed a bunch of homophobic men a series of gay porn videos and then attached equipment to their—*ahem*—putters.

It turned out that those with the most homophobic beliefs had the biggest "reactions" to the films. Talk about paradoxical response!

In short, the Imp has a sense of humor, and unconsciously trying to avoid any outcome can have a huge impact.

So what can you do about it? In general, it's best to avoid thinking about any unwanted outcome. When Sergio Garcia approached the 17th tee at the 2013 Players Championship at TPC Sawgrass, more than a decade after his earlier breakdown and again competing against Tiger Woods, all he needed was to land the ball on the green. The par three wasn't difficult except for a large water hazard between the tee box and the green. The biggest danger was to hit the ball soft. Unfortunately, Garcia's unconscious mind knew this too, and that's exactly what he did. An unfortunate quadruple-bogey later, and he ended up losing by six strokes—the same deficit he had suffered to Woods eleven years before.

As long as hazards are anywhere in our thoughts, we're screwed. So the solution is simple—don't think about them.

Starve the Imp of negative images, and you'll avoid its wrath.

The Angel of the Odd is a different beast from the Imp because it affects our intent, rather than our hidden unconscious. In Poe's story, the narrator openly questions the Angel's existence, claiming that he alone controls his destiny, not some strange being. As the man loses his clothes, his love, and then nearly his life, he finally accepts that his actual control is limited. Strange things sometimes happen, despite our struggles, and the more you try to stop them, the worse things get.

Golfers have a name for the Angel too, this impetus to overthink and overcontrol. They call it "the yips." Nearly every golfer has heard of the yips, though nobody knows what causes them. These are the mysterious, uncontrollable mental blocks that keep us from making a smooth swing. When Garcia became struck by the yips at the 2002 Open, the more pressure he experienced, the more he waggled and regripped his club. Thinking about it didn't help, and neither did pleas from the crowd to get on with his swing. Garcia was stuck in a vicious cycle, and it was the opposite of his unconscious mind leading him astray.

Yips affect between 25 percent and 50 percent of all players, including all ages and skill levels, adding an average 4.7 extra strokes per round. No biological cause has been found for their existence, and no treatment, either. They aren't limited to golfers, as billiard players, dart throwers, and even musicians routinely come under their power. It's as if, sometimes, golfers are simply possessed by the Angel of the Odd, a tendency to question strange occurrences and struggle to wrest back control. Eventually, even easy shots can become torture.

Though the origin of the yips is controversial, we know they come in two different varieties. The first is almost completely muscular, often appearing as freezing or muscular dystonia. These muscle jerks are often called golfers' cramps, and they lead to awkward backswings and abnormal club rotation. They're also not very interesting, at least from a psychological perspective.

The second form of the yips is the one most people are familiar with, and it's pure hell. It's caused by the same thing that led Poe's narrator to suffer at the hands of the Angel of the Odd—our need to control our fate, and the belief that we alone can fix perceived problems. Specifically, the yips strike when, after a miss or other failure, we overanalyze the error. This causes conscious awareness to take control of what should belong to muscle memory, and the result is always bad. We know these yips are psychological because they aren't random; they involve exaggeration of the same movements that are normally part of the swing. We don't spasm or lose control. We just amplify our mistakes, causing things like yanks, pulls, and other disasters.

One way to cause the yips, which is closely related to choking, is to ask players what they're thinking about during their misses. Surveys of yips-afflicted golfers show one thing in common—thoughts are almost always directed inward, like to clubface alignment during the takeaway. Contrast this with the thoughts of elite golfers, who almost never overthink. Instead, they focus on external factors like course conditions and even the hole itself. Conscious attention hurts because it gives control to higher-order areas of the brain like the frontal lobe, the part of the brain responsible for advanced problem solving. Unfortunately, that's like asking an MLB coach to take the mound in place of his star pitcher—the knowledge is there, but the skill is not.

It's also why thinking about the golf swing almost never helps. One study by researchers at University College Dublin found that focusing on technical adjustments during the putting stroke led to an almost 10 percent decrease in performance for elite players.[5]

If thinking about the swing is so dangerous, what should we think of? The general rule is to focus on something as far away from yourself as possible. When thirty golfers were asked to attempt a series of chip shots from roughly twenty yards, only one group landed the ball consistently within five feet of the pin.[6] Those were the players who were asked to think about the target exclusively—not their swing, not the ball . . . just the hole. Contrast this with those players who thought only about the club itself. They landed the ball five feet farther away.

That's not all. When the same experimenter told the players that a PGA professional was watching them play, and that money was at stake if they improved, players focusing on the pin landed it almost a foot closer. The pressure actually helped. By contrast, those thinking about the swing performed even worse, barely landing the ball on the green.

A curious golfer might be asking—then how do I get better? I know I need to keep my left wrist straight when I swing, so how do I improve if I'm only thinking about the pin?

It's a good question, and the answer is this—the middle of a golf swing is no time for thinking about improvements. That should come before you start that backswing, preferably before you even step to the tee. If you wait until the tee box to think about improvements, you might as well save your energy and toss the ball directly into the nearest water hazard.

But there's good news too, and it's that golf courses are filled with opportunities for thinking about your game. The greatest thing about the brain is we don't need a club in our hands to use it. For example, the next time you power up that golf cart, try giving yourself a "swing thought." It could be as simple as telling yourself to align shoulders with the target, and odds are it will improve your score by about a stroke per round. That's because these reminders harness both the Angel and the Imp; the Angel gets the instructions, but by the time you swing, it has become buried deep in the unconscious. This allows the Imp to have its way, except this time it's working for you, rather than against.

Another option is to use imagery before taking a stroke, but, again, that imagery should happen before teeing off. In one study, Robert Bell of Ball State University followed a group of golfers around a course, noting when they missed putts and from how far away.[7] Then he gave them a series of visualization exercises, asking them to imagine those shots having landed in the hole instead. When he followed them a second time, he saw that the players went from missing three or more "gimme" putts per round to none.

Which brings us to a final, counterintuitive solution. So far, we've seen that focusing on our target helps us avoid overanalyzing our swings. But there are other things we can do too, namely, closing our eyes. At first, that may seem crazy, but surprisingly, our eyes do very little for our stroke. Players completely blinded by artificial lenses still putt nearly as well as those with vision intact.[8] As long as you know where the hole is, most of your job is already done.

Technically, this is an oversimplification, and I wouldn't actually recommend closing your eyes anywhere on the course—mostly for safety reasons. One of the purposes of playing golf is to enjoy the outdoors, and it's probably not smart losing your vision when there are clubs and balls flying around you. Fortunately, research has shown there's another option, and it's to focus on the hole instead of the ball. Just like striking an approach shot with your iron, the trick is not to focus on the ball or your specific motions. When Eric Alpenfels of the Pinehurst Golf Academy and Bob Christina of the School of Health and Human Performance at the University of North Carolina had forty golfers attempt a series of putts of between three and 43 feet, they left the ball on average 37 inches away from the hole. However, when those players were told to look at the hole exclusively, not the ball, they left it nine inches closer, an improvement of 24 percent. Just by redirecting their eyes.[9]

Perhaps that's why successful putters see the hole as bigger than it actually is. Seriously, they do. When successful putters describe the size of the cup, they consistently overestimate, because to them the hole actually seems bigger.[10] When our imagination wants to see a larger target, why let our eyes get in the way? We might as well keep them closed or focus on the hole instead, allowing our imaginations to sink the putt.

So, to summarize, our minds need controlling like our bodies do. In future classes, we'll explore how anxiety and emotion impact our performance too, but for now, simply try practicing with a calm mind, or maybe tee off with a song playing in your head. Odds are it will help, but even if it doesn't, it will make your game more interesting. You might even pick up a few extra dollars from future playing partners who think they have the mental game mastered.

They don't, and to prove it, just remind them not to overhit their next putt. They might not thank you for the advice, but your point will be made.

READING LIST

Attention and Visualization

[9]Alpenfels, E., Christina, B., and Heath, C. (2008). *Instinct Putting*. New York: Gotham Books.

[6]Bell, J. and Hardy, J. (2009). Effects of Attentional Focus on Skilled Performance in Golf. *Journal of Applied Sport Psychology*, 21, 163–177

[7]Bell, R., Skinner, C., and Fisher, L. (2009). Decreasing Putting Yips in Accomplished Golfers via Solution-Focused Guided Imagery: A Single-Subject Research Design. *Journal of Applied Sport Psychology*, 21, 1–14.

[8]Bulsom, R., Ciuffreda, K., and Hung, G. (2008). The Effect of Retinal Defocus on Golf Putting. *Ophthalmic and Physiological Optics*, 28, 334–344.

Dusek, D. (2010). The New Way to Putt: Look at the Hole. *Golf Magazine*, March 6.

Jackson, R. and Morgan, P. (1998). Using Swing Thoughts to Prevent Paradoxical Performance in Golf Putting. In Farrally, M. and Cochran, A. (Ed.), *Science and Golf III: Proceedings of the World Scientific Congress of Golf* (pp. 166–173). Champaign, IL: Human Kinetics.

Kim, T. (2012). Effect of the Combined Practice of Visual Allowance and Occlusion on Learning to Golf Putt. *European Journal of Scientific Research*, 84, 328–335.

Malouff, J. and Murphy, C. (2006). Effects of Self-Instructions on Sport Performance. *Journal of Sport Behavior*, 29, 1–12.

Meacci, W. and Pastore, D. (1995). Effects of Occluded Vision and Imagery on Putting Golf Balls. *Perceptual and Motor Skills*, 80, 179–186.

Moffat, D., Collins, D., and Carson, H. (2017). Target Versus Ball Focused Aiming When Putting: What Has Been Done and What Has Been Missed. *International Journal of Golf Science*, 6, 35–55.

[5]Toner, J. and Moran, A. (2011). The Effects of Conscious Processing on

Golf Putting Proficiency and Kinematics. *Journal of Sports Sciences*, 29, 673–683.

[10]Witt, J., Linkenauger, S., Bakdash, J., and Proffitt, D. (2008). Putting to a Bigger Hole: Golf Performance Relates to Perceived Size. *Psychonomic Bulletin and Review*, 15, 581–585.

Wulf, G., Lauterbach, B., and Toole, T. (1999). The Learning Advantages of an External Focus of Attention in Golf. *Research Quarterly for Exercise and Sport*, 70, 120–126.

Ironic Control

[4]Adams, H., Wright, L., and Lohr, B. (1996). Is Homophobia Associated with Homosexual Arousal? *Journal of Abnormal Psychology*, 105, 440–445.

[2]Wegner, D. (1994). Ironic Processes of Mental Control. *Psychological Review*, 101, 34–52.

[1]Wegner, D., Ansfield, M., and Pilloff, D. (1998). The Putt and the Pendulum: Ironic Effects of the Mental Control of Action. *Psychological Science*, 9, 196–199.

[3]Wegner, D., Lane, J., and Dimitri, S. (1994). The Allure of Secret Relationships. *Journal of Personality and Social Psychology*, 66, 287–300.

Putting, general

Pelz, D. (2000). *Dave Pelz's Putting Bible: The Complete Guide to Mastering the Green*. New York: Doubleday.

Yips

Adler, C., Crews, D., Kahol, K., Santello, M., Noble, B., Hentz, J., and Caviness, J. (2011). Are the Yips a Task-Specific Dystonia of Golfer's Cramp? *Movement Disorders*, 26, 1993–1996.

Filmalter, P., Poppel, E., and Murthi, B. (2008). Motor Strategy Disturbances in Golf: The Effect of Yips on the Movement of the Putter Head. In D. Crews and R. Lutz (Eds.), *Science and Golf V: Proceedings of the World Scientific Congress of Golf* (pp. 353–359). Mesa, AZ: Energy in Motion, Inc.

Marquardt, C. (2009). The Vicious Circle Involved in the Development of the Yips. *Annual Review of Golf Coaching*, 67–78.

McDaniel, K., Cimmings, J. and Shain, S. (1989). The Yips: A Focal Dystonia in Golfers. *Neurology*, 39, 195–195.

Smith, A., Adler, C., Crews, D., Wharen, R., Laskowski, E., Barnes, K., Bell, C., Pelz, D., Brennan, R., Smith, J., Sorenson, M., and Kaufman, K. (2003). The Yips in Golf: A Continuum Between a Focal Dystonia and Choking. *Sports Medicine*, 33, 13–31.

Smith, A., Malo, S., Laskowski, E., Sabick, M., Cooney, W., Finnie, S., Crews, D., Eischen, J., Hay, H., Detline, N., and Kaufman, K. (2000). A Multidisciplinary Study of the Yips Phenomenon in Golf: An Exploratory Analysis. *Sports Medicine,* 30, 423–437.

Stinear, C., Coxon, J., Fleming, M., Lim, V., Prapavessis, H., and Byblow, W. (2006). The Yips in Golf: Multimodal Evidence for Two Subtypes. *Medicine and Science in Sports and Exercise,* 38, 1980–1999.

Introduction to Mathematics: Probability and Statistics

Prerequisites: None

On Friday, June 16, 1989, something happened that shouldn't be possible. The odds, about eight million to one, say that you could follow the PGA Tour for hundreds of years and still not expect such an event. For it to happen during a major championship was inconceivable.

The miracle began on the sixth hole of the Oak Hill Country Club in Rochester, New York, a 167-yard par three with a deep bunker to the right. It was the second day of the U.S. Open, and Doug Weaver, a newcomer to the tour, was first to play. When he launched his shot almost 15 feet past the hole, nearly everybody thought he had overshot. Then the ball bounced once and reversed direction, slowly rolling back toward the flag.

Closer and closer it inched until finally it fell into the hole. It was a hole in one.

The crowd erupted in applause. "That Weaver guy just knocked his ball into the hole!" one of the marshals told Mark Wiebe a short time later as he prepared his own shot. Wiebe nodded, then knocked his Titleist eight feet left of the pin with just a little spin. It also rolled directly into the hole.

Jerry Pate, former U.S. Amateur champion, was the next to record an ace that afternoon, his own ball landing seven feet past the pin. Just like the others, it rolled straight in. Two players later, when Nick Price's ball landed eight feet to the right and started rolling toward the flag, it seemed as if anything less would have been impossible.

In all, the four aces that day would constitute one-fifth of all holes-in-one ever scored at the U.S. Open. All within two hours. You almost had to pity Hubert Green, who teed off soon after Price. His strike stopped just inches from the pin, achingly close and enough to bring the crowd to a near frenzy. He had to settle for birdie and ninth place in the tournament.

Second only to baseball, golf is a game of math. For most of us, the odds of making a hole in one are about 12,000 to 1. For professionals, it's higher, but this still equates to scoring an ace only once every 3,500 holes, a rare event indeed. Some golfers go a lifetime without such luck. Others, like me, get lucky early in our playing careers, as I did on April 3, 2013. I was such a novice, I was still using a five iron on a 110-yard par three, yet somehow my ball landed just right and fell into the cup. Pure luck, I admit. Odds are I won't get so fortunate again.

Obviously, randomness plays a significant role in all sports. An excellent match today can be followed by a terrible one tomorrow, and even a sketchy player like me can get lucky sometimes. With such fluctuations, it can be difficult knowing how to assess our own skill. Is a winning streak due to a solid stroke, or just dumb luck?

Answering questions like this requires math, and in this class we'll address how to honestly measure our game. And let there be no mistake—there's a difference between skill and luck. Though Doug Weaver and the others who scored aces that day had a favorable pin location and perfect weather conditions, four amateurs surely wouldn't have fared as well. Math and statistics help us understand why.

The first thing all players should know is that golf isn't a streaky sport. It often feels like it is. Good days follow good, and bad days follow bad. Except—they don't. Statisticians have studied thousands of scorecards from players of all levels and found no signs of streakiness.[1] No matter how well you played the previous hole, your odds of getting a birdie on the next one are the same. Though players frequently feel like they have the "hot hand," or the opposite—that they are cursed—it's not true. If I bogie three holes in a row, odds are I'm not unlucky; I'm just not very good. Granted, changing your swing can have disastrous consequences on your score, but barring a complete breakdown, we're all generally consistent. With one exception.

This exception is pretty telling, because it pertains to a very specific part of the game. With putting, we sometimes do have hot and cold streaks, but only under specific circumstances. To understand those circumstances and how they arise, it helps to first understand the concept of noise and how it relates to streaky play, and perhaps the nature of statistics itself.

"Streaky performance is almost impossible to spot, and completely outside your control," says David Gilden, and he should know. He is the psychologist and astronomer who discovered the phenomenon. Seriously—he studies things like black holes too, not just golfers: "I developed my interest in streaks and clustering while looking at 1/f noise and the emissions of quasars."

Who knew that putting was related to the electromagnetic storms at the center of our galaxy? It turns out that the energy produced by rapidly spinning black holes isn't spewed out randomly. There's a pattern, with greater energy at lower frequencies. Those energies fluctuate like our own bodies fluctuate, and that pattern is called pink noise. We call it pink because it's almost like white noise, but not quite. White noise is all over the place, like what our radios play when tuned off-station. Pink noise follows a pattern, though the pattern isn't uncovered very easily, which is why astronomers sometimes spend entire careers studying it from sources like black holes.

Don't worry, because this isn't an astrophysics class (thankfully), but it's worth noting that streakiness can be hard to spot, and it's not completely random. Gilden prefers to talk about streakiness in terms of drummers, who act like quasars and golfers too but are a little easier to understand.

"Even a steady drummer shows fluctuations," explains Gilden. He means the tiny variations in beat, sometimes just lasting a millisecond, that can seem impossible to notice. "Hitting a little late, or a little early. Everybody does it, and it would be easy to assume these fluctuations are random. But they aren't. They depend on how long the pauses are between strikes, along with several other things. They're part of play."

The key thing to understand about streakiness is that our nervous systems don't work like computers. Machines are sure and steady. A computer doesn't get distracted or lose attention, and it certainly doesn't fluctuate based on circadian or hormonal rhythms. Bodies, however, experience constant background noise. That noise distracts our attention and throws off the timing of an otherwise steady beat. It's not something we can control, any more than we can control the frequency of light emitted from cosmic objects. It's the nature of math and the universe itself.

How does this affect your game? Let's send some players to the putting green to see for ourselves.

Gilden's discovery of attentional noise came when he had forty people attempt hundreds of golf putts on a laboratory-controlled green.[2] They hit from varying distances, sometimes short and sometimes from as far as twelve feet. The subjects usually made the short ones, of course, and seldom succeeded with the long ones. The surprise came when Gilden analyzed the success rates of the putts in between, just at the edge of players' ability levels.

Not only were the players streaky, but these were the only shots where good putts followed good, and bad followed bad. The randomness went away.

Actually, to be technical, randomness never goes away, but it can lose a bit of its edge. So the players were definitely streaky, though only when their own unsteady rhythms took control. We've all experienced such moments on the course, when we attempt a shot just within our skill level. We may not be able to feel it, but our bodies enter a state of stable disorder. Even our heartbeats come a little late, or a little early, just enough to put our nervous systems off balance. It's the same chaotic design you see in traffic patterns and the rise and fall of the tides. And it's inevitable.

Which tells us a lot about the nature of missed shots in general. For easy putts, we only miss when we become distracted. For hard ones, we miss because we never had the skill in the first place. It's the ones in between that get us, when the hits and misses come in streaks. They're special because they're most vulnerable to the natural fluctuations in our attention and physiological control. "It's like milk and cream separating," explains Gilden, referring to the way our attention fades in and out over the course of the day. "Hits and misses start to form clumps, which means longer runs. They separate, meaning you're more likely to see a failure following another failure, and vice versa."

And what can we do about it? Absolutely nothing.

But that's useful to know too. Just because you missed that eight-foot putt, that doesn't mean you should change your stroke. In fact, just the opposite. Even professional golfers miss that putt half of the time.

So move on.

God bless fellow Arkansas golfer John Daly.

Daly and I have almost nothing in common except our home state, but I find him fascinating because there are few professional golfers—nay, professional athletes—with more personality. When Daly won the 1991 PGA Championship, he was playing as ninth alternate. *Ninth.* When he won the British Open four years later, he was a 66–1 underdog.

Yet, despite his tour success, Daly has a bit of a wild side. In the 1998 Bay Hill Invitational, he incurred six straight penalties while trying to clear a 270-yard water hazard. Two years later at the U.S. Open, he hit three balls into the Pacific Ocean and one in someone's backyard. Daly has been fined nearly $100,000 in his career for cursing or otherwise bad behavior and has been cited twenty-one times—twenty-one!—for what the PGA calls "failure to give best efforts."

Daly is world-renowned for being a wild card both on and off the course, and we all know players like this—those who frequently win but seldom settle for par. That's why a player's handicap is a poor measure of skill; a single number can only tell you so much. Which leads to some interesting questions—if given the choice of John Daly or Nick Faldo, who would you rather play against? Both have similar pedigrees and scoring averages. Yet, Faldo never hit the famous 17th green of Baltusrol Golf Club in Springfield, New Jersey—630 yards total—in just two strokes.

He never also never teed off on a beer can at a sponsored event, or intentionally hit his ball over a crowd of spectators just to see if he could do it or if it would get him into trouble. (Seriously . . . in 1993, Daly was fined for $30,000 by the PGA for hitting a ball over a bleacher full of fans during a clinic at the Fred Meyer Challenge at the Oregon Golf Club in West Linn.) Consider Nick Faldo's final round during the 1987 British Open, a match where he shot straight par. As in, for every hole he scored exactly as course designers expected—no birdies, no bogies, just par. He won, thanks to a couple of late bogies by his closest competitor, Paul Azinger, but usually such conservative play doesn't win. When Rory McIlroy won the same tournament twenty-seven years later, he shot the same score, except he had an equal mix of bogeys and birdies. In the end, both won the tournament, but in very different ways.

So, which game is better in the long run—slow and steady, or wild and free? Enter the first and most important scientific paper on golf that you've never heard of: Godfrey Harold "G.H." Hardy's 1945 paper, "A Mathematical Theorem About Golf." My favorite thing about G.H. Hardy is that he didn't like golf, not even a little bit. "I am no golfer," he actually says in the otherwise very formal paper, explaining later that he found the game rather dull compared to his favored sport, cricket. His curiosity was purely mathematical, focused on the benefit of playing like John Daly, compared to Nick Faldo. Except, since the paper was written in 1945, the names were Bobby Jones and Walter Hagen. But you get the idea.

The question isn't that hard to measure, actually. All you need is a little math. Let's imagine two hypothetical players, one steady and consistent, the other wild and unpredictable, to see what I mean.

First, let's address the steady player; he only shoots par and never makes a mistake, but at the cost of never making a birdie. He's not so interesting. His partner is a little different; she hits a great shot 10 percent of the time, but at the cost of fouling things up just as often. Who should do better? (You shouldn't assume anything about my gender pronouns, other than I'm trying to remain grammatically neutral. There's no evidence that men and women play differently in that regard, and even if they did, that would be a different chapter.)

Anyway, Hardy actually did the math—algebra, technically—and computed the expected scoring averages for these two players. The short answer is that unpredictability isn't good. Specifically, it costs an average player 1.8 strokes per hole. Being twice as erratic adds 1.8 strokes more.

The reason for the difference is that bad shots tend to multiply, while great shots don't always help that much. Which is useful to know, because it means that sometimes we're best playing it cautious. Nick Faldo's British Open win might not make many highlight reels, but it's a good way to keep a lead. John Daly makes for great television, but not consistent wins.

However, there's an exception to this rule about careful play, and it can't be overlooked. The exception has to do with large tournaments where a little unpredictability is a good thing. Something curious happens when you get lots of golfers together, and I don't mean huge beer tabs and questionable side bets. I mean that having a wild side helps. When the field is large and the goal is to stand out, sometimes you have to take risks. Play it safe, and you'll go home in tenth place.

Let's imagine a hypothetical tournament to see what I mean.

Say we have a tournament of thirty players. Ten of them are steady as can be, like Nick Faldo except more so. They only shoot par, ever, and though they're not much fun to watch, at least they don't yell "fore" after every tee shot. Then there are the wild cards. These players are like Hardy's erratic players, making a miracle shot 10 percent of the time but fouling things up just as often. Let's say ten of the tournament players are like wild cards, and another ten are twice as erratic. These are the players who occasionally strike a hole in one but then hook the ball into the clubhouse parking lot immediately after.

Who would you bet on to win the tournament? Let's park our car at the far end of the lot and find out.

It turns out that the winner of the tournament will most likely be one of the most erratic players. If we do the algebra, we see that the winner for the tournament will likely average about a 67. That score will belong to one of the most erratic of players, though there's a catch—there's no telling which one. The most erratic players will average about a 76, well above par, but those are averages, not individual scorecards. When the field is large, you need to take risks, and for one or two players, those risks will pay off. For everybody else, they won't.

These results aren't isolated to mathematics laboratories either (are there such things?), because we see the same thing on the PGA Tour. Let's look at the 2006 PGA season, arguably the height of Tiger Woods's career, to see what I mean.

In 2006, Tiger Woods won eight of his fifteen tournaments. This earned him over nine million dollars in award money and enough sponsorship support to fund a small European economy. But he was far from the best player that year. We know this because Matthew Hood, a professor of finance from the University of Southern Mississippi, actually measured it. Specifically, he developed a complex mathematical algorithm to identify each PGA player's average ability level, and also his consistency.[3]

It turns out that Zach Johnson actually had a better year, at least in terms of consistent, high-level play. He made twenty cuts, compared to Woods's twelve, and never completely played himself out of a match or a tournament. Yet, he didn't win a single one. In other words, he didn't take enough risks to come in first place. Jim Furyk, Luke Donald, and K.J. Choi all had better seasons too, at least mathematically. Too bad math doesn't win golf tournaments.

Hood even had Tiger Woods play Johnson, Furyk, and Choi in a series of computer-simulated tournaments, based on their average ability, and saw the same results. Tiger won a lot, more than anyone else, despite Johnson playing more reliably day after day, week after week. Risks often hurt, but when you need to win it all, they're an essential part of the game.

This may make you wonder why we bother keeping handicaps when variability matters so much. Our handicaps measure the quality of our play, often leading to love/hate relationships. Some wear the number like a badge of honor ("Your daughter just turned nine? What a coincidence, that's my golf handicap!"). Others hide it like their age, hoping that everybody will think it lower than it actually is.

It's true that handicaps measure only average score, not variability, and thus do little to differentiate John Daly or Zach Johnson. Still, they're quite useful. If you're making a side bet on the next hole, you better know your partner's handicap, because if you don't, you're likely to be hustled.

We should also recognize that high handicaps aren't always bad. As we've already seen, a little unpredictability is a good thing, at least when the competition is tough. And nobody can be counted on for unpredictability more than a high-handicap golfer. Mathematicians have examined databases of online scorecards and seen it for themselves—teams do best when at least one player has a high handicap.[4] That player won't help on most holes, but he or she can still be counted on for an occasional surprise.

Most players think of handicap as the number of "free swings" based on differences in skill level. Those swings are applied on the most difficult holes, which is nice, because we all like free things. For example, if my handicap is five higher than my friend's, I get a free stroke on the five most difficult holes. And I take them every time.

It turns out that this simple correction leads to lots of interesting effects. One is that there's an "optimal difference" in handicap pairing during team play.

Since handicap is applied in terms of free strokes, it's best for playing partners to have very different handicaps. Ideally, you'd like to receive a free stroke only when your partner doesn't, because any overlap is overkill; only one teammate needs to win a hole at a time. Algebra shows that having a handicap differential of 11 between partners is ideal, because this maximizes the distribution of free strokes. On a hole where you get a birdie due to that free stroke, your partner can bogie for all you care. Any free strokes then are just wasted.

From this discussion, it might seem that handicapping systems aren't fair, because they're supposed to equalize players, not give unfair advantages. They do, but no system is perfect. In fact, the golf handicapping system was designed to be imperfect. On purpose.

Recognizing that better players deserve some sort of advantage, designers of the handicap system included something else too, and it's called a "Bonus for Excellence." In mathematical terms, this means the handicap formula ends with a correction of 4 percent, making it smaller than it should be. For a player with a handicap of three, a 4 percent reduction isn't much, but for players like me, it can make a big difference. For beginning golfers, it can even mean being shortchanged a full stroke per match. That missing free stroke may not seem impressive, but when a beer tab is on the line, it can't be overlooked. So more skilled players do have an advantage, at least in match play.

The real message is to choose your partners wisely, and don't be afraid to take some risks. More important, always park your car at the far end of the clubhouse parking lot. Even if your playing partner doesn't get out of hand, somebody else's probably will. Winning your next golf bet may feel good, but it won't pay for a new windshield.

Ben Hogan once claimed that putting has no place in golf. The true measure of a player is his or her swing, and I don't mean with a putter.

Ben Hogan could say that because he was Ben Hogan. You and I, however, better pay attention to our short game. Still, Hogan had a point—driving, iron play, and putting can seem like different sports. We could spend a lifetime perfecting our full swing and still have no chance on the professional tour without a decent putt or chip shot.

Success takes a variety of skills, not to mention some strict game management.

Measuring performance is a challenge for everyone, amateurs and professionals alike. Take for example the Bobby Locke saying "You drive for show but putt for dough." This reflects the common belief that long hits look good on television, but putting wins tournaments. We've all seen players who hit the ball a mile but still lose because they miss those pesky three-foot putts. Is it true that the putter is the most important club in our bag?

The answer is both yes and no. If you look at specific skills alone, putting is indeed the most important. One analysis showed that if professionals improved their putting by just one stroke per round, they could earn $319,000 more per year.[5] By comparison, driving ten extra yards earns only about $117,000. Improving accuracy with the iron hardly helps at all.

The problem is that golf skills don't exist in isolation, and again let's take John Daly as an example. In 1995, the year Daly won the British Open, he ranked first in average driving distance, just shy of 300 yards. But his accuracy was ranked 184th. That means he barely hit the fairway half the time, and that wasn't unusual for the big hitters.

The real issue with driving is that it's measured by both distance and accuracy. Being good with one helps, but taking care of both is ideal. In fact, having a drive that's both long and accurate *is* more important than putting, because hitting the far end of the fairway helps every other part of the game. Landing closer to the green means shorter chip shots. Shorter chip shots mean shorter putts. Shorter putts mean fewer strokes. One skill feeds another.

Which brings us to our final, end-of-year project for our semester of mathematics, an alternate way of looking at golf scores. Though it's not complicated, it will make you think differently about how we measure the game.

Let's consider a simple putt from five feet. Professionals will make this shot 75 percent of the time. For those with handicaps like mine, the odds are closer to 50/50, making it a nail-biting endeavor. Let's say I miss this putt by an inch. Compare this with another putt missed from forty feet away.

What's the difference in value between these two shots? They ended up in the same place, and they both cost a stroke. Yet, clearly, they weren't the same. Both failed, yet one wasn't as disappointing because it wasn't expected to go in. The other was. The value of these shots depends on the difference between expectations and outcome. The end result of both is a gimme putt, but the easier shot had the opportunity to be much, much more.

Here we're confronted with our biggest math challenge yet—how to measure the value of each swing—which led researchers from MIT and Harvard to develop a "putts to go" system.[6] This measures how many strokes you'd expect to have remaining from every distance to the hole, allowing you to measure the value of each shot.

Let's take two professional golfers as an example to see how they compare, based on data available to the researchers in 2011. At the time, Ernie Els was considered one of the greatest putters in the PGA, well in the top 5 percent, while Stephen Leaney was one of the worst. You'd expect Els to be the clear favorite in putting efficiency, based on his 1.75 average putts per hole, but this wasn't the case. Actually, he was at the bottom of the rankings in that category. Why? Because his approach shots were so consistently good. While Leaney often struggled to reach the green in regulation, Els consistently landed his ball so close to the hole that he hardly needed the putter. Math showed that Els was good on the green mostly because he was so good everywhere else.

The same type of analysis has been applied to driving and iron play too, sometimes called the Personal Par system, and it works the same way.[7, 8] Every stroke has an expected value, based on your average game and how many strokes the swing leaves you afterward. Do you drive 300 yards off the tee but take two more strokes to reach the green after that? If so, you're probably better off practicing with your irons. Are you decent landing on the green with your irons but take three putts or more after that? Well, your putting probably needs work, but more likely you're not as decent with your irons as you thought. You should land the ball near the hole more often than you are, even if by accident, suggesting you might want to hit the driving range, too. Though these may seem like obvious observations, it's easy on the course to forget that every shot depends on the one that came before it, and that counting strokes is a poor way of measuring performance.

For the record, the most consistent putter at the turn of the century, as measured by the MIT system, was Tiger Woods. Actually, he was best no matter how you measure, gaining on average 0.69 strokes on the green, compared to his competitors. As for the least consistent players, that's hard to say, but Vijay Singh was especially good at giving himself short putts from his approaches, only to squander the advantage. Don't feel too bad for them, though. They still did pretty well.

This isn't to say that putting is the only thing differentiating amateurs and professionals. Once you make the PGA Tour, putting becomes pretty important, but it's still only a part of the game. In fact, scientists have recently developed something called the Golfmetrics system to see how professionals and amateurs compare, a little like Jonah Hill did for baseball in the movie adaptation of *Moneyball,* except now we're talking drives rather than fastballs. (Jonah's character isn't in the book, by the way, which is why I recommend the movie. They're both fantastic, though.) They looked at accuracy and distance for all types of shots, and for all types of players, and it turns out that the biggest difference between professionals and others isn't the putter. Not even close.

The biggest challenge for most amateurs, at least according to the math, is the frequency of "disaster shots." These are the failures that will crush you, like missing the ball altogether or topping it when you need to clear an otherwise easy 50-yard water hazard. They not only add strokes, they leave you in difficult lies too, leading to a cascading effect. In fact, reliability and accuracy seem to be the biggest hindrances for most beginners, not one-inch misses on the green. That's because for amateurs, the game is much more about disaster management than optimization.

Looking at strokes as a kind of currency has its benefits. The game depends a lot on chance, but we can all benefit from knowing our own baseline odds. A good Texas Hold 'em player always keeps close track of his or her chances at the table, no matter the pressure. And when the odds are in his or her favor, he or she will put all her chips in. For golfers, the equivalent of going "all in" is knowing when to hit over that huge water hazard, and when to lay up. Playing our best means knowing what we can consistently do, and what requires some extra luck.

We've already seen that the sport is inherently random, but our game management doesn't have to be. There's always room for improvement, and that starts with knowing our game. Even if you've never hit a hole in one before, that doesn't mean you can't on your next shot. You aren't likely to see four aces in a single day, but you can understand how they happen and make them a more likely part of your game.

That's why golf is played one stroke at a time.

READING LIST

Assessing Performance

Broadie, M. (2008). Assessing Golfer Performance Using Golfmetrics. In D. Crews and R. Lutz (Eds.), *Science and Golf V: Proceedings of the World Scientific Congress of Golf* (pp. 253–262). Mesa, AZ: Energy in Motion, Inc.

[8]Cochran, A. and Stobbs, J. (1968). *The Search for the Perfect Swing*. Grass Valley, CA: The Booklegger.

[6]Fearing, D., Acimovic, J., and Graves, S. (2011). How to Catch a Tiger: Understanding Putting Performance on the PGA Tour. *Journal of Quantitative Analysis in Sports*, 7, 1–45.

[7]Landsberger, L. (1994). A Unified Golf Stroke Value Scale for Quantitative Stroke-by-Stroke Assessment. In A.J. Cochran and M. Farrally (Eds.), *Science and Golf II: Proceedings of the World Scientific Congress of Golf* (pp. 216–221). Grass Valley, CA: The Booklegger.

Player Variability and Handicaps

Hardy, G. (1945). A Mathematical Theorem About Golf. *The Mathematical Gazette*, 29, 226–227.

[3]Hood, M. (2008). Consistency on the PGA Tour. *Journal of Sports Economics*, 9, 504–519.

Minton, R. (2010). Lipping Out and Laying Up: G.H. Hardy and J.E. Littlewood's Curious Encounters with the Mathematics of Golf. *Math Horizons*, 5–19.

[4]Siegbahn, P. and Hearn, D. (2010). A Study of Fairness in Fourball Golf Competition. In S. Butenkjo (Ed.), *Optimal Strategies in Sports Economics and Management* (pp. 143–170). Heidelberg: Springer-Verlag Berlin.

Skills and Money

[5]Alexander, D. and Kern, W. (2005). Drive for Show and Putt for Dough? An Analysis of the Earnings of PGA Tour Golfers. *Journal of Sports Economics*, 6, 46–60.

Dorsel, T. and Rotunda, R. (2001). Low Scores, Top 10 Finishes, and Big Money: An Analysis of Professional Golf Association Tour Statistics and How They Relate to Overall Performance. *Perceptual and Motor Skills*, 92, 575–585.

Finley, P. and Halsey, J. (2004). Determinants of PGA Tour Success: An Examination of Relationships Among Performance, Scoring, and Earnings. *Perceptual and Motor Skills*, 98, 1100–1106.

Wiseman, F. and Chatterjee, S. (2006). Comprehensive Analysis of Golf Performance on the PGA Tour 1990–2004. *Perceptual and Motor Skills*, 102, 109–117.

Streakiness

Clark, R. (2004). On the Independence of Golf Scores For Professional Golfers. *Perceptual and Motor Skills*, 98, 675–681.

Clark, R. (2005). Examination of Hole-To-Hole Streakiness on the PGA Tour. *Perceptual and Motor Skills*, 100, 806–814.

[1]Clark, R. (2005). An Examination of the Hot Hand in Professional Golfers. *Perceptual and Motor Skills*, 101, 935–942.

[2]Gilden, D. and Wilson, S. (1995). Streaks in Skilled Performance. *Psychonomic Bulletin and Review*, 2, 260–265.

Premedicine: Kinematics and Human Anatomy

Prerequisites: None

We expect professional athletes to be big and strong. Babe Ruth stood over six feet tall, with 215 pounds to back it up. That may sound big, but it's nothing compared to sluggers of today. Alex Rodriguez bests him by an inch in height and fifteen pounds, and he isn't far from the MLB average. Zdeno Chara, world record holder for strongest shot in hockey, stands 6'9" tall. Ivo Karlovic, the Croatian tennis player who holds the recognized record for most aces in a career and second-fastest serve, is just shy of seven feet.

Being large helps, especially when your sport involves hitting things with clubs, bats, or sticks. Perhaps that's why professional baseball players are five inches taller now than they were a hundred years ago. Power comes from muscle, and the best way to get that is to be bigger.

Yet this doesn't explain Hidemichi Tanaka.

Born in Japan and golfing professionally by the age of twenty, Tanaka is the antithesis of Babe Ruth. At barely five feet tall, Tanaka is far from muscle-bound. His 135-pound frame doesn't strike an imposing figure either, but for over ten years, he made a huge impression on the PGA Tour. When he entered the 2000 PGA Championship, he was among the longer hitters of the field and even hit one drive over 330 yards. Known in Japan as "Chibbiko," meaning little golfer, he earned nearly three million dollars overall.

Very few professional golfers are below-average height (an informal analysis from 2013 showed the number to be roughly 10%) yet hitters like Tanaka show that size isn't everything. To see where such power comes from, researchers from the University of Toledo even videotaped his swing with electromyography sensors along his torso and force plates below his feet.[1] Analysis showed that at time of impact, Tanaka exerted over 263 pounds of pressure against the ground, almost double his actual weight. Since most of that pressure fell on the left foot, his body generated three times more pressure than the force of gravity while at address.

A great thing about golf is that nearly anyone can play. Although size and power help, technique is a lot more important, which is why players like Tanaka post such amazing drives. It's also why no two swings are alike. One comprehensive analysis of over a hundred expert golfers, including such icons as Bobby Jones and Arnold Palmer, found that no two professionals swung the same.[2] One player cocked his left wrist 70 degrees, another half that amount. One player hardly shifted his weight during the backswing, another did so drastically. Everybody hit the ball well, but since all bodies were different, so were the swings.

In this class, we'll explore why hitting a golf ball is so difficult, and why everybody does it differently. There is no such thing as a perfect swing, which is why no lesson or piece of advice works for everybody. Still, we can all learn more about balance and timing. Tanaka got a lot out of his modest frame, and so can you with a little understanding of how the body operates.

The average golfer drives the ball roughly 200 yards from the tee. For professionals, that number is higher, though there's plenty of variation. In 2017, Rory McIlroy led all pros by striking the ball on average 317 yards. Jim Furyk barely reached 270.

Long-ball competitions are particularly interesting because they waste no time with trivialities like putting. The goal is to hit the ball far, like with the 2017 "Mile High Showdown" in Denver, Colorado. That competition began with both Ryan Reisbeck and Maurice Allen each driving their ball 483 yards to move on to the semifinals. More long hits followed until they met in the finals, where Reisbeck landed his ball outside the allowable field, leading to disqualification. Allen, who simply had to hit in bounds, walked away with the honor of long drive champion after hitting *only* 436 yards.

Such feats sound impressive until you consider the strike Dustin Johnson laid on his TaylorMade TP5x at the 12th hole of the Austin

Country Club course in March 2018. That went 489 yards, and it was during actual play.

Who knows what records the future will bring.

One thing all long hits have in common is that they start with the feet. That's where the player makes contact with the ground, so all force starts at this point. This makes balance especially important, because torque requires a solid foundation. It's also why skilled golfers have better balance than amateurs. One study found that when golfers stand on one leg atop a force plate, they sway less than nonplayers.[3] Higher handicaps mean more swaying, proving that balance is a big part of your golf score.

The reason for this is that the swing requires us to shift balance. That shift is an easy way to distinguish amateurs from professionals, which led James Wrobel of the University of Michigan to ask—how does balance help our game? As a podiatrist and balance specialist, he knew that posture can be trained. He also knew that improved balance reduces other movements, like sway and jitter. Does improved balance lengthen driving distance by increasing power, or does it simply minimize other movements?

Wrobel started by placing a series of sensors on players' bodies.[4] As his subjects began swinging, he measured how their balance shifted. The differences were striking. All players shifted their weight forward during the swing, though the paths varied widely. Skilled players transitioned their weight in a smooth motion. Others wobbled. Eventually, a pattern emerged, and Wrobel saw that talented players transitioned closer to a straight line. Those who were beginners moved their body like a new driver navigates a freeway—their path weaved and meandered and lacked general self-control.

There's a story, probably apocryphal, of a student who once asked Michelangelo how he carved his famous statue *David*. Perplexed by the question, Michelangelo replied, "It's easy. You start with a large block of marble, then chip away everything that doesn't belong."

I have no idea if Michelangelo ever played golf—it existed back then, though almost surely not in Florence—but his observation says a lot about the swing. When we start playing, our game is like an uncarved block of marble. The longer we play, the more we chip away at bad habits until what remains is smooth and linear. When our bodies are steady, the rest of the game follows.

This means that golf depends more on what we *don't* do than what we do. This surprises many people, because it feels like a fast swing is a better one. Professionals *do* swing faster, but that's deceptive. What actually travels faster is the clubface, which may reach speeds of 125 miles an hour for a professional. For an amateur, that number is closer to 100, though in the end the difference is minor. If you look at the bodies of amateurs, rather than the clubface, that's where the true story is told.

To see how, let's look at another study of the golf swing, this one by professionals at the Coeur d'Alene Golf Club in Idaho, in coordination with researchers from Pennsylvania State University.[5] Like Wrobel, they also placed sensors on golfers during the swing, except here they measured force from backswing to follow-through. The first thing they found was that neither player hit the ball with weight shifted fully to the front foot. However, the amateur was especially unsteady, with a long, unbalanced phase between setup and top of the backswing. Even the follow-through included wobbling. By contrast, the professional swung surely and without hesitation. It wasn't even until the end of the follow-through that balance between the feet was restored.

Most instruction books don't emphasize balance because it's not easily practiced, but that doesn't mean we can't improve. Many training programs include drills like remaining motionless in your follow-through until the ball hits the ground. Some drills are even fun, like taking off your shoes when you swing. That also helps give immediate feedback from your feet. Seve Ballesteros, the beloved phenomenon who placed second at the British Open at age 19, grew up playing barefoot on the sandy beaches of Pedrena, Spain. Sam Snead supposedly learned to play while barefoot in backwoods Virginia. Being poor helped these future greats develop a feel for where their bodies stood, though you don't need to lack money to gain the same benefits. You just need to risk a warning from clubhouse managers about proper dress code.

So, the next time your swing seems off, consider reevaluating your balance. Did your swing end with a nice, steady shift forward? Or did it feel more like your first time riding a surfboard—lots of wobbling, unsteadiness, and in the end more sand between your toes than you'd like to admit?

Surfing is great, but it has no place on the golf course.

Something impressive happened to golf at the end of 1992. The professional season was over, and most golfers had packed up their clubs for the season. Yet, Jim McLean was still hard at work. One of the world's greatest instructors, he was about to publish a piece for *Golf Magazine*, one that would revolutionize the swing. That revolution was called the X-Factor.

Though most nongolfers think of "X-Factor" as the popular television show produced by Simon Cowell, where young twenty-somethings get berated while desperately trying to become famous, years before, it meant something else. This was the term McLean gave to the difference in rotation between a golfer's waist and shoulders, and it was a revolutionary idea. Though he'd been teaching the concept for years, his magazine article introduced it to the masses, and they loved it. More magazine articles followed, and a swing revolution was born.

The general idea behind the X-Factor is simple. Power in the golf swing comes from torque, and as long as that torque doesn't accompany a loss of balance, power follows. Measuring torque is difficult, at least without electronic sensors, though the simplest approach is to measure the rotational difference between the hips and shoulders, or X-Factor. This tells you how "wound up" your spine is during the backswing, like coil in a spring. If a golfer turns neither hips nor shoulders, there's no rotation at all. Turning both equally doesn't produce torque either, because there's nothing to unwind. It's the difference that matters.

Probably the best example of maximizing X-Factor is Tiger Woods. At his prime, Woods averaged a hip rotation of about 35 degrees, and his shoulders roughly 100. That made a difference of 65 degrees, enough to rank him near the top of all professionals. John Daly, another notorious long hitter, turned his shoulders even more, over 120 degrees, though his massive hip rotation (66 degrees) led to slightly lower X-Factor. Even Jack Nicklaus, who wasn't particularly known for his flexibility, still managed an impressive 40-degree X-Factor.

When discussing X-Factor, we can't forget Michelle Wei. With a 45-degree hip turn and shoulder rotation greater than 110, she matches Tiger Woods. This might explain how she managed to hit 300-yard drives as a teenager.

Proof that the X-Factor matters can be seen in the laboratory, too. When Joseph Myers of the University of North Carolina attached sensors to golfers' bodies, he expected to find that body rotation was key.[6] Yet, when he examined the relationship between torso rotation and ball velocity, there was none. Nor was there a relationship between pelvic rotation and ball speed. In fact, no relationship existed until their difference was considered as a single variable—the X-Factor. Then he observed a significant correlation between X-Factor and ball speed, enough to indicate that almost a quarter of our hitting power depends on this alone.

From this it may seem that we should rotate as much as possible, but again that would be a mistake. The problem is that power isn't everything. Rotation is important, but surprisingly amateurs don't lack flexibility. When Michael McTeigue of SportSense Incorporated compared the rotation of male amateurs and professionals, he found that the average professional turned his hips 55 degrees and his upper body 87 degrees.[7] This provided an X-factor of 32 degrees. And the amateurs? The rotation in their hips and torso were 53 and 87 degrees, respectively, an X-factor of 34. Almost identical to the professionals!

So amateurs don't necessarily suffer from poor flexibility. Granted, long hitters like Tanaka rotate more than amateurs, but on average the difference isn't significant. In fact, the only difference McTeigue found was that professionals progressed faster through their swing, to the tune of about a quarter of a second.

This slowness wasn't isolated to any specific part of the swing either. Amateurs took longer on their backswing. And downswing. And nearly everything else. Separate studies have broken the swing down further, from takeaway to finish position and five points in between and confirmed that amateurs are slower at every stage.[8] In short, amateurs take longer to swing the club.

This presents a dilemma for the average player, because faster swings produce longer hits, but they also mean less stability. Amateurs simply don't have the muscle memory to swing any faster without losing balance and control.

If only our golf swings were as reliable as those of Iron Byron. That's the name of the robot developed by George Manning for the club manufacturer *True Temper*. It swings clubs just like people do, with a rotating shoulder and wrist, though its body is metal and stands only a few feet tall. Named for the legend Byron Nelson, who was so reliable only a machine could recreate his swing, Iron Byron was regularly used by the United States Golf Association (USGA) to test equipment for conformity standards. It worked, as the turf along the centerline of the USGA testing fairway had to be replaced every couple of years. Apparently, having a golf ball land on the same spot over and over again, day after day, isn't good for carpets or rugs, no matter how well they tie the room together.

The amazing thing about Iron Byron is that it uses a double-pendulum motion to swing, just like people. This means that it exhibits the same rotation as humans, with articulated elbow and wrist hinges to simulate an actual swing. If humans didn't have wrists, the golf swing would involve only a single pendulum (we'd also be unable to record our score, but that's another matter). If we lacked shoulders, again we'd be left with a single pendulum. Having both vastly increases our driving distances, but at the cost of more ways to screw up.

To see how the double pendulum is important for the golf swing, consider rotation speed for various body parts during the swing. Each part reaches peak speed at a different time. The hips start rotating first, and when the hips reach maximum rotation speed, the arms take over. Then, once they've reached top speed, all that's left is the club. If everything works properly, the club reaches maximum speed just as it strikes the ball.

Thinking of the swing in terms of multiple pendulums shows how important timing is for successful contact. If one part of the body gets ahead, the entire swing falls apart. Some even describe the swing as a triple pendulum, with the torso and upper arms being the first link, the lower arms being the second, and the club being the third. Each of those links possesses its own rotational velocity, and when everything is combined, magic happens.

Unfortunately, it's also easy to take this knowledge and simplify the game to adages like "always swing with the hips." Though the swing does start with the hips, this undervalues later parts of the swing. Beginners often break their wrists early because they're told to focus on body rotation instead. Some instructors even tell beginners to consider the arms an extension of the club. Their justification is that the wrists aren't very important, and they're right because relative to the rest of the body, the wrists don't generate much power. One mathematical analysis of the swing found that the shoulders contribute most to the swing, followed by the arms. The wrists hardly mattered at all.[9]

Yet, the wrists *are* important. Even when wrists are passive hinges, they generate incredible power. Although the exact timing of the wrist turn doesn't have a huge impact, if it's taken away altogether, the result can be disastrous. When the body motions of 45 scratch golfers were analyzed using a kinematic motional analysis system, scientists found that approximately 15 percent of the club's kinetic energy was generated by the hips.[10] Roughly 20 percent came from the torso. Over 60 percent came from the wrists.

When that energy is converted to ball speed, we can see that removing trunk rotation slows club speed from 107 mph to 97 mph.[11] That's a 10 percent drop, which isn't much. Yet, when we fix the wrists, meaning we don't let them bend at all, speed plummets to 57 mph. That's a drop of about half.

If only things were as simple as *always swing with the hips*. The problem is that there are an infinite number of such adages. *Always keep your head steady*—check. *Let your weight move forward*—check. *Keep the left wrist flat*—check. Each of these reminders makes us forget that reliability on the course is about removing, not adding. Hidemichi Tanaka didn't master the swing because he broke his wrist at the perfect time. He did so because his movements were smooth and coordinated. His strength came from efficiency and control.

Though this could easily seem frustrating, it should instead feel promising. We're never far away from a perfect swing. Our goal shouldn't be to speed things up, or master some new skill. It should be to carve away our bad habits by slowing things down. We must never swing so fast that we lose control.

How do we do that? It starts by working on our consistency.

It's easy to get the impression from reading scholarly articles on golf that at any given moment, hundreds of golfers are swinging clubs with sensors attached to their backs. With cameras recording every move, these golfers are like lab rats in spiked shoes. In fact, the entire rat species should be happy that they can't play golf, because there's no telling how many experiments there would be in which they'd be enlisted. That being said, let's visit one more study where—you guessed it—golfers had their swing recorded while being monitored by high-tech AV equipment.

So far, we've explored the important role of balance and torque. We've also shown how amateurs swing slower than professionals, which is probably good because these players also lack control. We generally don't miss shots because we're too slow, or we forget to bend our wrists. We fail because we allow our inexperience to screw up what should have been a smooth and steady motion.

This led Justin Keogh of the Aukland University of Technology to ask a question—what about variability?[12] In other words, if your first backswing takes eight-tenths of a second, how long will the next one take? How about the third? We already know that amateurs take longer to strike the ball, but are they also more variable?

The first thing Keogh did was measure the speed of amateur and professional players, but he didn't stop there. He also measured variability, defined as how consistent (or inconsistent) players were on average from one swing to the next. Keogh found that when you look at the raw numbers alone, amateurs and professionals aren't very different. The pros rotate their hips 99 degrees during the backswing, amateurs 100. The pros keep their feet half a meter apart, and so do amateurs. In fact, the only reliable difference between the groups is their variability, and it's drastic. Of the 13 measures collected, amateurs varied more on nearly every measure.

Achieving greater consistency depends on practice and not fixing things that aren't broken. Often we self-diagnose bad hits, looking for which body movement failed us. Yet, odds are that the mistake was simply part of learning. When golfers are asked to identify their bad hits using body awareness alone, they generally fail. One study compared self-reported "mishits" with well-struck balls and found that there were actually no significant differences in the swings themselves.[13] Not only are amateur golfers variable hitters, they don't even know when they got it right. The best that any of us can do is slow ourselves down until every swing is under control.

Hitting a golf ball is difficult. When *USA Today* listed the ten most difficult maneuvers in sports, hitting a straight drive off the tee ranked fourth, behind only hitting a fastball, race-car driving, and pole vaulting. This should help us appreciate just how difficult golf is. Perhaps that's why consistency ranks as one of the top frustrations with the sport. Why shouldn't it be? Studies show that having an unreliable stance width, even if that variability is just 1 percent, is enough to ruin an otherwise perfect shot.[14] With such minor differences having such big effects, who wouldn't get frustrated?

The best we can do is practice, trying to make our swing as replicable as possible. Every body is different, but there's certainly a perfect swing for you. Hidemichi Tanaka got a lot out of his swing, and so can anyone else.

It just takes practice.

READING LIST

Balance and Weight Shifts

[8]Healy, A., Moran, K., Dickson, J., Hurley, C., Smeaton, A., O'Connor, N., Kelly, P., Haahr, M., and Chockalingam, N. (2011). Analysis of the 5 Iron Golf Swing When Hitting for Maximum Distance. *Journal of Sports Sciences*, 29, 1079–1088.

[6]Myers, J., Lephart, S., Tsai, Y., Sell, T., Smoliga, J., and Jolly, J. (2008). The Role of Upper Torso and Pelvis Rotation in Driving Performance during the Golf Swing. *Journal of Sports Science*, 26, 181–188.

[7]McTeigue, M. (1994). Spine and Hip Motion Analysis During the Golf Swing. In A.J. Cochran and M. Farrally (Eds.), *Science and Golf II: Proceedings of the World Scientific Congress of Golf* (pp. 50–58). Grass Valley, CA: The Booklegger.

[5]Robinson, R. (1994). A Study of the Correlation Between Swing Characteristics and Club Head Velocity. In A.J. Cochran and M. Farrally (Eds.), *Science and Golf II: Proceedings of the World Scientific Congress of Golf* (pp. 84–90). Grass Valley, CA: The Booklegger.

[3]Sell, T., Tsai, Y., Smoliga, J., Myers, J., and Lephart, S. (2007). Strength, Flexibility, and Balance Characteristics of Highly Proficient Golfers. *Journal of Strength and Conditioning Research*, 21, 1166–1171.

[4]Wrobel, J., Marclay, S., and Najafi, B. (2012). Golfing Skill Level Postural Control Differences: A Brief Report. *Journal of Sports Science and Medicine*, 11, 452–458.

Consistency

[12]Keough, J., Bradshaw, E., Hume, P., Maulder, P., Marnewick, M., and Nortje, J. (2007). Biological Movement Variability during the Golf Swing. *Paper presented at the 25th Annual Conference of the International Society of Biomechanics in Sports, Ouro, Brazil.*

[13]Neal, R., Lumsden, R., Holland, M., and Mason, B. (2008). Segment Interactions: Sequencing and Timing in the Downswing. In D. Crews and R. Lutz (Eds.), *Science and Golf V: Proceedings of the World Scientific Congress of Golf* (pp. 21–29). Mesa, AZ: Energy in Motion, Inc.

[14]Shan, G. and Zhang, X. (2011). How Tough is it to Repeatedly Hit the Ball in Golf? *Biomechanics in Sports*, 29, 377–380.

Rotation and Kinetic Energy

[10]Anderson, B., Wright, I., and Stefanyshyn, D. (2006). Segmental Sequencing of Kinetic Energy in the Golf Swing, *The Engineering of Sport Six*, 167–172.

Cheetham, P., Rose, G., Hinrichs, R., Neal, R., Mottram, R., Hurrion, P., and Vint, P. (2008). Comparison of Kinematic Sequence Parameters between Amateur and Professional Golfers. In D. Crews and R. Lutz (Eds.), *Science and Golf V: Proceedings of the World Scientific Congress of Golf* (pp. 30–36). Mesa, AZ: Energy in Motion, Inc.

[9]Sharp, R. (2009). On the Mechanics of the Golf Swing. *Proceedings of the Royal Society A*, 465, 551–570.

[11]Sweeney, M., Mills, P., Alderson, J., and Elliott, B. (2011). The Importance of Wrist Flexion and X-Factor in the Golf Swing: A Forward Kinematic Approach. *Biomechanics in Sports*, 29, 945–948.

Swing Power

[1]Okuda, I., Armstrong, C., Tsunezumi, H., and Yoshiike, H. (2002). Biomechanical Analysis of Professional Golfer's Swing: Hidemichi Tanaka. In Thain, E. (Ed.), *Science and Golf IV: Proceedings of the World Scientific Congress of Golf* (pp. 18–27). New York: Routledge.

[2]Plagenhoef, S. (1983). Golf Research Projects. *Paper presented for the International Symposium on Biomechanics in Sports, San Diego*.

Introduction to Business and Economics

Prerequisites: None

Something strange happened at 11 a.m., February 18, 2010. In the course of just minutes, volume on the New York Stock Exchange froze. That is, for a quarter of an hour, stockbrokers across the country stopped trading, and the country's financial backbone turned into a possum playing dead on a busy freeway.

Then, at 11:14 a.m., everything exploded.

The day had started normally, with activity being slow but steady. The afternoon before, Federal Reserve Chairman Ben Bernanke had raised emergency funding interest rates by a quarter of a percentage point, a minor correction but enough to make the news. Still, the move was expected, and the market seemed unconcerned. Then things started slowing. By 11 a.m., the American economy had fallen asleep, though everybody suspected a violent awakening was in the works. They were right. When trading resumed, what had been a modest 100,000 shares traded per minute became six times that amount.

At that moment, Tiger Woods was hugging his mother, having concluded the most difficult press conference of his life.

What had slowed the entire country's stock market wasn't news of a corporate merger or tax hike, but an admission by the world's most famous golfer that he had engaged in marital infidelity. "I want to say to each of you, simply and directly, I am deeply sorry for my irresponsible and selfish behavior," Woods said to the camera, reading from a prepared statement. "I have let you down, and I have let down my fans . . . I do plan to return to golf one day, I just don't know when that day will be."

For those unfamiliar with the scandal, several months before, Tiger Woods had crashed his Cadillac Escalade in the middle of the night just a short distance from his house. An investigation revealed that he'd had a confrontation with his wife, Elin Nordegren, who had apparently chased him from their house with a nine iron. Though Woods asked for privacy, rumors of an affair quickly made that impossible. Next came leaked voicemails from an alleged mistress and rumors of a divorce. By the time Woods finally spoke about the incident on February 19, a speech that ended around 11:14 a.m., fans across the world—even busy stockbrokers—stopped everything just to hear from the man himself.

After the news conference was over, stocks immediately plummeted, especially companies sponsoring the famous athlete. In the end, Nike and Electronic Arts saw their overall values drop over $10 billion. All because of a single news conference.

If it seems hard to believe that a routine news conference could impact an entire nation's economy, think again. Superstitious economists have followed golf for years, many drawing connections that approach ridiculous. When Woods first turned pro, the NASDAQ hovered around 1,100, but less than a year after he won his first Masters, it had already skyrocketed past 1,700. In May 2000, when Tiger was busy winning five of six majors, it set records by passing 5,000. All seemed good until he switched coaches and went on a ten-major losing streak. That's when the NASDAQ tumbled back down to 1,200. Was Tiger responsible?

I doubt it, because by the same logic, you could just as easily call Tom Watson a stocks killer. After all, each of his Masters wins was followed by S&P losses of more than 6 percent. I have no reason to believe Watson had some magic influence over the American stock market, so such correlations are probably spurious, but there's no arguing that golf still has a huge economic impact, especially when it comes to scandals and sponsorship deals. Celebrity endorsements aside, golf and money have had a long and interesting relationship, and in this class, we'll explore the important role money plays in the sport. Let there be no mistake: golf isn't cheap. With the average golfer spending $2,700 per year on the game, with many spending over double that amount, nobody is hitting the links without a few dollars in their pockets. In this class, we'll see how these dollars are being spent, and how money has become an important part of the game.

Golf is not for those without disposable income. Rounds can cost as little as $10, or as much as $300, depending on your ambition. If you live in Kentucky or West Virginia, consider yourself lucky. These are the cheapest places to play according to the National Golf Foundation, the average cost there being about $30. The most expensive state surprises many people—Nevada. There you can play for an average greens fee of $110, though prices range widely. If you want to play at Shadow Creek or Wynn Golf Club, expect to pay several hundred dollars or more. If you're closer to Reno, where vacations are less costly, you're a little luckier. Just don't try to play in the middle of summer.

The most expensive course in America? Well, that depends on the day or season, but near the top of the list has to be Pebble Beach. If you want to enjoy this sprawling 18-hole public course along the coast in Monterey, California, you'd better start saving now. It will cost you over $500 just to tee off, and that's not counting tax or caddie fees (you're not seriously carrying your own bag, are you?).

Golf has an annual economic impact of over $176 billion, supporting just shy of two million jobs in the United States alone. That's a huge number, with only half that amount being spent at the course. The rest comes from tourism, supplies, and even real estate. If you compare the economic impact of all sports, golf comes in higher than such spectator sports as baseball and basketball, and just below going to the movies. That's impressive.

Let's not forget other countries, too. In Japan, the sport's second largest market, over ten million people enjoy the sport, though this is nothing compared to the 1990s. Back then, golf was so popular—and so expensive—that club memberships were traded like stocks, rising and falling with the state of the economy. According to one often-shared story, a Japanese Yakuza (think "mafia gangster," except more badass) once wanted to join the exclusive Koganei Country Club outside Tokyo, offering over three million dollars for a membership. His only problem was that nobody would sell him a spot. The issue wasn't his illicit business, or fear that other gangsters might follow. It was that his offering price wasn't high enough.

Also in Japan is the problem of hitting a hole in one. Most golfers don't worry about such things, despite the tradition of covering your group's bar tab. But in Japan, this tradition also covers greens fees and dinner, which can cost a thousand dollars or more. As a result, many pay for "Hole in One Insurance," which covers the player during such fortunate events, for the modest cost of 50 dollars annually. I have no idea if insurance companies treat handicaps like actuarial tables, but it's fun imagining insurance agents following top golfers around the course, calculating the odds they'll have to pay out before signing on to a policy.

If it feels like the game has become too expensive, know that owning a course isn't cheap, either. The average course requires between 50 and 150 acres, with each hole costing upward of half a million dollars to develop. And that's not even counting the price of the land, which can vary widely. Add in drainage, landscaping, and building a clubhouse, and the investment becomes huge.

Course designers can cost a pretty penny too, especially for the big names. Jack Nicklaus charges up to five million dollars for a signature course, and if that seems ridiculous, know that it's worth it. Studies show that a course by a well-known designer is worth twice as much as one with a lesser name, and four times more than one not designed by an architect at all.

With all these numbers, this is beginning to sound like a math class, I know. That's because it basically is. For course designers, math matters a lot, because without close management, it's easy to go bankrupt. An average course requires roughly 25,000 to 35,000 rounds per year to make a profit, though a lot depends on weather and the economy. For any individual greens fee, about half will go to maintenance, which includes labor and materials. Then another quarter will keep up the clubhouse and other services, such as food. What's left will be spent on salaries and cart maintenance, leaving—if the course is lucky—a small bit to tuck away. Which is important, because a single long winter or rainy summer can make profits quickly disappear.

At least there's plenty of choice. There are private courses and public. There are also semiprivate and nontraditional courses, for example, par-three courses, which can be played with just a wedge and a putter. With so much variety, the closest business comparison in terms of cost and land is the ski industry. Yet, even that is vastly different, since these only run part of the year. Not to mention that for every ski resort, you'll find over thirty golf courses.

The most important thing a golfer should know is that golf courses are generally priced appropriately, though we can all pay attention to how our home course operates. Certain rules are fair, like higher rates for peak playing times and discounted rates for weekday play. Others aren't, like charging rates not matching course quality. One survey by Sheryl Kimes of Cornell University asked several hundred golfers what they thought were fair practices, and the results were interesting.[1] Generally, golfers are willing to pay so long as the price matches the value. They're even willing to incur penalties for missed tee times, so long as the rules are clear. However, some practices are clearly inappropriate, like "airline pricing." This is the process of varying rates depending on when you book, like airlines do for seats. Interested in playing that fabulous new course with the water hazard modeled after TPC Sawgrass? If the course charges an extra $50 to reserve a tee time a month in advance, stick with the local municipal course instead.

Sometimes it's difficult knowing how fairly a course is truly being managed. Take for example tee times, perhaps the most complex problem in golf management. Though the average golf game lasts approximately four-and-a-half hours, or 15 minutes per hole, there's incredible variation. This can make scheduling difficult, as managers need to optimize number of players while avoiding congestion. Complex mathematical models have even been developed to solve the problem, taking into consideration varying group sizes, and as you'd expect, the analyses can be complex.

Which brings us to another study by Sheryl Kimes, this one with Lee Schruben, a professor of industrial engineering from the University of California at Berkeley.[2] They wanted to know if the problem could be solved by watching golfers play at different speeds, but since that seemed like a lot of work, they set up a simulated course on their computer instead. This involved sending thousands of virtual golfers out to play each day for hundreds of days, with spacing between groups varied and carefully measured. Just like real golf, everybody played at different speeds and waited patiently for those in front of them to move on before teeing off. Simulated players who didn't finish by the end of the day had their game cut short.

By controlling the players' environment, Kimes was able to examine all aspects of their play, from length of delays to the number of players finishing all 18 holes. They found that there actually *does* exist an optimal tee-time interval—about 12 minutes. This doesn't mean more players can't tee off in a day, because at shorter intervals, over 80 groups can be squeezed in before sunset. It's just that the club will be so backed up that few will reach the eighteenth hole with any daylight remaining. They'll be frustrated too, because what should have been a four-hour round (actually, a 4.16-hour round, according to Kimes) instead lasts over seven.

So next time you go to the course and see that you're set to tee off at 8:35, between a group of four at 8:28 and another at 8:42, be thankful you're not starting in the late afternoon. You might also want to bring some lunch, and maybe some dinner, too.

We can't blame courses for accommodating as many players in a day as they can, just as we can't blame them for trying to make their business succeed. However, we can learn more about how competitive pricing works. Take for example course quality, so hard to define yet so important. Does a course have any scenic views? Are the fairways maintained properly, without bare spots or grounds under repair? Are greens cut regularly and maintained even during low water? These are the questions that distinguish a regular course from an exceptional one, and also what separates a 30-dollar round—cart included—from one ten times that amount.

Surveys show that as quality of course increases, so does cost at a relatively constant ratio.[3] In other words, the more money a course spends on maintaining its grounds, the more it earns, in roughly equal amounts. Granted, some factors like location, design, and view are beyond a manager's control, but almost everything else can be improved; and when it is, the cost is generally passed on fairly to the consumer. This means that golf may be expensive to play, but we get what we pay for. The vast differences in quality don't represent laziness (on one hand) or desire to gouge the player (on the other). They're simply choices all owners make regarding their personal supply-and-demand curve.

Thinking of golf course maintenance in terms of supply and demand can also help us decide where to take our game. And there are choices. Today, there are roughly 15,000 golf courses in the United States, or about one course for every 21,000 players. If you're like me, you have no idea what that means, so let's see that number visually as a function of time.

From Figure 1, which shows number of golf courses per million

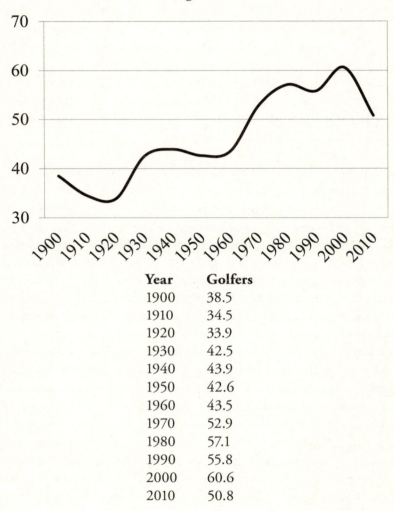

Figure 1

Year	Golfers
1900	38.5
1910	34.5
1920	33.9
1930	42.5
1940	43.9
1950	42.6
1960	43.5
1970	52.9
1980	57.1
1990	55.8
2000	60.6
2010	50.8

people in the United States, we see that there have been three "booms" in the sport. The first occurred in the 1920s, otherwise known as the Roaring Twenties, when dancing, sport, and liquor (despite prohibition) were in abundance. Good times, at least until Jesse Livermore reinvented short-selling stocks and the market crashed in 1929. But that's another book. Next came the late 1960s, followed by the economic boom of the 1990s. We are currently in a golfing recession, with between 150 and 250 courses closing per year. This decline matches a decrease in players, which the PGA says is due to slow play, cost, and overall difficulty of the sport.

In some ways, the boom of the 1990s is responsible for this decline. At the time, developers became obsessed with longer, harder-to-play courses, and so many regular golfers became forgotten. Take for example the relatively new Farmstead Golf Links, which includes a 767-yard final hole covering two states. In other words, it starts in South Carolina and ends in North Carolina. Or take for example the Coeur d'Alene Golf and Spa Resort in northern Idaho, built at the beginning of the 1990s boom and including a floating 14th green. You read right—the green actually floats atop Lake Coeur d'Alene, having been built on a specialized raft. If you're lucky enough to hit the green, you'll need a boat if you want your ball back. Costing three times more than any other green in history, the hole makes the resort's heated golf cart seats and walnut dashboards seem almost pedestrian. Let's face it—though some golfers love such amenities, they're probably not the best way to draw in new participants to the sport.

Regular golfers may sometimes feel overwhelmed by these exotic choices, but at least traditional, public courses are still the majority. Though a select few golfers do play only at high-end resorts, most still frequent locations built in the 1960s and earlier. As a result, most courses have found themselves catering to this core group of players, and their rounds are still increasing. According to one survey, over 80 percent of serious golfers report they still play as much as or more than they did the previous year, with only 11 percent saying their game is in decline.[4] That's why one quarter of all golfers account for more than three quarters of all spending for the sport; people who catch the bug don't give it up easily.

Nowhere is the growing emphasis on playable courses and reasonable prices more apparent than the shift from private clubs to public courses. With initiation fees averaging $21,000 and annual dues over $5,000, private facilities are hardest hit during economic struggle. As a result, they now make up only a quarter of all golfing facilities, down from half in 1970 and almost the entire market 40 years before that. By contrast, public courses are as healthy as ever, as are nonstandard courses, such as par-three courses and those with nontraditional length (for example, fewer than 18 holes). When these facilities are also considered, we see that golf is as strong as ever.

The amazing thing about golf is that you don't even have to play to see its economic impact, especially if you live near a course. Nearly half of the surge of the 1990s was due to planned golfing communities, meaning it's now common to live by a course. And if you do, then you're in luck, because courses can raise a home's value between 6 percent and 12 percent. Still, value depends on location. Just as homes on creeks can ask double the ordinary price, and those with ocean views even more, location by a fairway is key. For every foot your house is away from the clubhouse, value drops roughly $10. That may not sound like much, but it adds up fast. By the time you're a tenth of a mile from a tee box, your home value is lower than normal, not higher, because of increased clubhouse traffic. That can be expensive, especially since one in four families living on a course don't even play once a month.

As we end this class, it's time to return to the man who started things off, Tiger Woods. Though most of us don't play for money, or maybe just small Nassau bets, some live or die by their score. For them, golf keeps their families from starving, so it's worth appreciating just how difficult it is to make a living on the tour. If this is something you're considering, I don't want to ruin your dreams. But I do want you to know that it's almost surely a terrible idea.

Make no mistake, PGA Tour pros play for big money. When Patrick Reed took home the green jacket from his 2018 Masters Tournament victory in Augusta, he earned just shy of two million dollars. That's a lot of money, so much that the player who earns 36th place today earns roughly as much as the winner did in the 1980s. Purse sizes continue growing, too. Yet, this shouldn't encourage you to quit your day job, because of the eighty million golfers in the world, only 245 play the PGA Tour in a season. That puts your odds at about 1 in 326,000. By comparison, that's about the same odds as dying from a fireworks accident. Even if you make one of the other tours, like the Mackenzie Tour of Canada, your chances for advancing to the PGA are about the same as your chances of meeting an eventual life partner on a blind date.

I don't know about your past dating history, but that doesn't make me feel very optimistic.

There's also the problem of competition once you make the tour, which is fierce. On any given weekend, about seventy players compete for a total purse of up to eight million dollars, depending on the event. Except there won't really be just 70 players, because half the field will already be cut. As if that's not enough, the purse won't really be eight million dollars.

Don't get me wrong: when the Masters Tournament says it awards millions of dollars, they're telling the truth. This amount is just distributed rather cruelly. The breakdown follows an exponential decrease function, with prizes dropping quite sharply after first place. Traditionally, first place receives 18 percent of the take, which for a competition like the Masters means close to two million dollars. Second place receives 10.8 percent. Third, 6.8 percent. From there, it keeps dropping rapidly, so that the player who comes in 70th, usually the last to get a cut, might earn as little as $15,000 for making it that far, minus caddie, hotels, and other expenses. If that sounds low, that's because it is, but it's nothing compared to the poor slob who finishes 71st. Though the traditional weekend cutoff for a PGA tournament is 70, if two or more players are tied at 70th, the PGA mercifully lets them all in. Except whoever finishes last is promised nothing at all. He or she is likely to go home empty-handed.

The drop in prize money is especially brutal given the actual distribution of scores. Analysis of PGA scorecards shows that for all tournaments, there's some average score that nearly all players are crowded around. As with any average, there are outliers, and these are the players who earn the big money, or none at all. This means that the wealth is spread differently from skill, with exceptional cases like Phil Mickelson and Dustin Johnson enjoying the lion's share of the rewards. Economists even have a name for this pattern, and it's called the backward-bend of the labor supply curve. For the professionals you see frequently—Mickelson, McIlroy, Fowler—their pay is so skewed, relative to the rest of the field, that money no longer becomes a primary motivator. They actually have a disincentive to play each week. So a player like Tiger Woods probably doesn't care how many millions, or billions, a recent affair might have cost him, simply because the money isn't why he plays. Studies even show that successful players are less likely to enter large numbers of tournaments, compared to the struggling masses, because the payoff isn't worth it. By awarding money so handsomely only to the top players, the PGA is actually reducing the chances you'll see your favorite player on television.

So, the next time you see that Dustin Johnson has just won another tournament, know that many want to be in his place. Also know that Johnson isn't the only one who is celebrating, as his sponsors will see even greater revenue than he will. Even course managers will enjoy the publicity, knowing that lots of people will hit the links the following day hoping to hit that same great shot they just saw on television.

And there's no shame in being one of them.

READING LIST

Course Cost and Revenue Control

Hirsh, L. (1991). Golf Courses: Valuation and Evaluation. *Appraisal Journal*, 59, 1–8.

Judge, M. (1998). An Architect's Name: What's It Worth? In Farrally, M. and Cochran, A. (Ed.), *Science and Golf III: Proceedings of the World Scientific Congress of Golf* (pp. 587–593). Champaign, IL: Human Kinetics.

[2]Kimes, S.and Schruben, L. (2002). Golf Course Revenue Management: A Study of Tee Time Intervals. *Journal of Revenue and Pricing Management*, 1, 111–120.

[1]Kimes, S. and Wirtz, J. (2003). Perceived Fairness of Revenue Management in the U.S. Golf Industry. *Journal of Revenue and Pricing Management*, 1, 332–344.

Rasekh, L. and Li, Y. (2001). Golf Course Revenue Management. *Journal of Revenue and Pricing Management*, 10, 105–111.

Earning a Living on the PGA

Ehrenberg, R. and Bognanno, M. (1990). Do Tournaments Have Incentive Effects? *Journal of Political Economy*, 98, 1307–1324.

Gilley, O. and Chopin, M. (2000). Professional Golf: Labor or Leisure. *Managerial Finance*, 26, 33–45.

Rinehart, K. (2009). The Economics of Golf: An Investigation of the Returns to Skill of PGA Tour Golfers. *Major Themes in Economics*, 2, 57–70.

Scully, G. (2002). The Distribution of Performance and Earnings in a Prize Economy. *Journal of Sports Economics*, 3, 235–245.

Golf Course Management and Industry Growth

Adams, R. and Rooney, J. (1985). Evolution of American Golf Facilities. *Geographical Review*, 75, 419–438.

[4]Latta, M., Taylor, A., Mitchell, M., and Thrash, C. (2007). Retaining Current Vs. Attracting New Golfers: Practices among the Class A Carolinas Professional Golf Association Membership. *Sport Journal*, 10, 1–8.

O'Hara, J. (2002). Golf Participation Growth Feasibility Assessment: Identifying the Growth Potential for Golf Participation and Golf Related Spending. In Thain, E. (Ed.), *Science and Golf IV: Proceedings of the World Scientific Congress of Golf* (pp. 1763–1769). New York: Routledge.

Sheets, B., Roach-Humphreys, J., and Johnson, T. (2016). Turnaround Strategy: Overview of the Business and Marketing Challenges Facing the Golf Industry and Initiatives to Reinvigorate the Game. *Business Education Innovation Journal*, 8, 161–171.

[3]Shmanske, S. (1999). The Economics of Golf Course Condition and Beauty. *Atlantic Economics Journal*, 27, 301–313.

Residential Property Values

Grudnitski, G. (2003). Golf Course Communities: The Effect of Course Type on Housing Prices. *Appraisal Journal*, 71, 145–149.

Nicholls, S. and Crompton, J. (2007). The Impact of a Golf Course on Residential Property Values. *Journal of Sport Management*, 21, 555–570.

Nicholls, S. and Crompton, J. (2005). Why Do People Choose to Live in Golf Course Communities? *Journal of Park and Recreation Administration*, 23, 37–52.

Quang Do, A. and Grudnitski, G. (1995). Golf Courses and Residential House Prices: An Empirical Examination. *Journal of Real Estate Finance and Economics*, 10, 261–270.

Wyman, D. and Sperry, S. (2010). The Million Dollar View: A Study of Golf Course, Mountain, and Lake Lots. *The Appraisal Journal*, 1, 159–167.

Sophomore Year

Congratulations on advancing to the next year of *Golf University*! So far, you've been introduced to topics like physiology, math, and psychology and even learned how factors like money influence the game. Now it's time to move on to more advanced subjects. You're no longer a new student to the sport, so let's delve deeper.

Sophomore year is typically when students get a groove for school and develop a personal connection with the topics that interest them. Fortunately, you already know that golf is something you enjoy. What comes next are topics you probably haven't thought much about: How does playing with partners or in front of crowds influence performance? How do weather and time of day change the way the ball flies or bounces, and why do drives travel farther in the Deep South than in colder climates? Why do beginners learn faster when they model the finish position of the swing, rather than study individual muscle movements?

These are the kinds of questions you will answer your sophomore year, as you transition from new learner to burgeoning expert. We start with a discussion of physics, probably the least understood part of the game. Without understanding concepts like lift or spin, reliable control on the course is unlikely. So let's take a trip to the moon and see just how important these concepts really are.

Physics 101:
Forces and Inertia

Prerequisites: None

Odds are that you'll never play Augusta National Golf Club. Sorry, but it's true, just like you'll never play Oakmont or Shinnecock Hills, either. These clubs are so exclusive that money alone can't promise membership. Augusta doesn't even have an application process; you practically have to wait for one of its three hundred members to die or get thrown in jail. Then, in a few weeks you might get an invitation in the mail.

But probably not.

Still, these aren't the most difficult courses to get into. In fact, there's one course that has been played only once, and by only a single player. Membership has been closed for over 40 years, and cost to play wasn't just high, it was in the millions. That course is the Fra Mauro Country Club, and it's located 240,000 miles away on the south side of the moon.

Many people know that Alan Shepard once hit a golf ball on the moon, but few are aware of how difficult the shot was. Shepard had just finished taking rock samples from a nearby crater, having returned to the landing module to perform routine chores. His golf adventure hadn't been approved by NASA, and he certainly didn't have room to bring a full bag, so he was forced to attach the bottom of a six iron to a soil sample pole. With a golf ball secretly shoved into his spacesuit pocket, he waited for a television camera to be turned on. Then he revealed his intentions.

"In my left hand I have a little white pellet that's familiar to millions of Americans. I'll drop it down."

At this point, Shepard dropped a single golf ball next to his left foot, then looked to the distance for a target. There were no nearby greens, but thanks to eons of meteorite collisions, there were plenty of holes at which to aim. Unable to rotate his torso, Shepard swung back with a single arm as far as he could. Then, when contact came, all that followed were scattered moondust and a buried golf ball.

"You got more dirt than ball that time," Ed Mitchell exclaimed. Mitchell was Shepard's landing partner, and his voice sounded more than a little jealous.

Shepard paused a moment, then tried again. This time he made contact, but it wasn't solid. The ball bounced harmlessly toward the camera.

"That looked like a slice to me, Al," remarked ground control. Shepard was now getting grief from his gallery, too.

Astronauts aren't known for accepting failure easily, so Shepard dropped another ball, this time with conviction. His next hit would go far, he decided. With another one-handed swing, Shepard finally made solid contact, then he watched the ball sail into the distance. Without any air resistance, there was nothing to slow it down, so the ball kept going, and going, with nothing but a tiny bit of gravity to eventually bring it back home.

"Miles and miles and miles," Shepard exclaimed with pride as he watched the ball fade out of sight.

Sadly, the ball didn't actually go miles. The moon is notorious for giving false perspective, and so the ball probably only traveled a few hundred yards. But you can't blame Shepard for his enthusiasm. The ball had remained airborne (or vacuumborne) for seemingly forever before finally falling back to the moondust, by some estimates over half a minute. The sight must have been incredible.

In this chapter, we'll explore the physics of ball flight and what makes a great shot. Most of us will never play on the moon, but with a little knowledge about bounce and roll, you'd be surprised what is possible. Take for example Nils Lied, who once hit a 2,600-yard drive. An amateur golfer and professional meteorologist, he had the advantage of working at the Mawson Research Station in Antarctica, with a nearly endless ice sheet as his fairway. It's not surprising he hit it over a mile. The American sailor Bill Ice had a similar idea, except he took advantage of the Pacific Ocean. Specifically, his chip shot over the Mariana

Trench probably didn't stop before sinking the entire six-mile depth to the ocean floor. It's just a shame he had to take a penalty for a lost ball.

Last, there's the longest golf hit in history, as recorded by Russian engineer Mikhail Tyurin. Like Shepard, his strike took place in space, except he didn't have any moon gravity to deal with. With a single strike off the International Space Station, his drive sped ahead and orbited the planet for several days before making reentry. Physicists believe it traveled close to a million miles before burning up in the atmosphere.

Silly stories aside, we can all use physics to benefit our game, and this chapter starts with the moment of the swing's impact. This is the point where all kinetic energy is transferred from the player to the ball, and since everything stems from that moment, let's explore that half millisecond in detail to see what happens next.

Striking a golf ball is an incredibly violent act. Contact lasts only about 400 microseconds, so fast that the ball is long gone before sound of the strike reaches our ears. In that brief interval, over 10,000 Newtons of force is sent from club to ball, equivalent to the force of gravity on a light car. That's enough to compress the ball nearly half an inch before it bounces back and speeds away.

The amazing thing about this contact is that it determines everything the ball does next. Weather and ground conditions matter, but they don't add any new energy. They only alter already established spin and velocity. Everything else depends on this moment of collision, with even minor changes having huge impacts on where the ball goes. This makes the game difficult for beginners, but also satisfying for experts. These are the players who know how to use subtle changes to their advantage, because the same forces that cause a beginner to slice allow a professional to fade or draw.

The most important issue for most players is efficiency, which determines how well energy is transferred from body to ball. In a perfect world, every bit of the club's momentum translates forward ball velocity, but we don't live in a perfect world. Several factors reduce ball speed, including squareness of contact, angle of approach, and even the club itself. One very complicated mathematical analysis found that hitting the ball with maximum efficiency would require a club length of 16 feet.[1] That's not going to happen for many reasons, just one being that they don't make golf bags that tall. Add to that the inevitable loss from compression and sound, and no hit will ever be perfect.

But this doesn't mean that we can't be as efficient as possible, starting with solid contact. When the swings of amateur and professional golfers were examined using high-speed cameras, scientists observed that amateurs transfer about 67 percent of their kinetic energy from club to ball.[2] That's a lot of waste. Professionals don't do much better, transferring only about 5 percent more. Which begs the question—where does the other energy go?

One answer is that energy comes in many forms. Forward ball speed is what's called translational kinetic energy, the same for any object traveling forward through space. But there's also rotational kinetic energy, which leads to turning about an axis. When a strike isn't head-on—and we'll discuss what that means soon—some energy becomes rotational, leading to spin. This translates to slices and hooks, and unless it's done on purpose, a lot of energy is wasted.

To understand how contact with the ball matters, it's worth seeing the process visually. This brings us to the most important concept in golf, at least in terms of physics—the D-plane (see Figure 2).

The D-plane is actually a very simple way of looking at how two primary forces influence the path of the ball. First is the direction of the clubface itself. In physics, any vector perpendicular to a plane is called its "normal," so here we're talking about a vector normal to the flat clubface. If we hit the ball with the club turned 45 degrees away from the target, this will be the direction of your translational force.

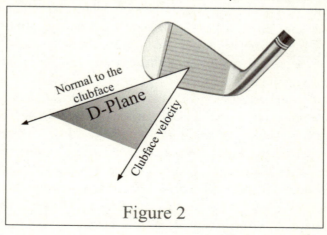

Figure 2

The ball will start traveling perpendicular to the clubface, and you'll be stuck searching through weeds to avoid a costly penalty.

The second factor is the direction of the swing itself. This is different from the face of the club, because now we're talking about the path of the club. If that direction is out-to-in, then the track of the club will be to the left of the target, assuming you're a right-handed golfer. This has the greatest impact on rotational force, meaning spin. Ironically, the spin works counter to the club's path, so if you swing out-to-in (or to the left as you're facing your target), this imparts clockwise spin looking down on the ball, curving the ball to the right.

The plane formed by these two vectors is called the D-plane, named for the Greek letter *delta* representing the direction of movement. The benefit of thinking about ball contact in terms of the D-plane is that it helps us recognize our errors. If a drive starts by going to the right, the clubface was probably open (i.e., right-facing) when it hit the ball. However, if the ball starts curving back to the left, your swing path was probably inside to out. It can be a challenge recognizing these paths in real time, though it's much easier when things go drastically wrong. Most beginners start off with a bad slice, because we naturally want to swing out-to-in. This leads to lots of spin, and much of the ball's energy is wasted. Then we waste our own energy apologizing to players on the adjacent fairway.

Every possible ball flight path can be traced back to these two factors, assuming we make solid contact with the ball. That last assumption is significant, because we don't always make solid contact. It's easy to hit the ball off-center of the clubface, and that can affect spin, too. When impact occurs on the club's toe, the outermost part of the clubface, the ball can roll off rather than fly straight ahead. That's because the club's center of mass doesn't lie directly behind the ball, and the result can be disastrous.

For the moment, though, let's assume we have a square hit. Even then, there are many different paths a ball can take, depending on clubface direction and swing path. There are pulls, pushes, slices, and hooks, and all are a direct result of how we use the D-plane. Professionals know each path well and can adjust their feet at setup to maximize flight path depending on the situation.

Once the ball is in the air, there's nothing we can do to influence its path, but complex forces will still be at play. As Alan Shepard found on the moon, ball flight depends on more than the direction of the hit. Spin and lift play a big role, so long as you're on a planet with an actual atmosphere. The 19th-century Scottish physicist Peter Guthrie Tait was the first to question why golf balls fly farther in solid air, compared to a vacuum. Before Tait, it was almost universally accepted that spin was bad. Everybody knew that our atmosphere slows harder hits, but nobody knew why balls spend so much time airborne before returning to the ground. At times, they even seem to ignore the effects of gravity. The answer, Tait concluded, had to do with vertical spin. When the top of the ball rotates toward the player, a low-pressure pocket is formed on its surface. Just as aircraft wings create low pressure along their tops, the result is lift.

Even when contact with the ball is solid, some spin is inevitable. That spin occurs because all clubs are built with angled faces, and this angle produces vertical spin. This spin provides lift, staving off gravity and keeping our hit from being a worm burner.

It's important to recognize that gravity isn't the only vertical force acting on the ball. Just like an airplane wing is lifted by faster air along its surface, the ball is also pulled up by this lower pressure. And it can have a big impact on distance. Let's say a ball leaves the clubface traveling about 160 miles per hour. That sounds fast, and it is, but remember that this is the exact moment of impact. Soon the ball will slow down, losing a third of its speed within only a second. Still, at launch, it will be traveling with a spin of roughly 3,000 revolutions per minute. That spin can create enough lift to increase launch angle to 25 percent. So even though gravity is trying to pull the ball down, spin more than compensates. Eventually, gravity will win, of course, but even then, the fall of the ball will be softened. By the time the ball hits the ground, over 60 percent of the spin will remain. By comparison, if you're lucky, forward speed is a third of when the ball left your club.

All this means that although Shepard's hit on the moon was impressive, his ball would have still traveled higher on Earth.

We can't blame Shepard for being optimistic about hitting in a vacuum. After all, air does slow the ball down. It just lifts it up, too. The reason golf balls have irregular surfaces is they smooth their paths through the air. The physics behind the interaction between ball and air is complex, the primary influence being something called a separation layer. This layer forms when smooth surfaces travel through fluids like our atmosphere. Due to the way air hugs these surfaces, eddies form in their wake, creating drag. To overcome this drag, it helps to create a turbulent layer along the object's surface to discourage such eddies from forming. This is why golf balls have dimples, because they produce turbulence. On airplane flights, turbulence may be a nuisance, but on the golf course, it saves our drives.

The speed at which this turbulent layer forms depends on an object's surface, and for golf balls, it's about 55 miles per hour. Balls traveling at least this fast experience half the drag than if they were perfectly smooth. If golf balls didn't have dimples, drag would increase significantly based on their speed. This interaction between lift and drag is also why it's so difficult knowing what loft of driver is best. For Alan Shepard, the decision was simple, since in a vacuum the optimum loft is 45 degrees. Not so on Earth. This is why researchers from *Golf Digest* conducted their own experiment using a variety of golfers and drivers.[3] Through extensive testing, they found that unless you swing pretty fast (say, 85 mph or more), you're best off with a high-loft driver. At these lower speeds, we don't get enough lift to raise the ball from the ground, so a driver of 16-degree loft or so is needed. At faster speeds, this becomes less of a problem, and as a result we're better off with drivers closer to 11 degrees. That's because getting the ball into the air isn't as important as ensuring its energy is spent going forward. These findings match results using simulated clubfaces and complex mathematical models, suggesting that altitude tends to take care of itself.

As P.G. Tait found over a century before, distance and lift work together so energy isn't wasted.

As Rory McIlroy approached the 10th hole of Congressional Country Club in Bethesda, Maryland, just hours away from winning the 111th U.S. Open, there wasn't much doubt regarding the day's outcome. He had started the morning eight strokes ahead of his closest competitor, and a couple of birdies had already provided an additional buffer. All he needed to do was reach the green on the simple par three, but great winners don't play it safe. He'd shot aggressively so far, having put behind him all memories of a disastrous Masters Tournament a few months before. This was the time for finishing everybody off.

At first, McIlroy's tee shot looked long. But then it hit the ground and bounced and . . .

Then it stuck. Having already traveled 218 yards, the ball bounced once, then gripped the grass like it was clinging for dear life. It didn't hesitate or trickle forward. Instead, it gripped the green and rolled almost immediately backward, directly toward the hole. Though it didn't go in, stopping about three inches away instead, it still meant one more birdie for the record books and a memory that's still talked about today. By the end of the day, McIlroy held eleven U.S. Open records, including lowest score (268) and most holes under par (16).

McIlroy's ball stuck the ground so firmly because of spin, which does more than simply lift our drives. It also allows professionals to stick balls ten feet or more past the hole, then see near-miraculous finishes. What can't it do?

Once the ball finishes its flight and hits the ground, things get complicated. What happens next depends not just on ball speed, but the nature of the ground itself. For driver hits, relatively flat clubfaces mean that rotation will be minimal. As a result, the ball lands and bounces, then comes to rest after friction takes its toll. The length of roll depends almost entirely on the ground's surface and the angle of the ball's landing, with steeper landings and softer grass meaning less roll. For iron shots, it's a different story. For those hits, spin is much greater, and there are dozens of things the ball can do.

We've all seen professional shots on television that seem impossible. Somehow the ball lands five feet past the hole, then suddenly it rolls backward toward the cup. These shots are made possible by high-lofted clubs, which give the ball lots of spin to grip the surface. That grip can either slow the ball down or completely turn it around depending on spin and compactness of the turf.

Mathematical analyses have shown that as long as the ball has a certain amount of backspin, about 7,400 rpm, it will always roll backward.[4] The only question is how many bounces it takes first (usually only one). For firmer greens like those on the professional circuit, it will immediately roll backward. For softer ones, it might bounce twice or more, but still only two factors matter—the firmness of the green and rotation of the ball. Fortunately, modern clubs have deep grooves to help make spin possible, and therefore, with a little luck, anyone can look like a pro.

Now that the ball is finally on the green, all that's left is to put it in the hole. Again, it might seem like the physics should be simple—just putt the ball toward the hole and let gravity do the rest. Again, life isn't that simple.

No matter how well you aim, if you hit the ball too hard, it isn't falling in the hole. Balls can lip out, bounce off the opposite rim, and even enter the hole and spin back out. Just ask Joe Daly, who experienced all three during the 2000 Q-School PGA Tournament. Only a single stroke away from earning his PGA Tour card, the golfing equivalent of winning the lottery, all he had to do was make a five-foot putt. Unfortunately, he somehow bounced his ball off the opposite rim, saw it circle below the rim, and then saw it pop back out again. Odds are he could try the same shot a million times and not recreate the error. Sadly, life doesn't give second chances, and he failed to qualify. How fast is too fast? Well, most physicists agree that any ball rolling greater than five feet per second (about 3.5 mph) has zero chance of falling in the hole. Physics can be cruel.

The term "capture" refers to how most pros think about the hole's influence because that's what it does—capture the ball. For a ball to go in, it must reach the hole's capture radius. Under the best circumstances the capture zone is 2.125 inches, the diameter of the hole on all regulation courses. In reality, the radius is much smaller. As ball speed increases, so does momentum's inclination to pull the ball around the cup and back out again. Even at speeds of just one foot per second, the effective capture radius is cut by over 25 percent. The best any player can do is have speed be near zero by the time the ball reaches the hole. Just be careful not to hit *too* softly. An underhit ball has zero chance of going in, regardless of how lucky you are.

To see how putting speed affects accuracy, and how slope matters too, consider Figure 3. You'll notice that the horizontal axis represents aim relative to the cup.[5] The vertical axis represents the ball's speed, and shaded areas represent the size of the capture zone. From the graph, we see that slower hits are always better so long as they reach the hole. We also see that downhill putts are easiest because the capture zone area is largest. Most players hate downhill putts because misses leave difficult follow-ups, but technically they're easier because gravity pulls the ball toward the cup. By contrast, uphill puts are extremely unforgiving. Their capture radius hardly changes depending on speed, making uphill putts twice as cruel in terms of gravity being stubborn, compared to the alternative.

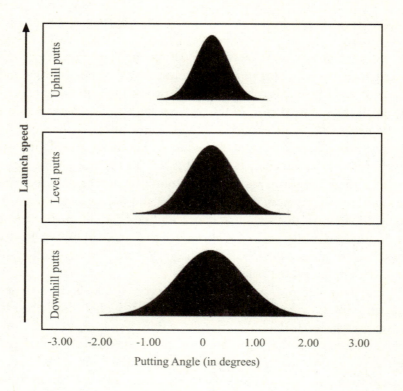

Figure 3

Returning to the issue of speed, it's a mistake to assume that every putt should stop exactly at the hole. If we did that, half our strikes would leave the ball short, assuming you're not a machine. Pros call this phenomenon *Never up, never in*. We're best always giving the ball enough speed to reach the hole, but not much more. How far past the hole should we aim? Dave Pelz, putting guru and founder of the Dave Pelz Golf Schools, recommends seventeen inches, which is a good rule, but that's still a shortcut. We can actually use math and physics to calculate optimum speed, and the solution is more complicated.

First, we must recognize that the cost of missing depends on from where you are putting. For a long putt, let's say 20 feet or more, your chance of success is small unless you're someone like Phil Mickelson. At the same time, the opportunity for an overhit and nasty follow-up shot is significant. In these cases, we don't need to aim past the hole because there's little to gain. Conversely, for a short putt of five feet or less, we might as well give the hit something extra, because if we miss, the follow-up *should* be a gimme. That's why we should always aim two feet past the hole, multiplied by the odds of making the putt.[6] Do you make five-foot putts half the time? If so, try giving the ball enough roll to stop roughly one foot past the cup. You'll seldom come up short and gain over a stroke a round compared to your math-challenged friends. It's a simple matter of risk management.

Finally, before we conclude this physics class, it's worth reexamining the idea of aim. So far, we've discussed aim as if it were straightforward—simply orient the putter toward the hole and swing. Sadly, even that isn't so simple. For the full swing, both clubface angle and swing path have their effects. Here's where we discuss our final study in physics, one performed by Jon Karlsen of the School of Sport and Health Sciences in Stockholm, Sweden.[7] He examined expert golfers holing out from about thirteen feet using ultrasound sensors to capture each swing. From his analysis, he studied three factors, the first being the putter's face angle. Second was the path of the swing, and third was the contact point with the club. Did the same rules about clubface angle and swing path apply for putters as they did for the driver?

Not surprisingly, they did. Karlsen found that the most important factor affecting putting was the face angle of the club. Like with driver hits, if the club's face isn't directed toward your goal, bad things happen. Karlsen found that 80 percent of the variability in the ball's roll depended entirely on aim. Swing path of the putter was a distant second factor at 17 percent, largely because spin doesn't matter much on a putting surface. The remaining 3 percent depended on how solidly the player strikes the ball.

This finding is particularly interesting because it means that direction of the clubface matters most for where the ball goes. Except there's a catch. Karlsen observed something else too, something both discouraging and enlightening. He found that we all aim relatively consistently, even if the ball doesn't go in the hole. The average variation of aim from stroke to stroke was only half a degree, meaning that we should sink over 90 percent of our putts from 12 feet. But we don't. Even PGA players miss from that distance over twice as often. What gives?

Quality of greens certainly matters, especially after a full day of play. Wind and other environmental factors such as dew and debris have their impact, too. But most important is the reading of the green. Studies show that even professionals guess wrong on their aim by a degree or more on average.[8] That's almost twice as much as Karlsen's swing-to-swing variability. This alone translates to missing the hole over half the time at ten feet. Add slant and difficulty reading distance, and long putts become almost a matter of chance. Even putts of five feet will miss a third of the time, simply because lining up the putt is so hard.

This means that the enemy isn't Newton's universal laws of motion. It's luck and our own perceptive skills. Physics may be an exact science, but some things are simply beyond our control.

Physics is messy, like golf. If it weren't, the sport wouldn't be nearly as fun.

Reading List

Aerodynamics of Golf Balls

Bearman, P. and Harvey, J. (1976). Golf Ball Aerodynamics. *Aeronautical Quarterly*, 27, 112–122.

Choi, J., Jeon, W., and Choi, H. (2006). Mechanism of Drag Reduction by Dimples on a Sphere. *Physics of Fluids*, 18, 18–21.

Lorenz, R. (2006). *Spinning Flight: Dynamics of Frisbees, Boomerangs, Samaras, and Skipping Stones*. New York: Springer.

[3]Stachura, M. (2003, November). Why everybody needs to try more loft—and that means you! *Golf Digest*, 12–15.

Stengel, R. (1992). On the Flight of a Golf Ball in the Vertical Plane. *Dynamics and Control*, 2, 147–159.

Winfield, D. and Tan, T. (1994). Optimization of Clubhead Loft and Swing Elevation for Maximum Distance on a Golf Drive. *Computers and Structures*, 53, 19–25.

Bouncing and Ground Conditions

Penner, A. (2002). The Run of a Golf Ball. *Canadian Journal of Physics*, 80, 931–940.

[4]Roh, W. and Lee, C. (2010). Golf Ball Landing, Bounce and Roll on Turf. *Procedia Engineering*, 2, 3237–3242.

The D-Plane

Jorgensen, T. (1994). *The Physics of Golf.* New York: American Institute of Physics.

Miura, K. (2003). Mapping Clubhead to Ball Impact and Estimating Trajectory. In Thain, E. (Ed.), *Science and Golf IV: Proceedings of the World Scientific Congress of Golf* (pp. 490–500). New York: Routledge.

Miura, K. and Sato, F. (1998). The Initial Trajectory Plane after Ball Impact. In Farrally, M. and Cochran, A. (Ed.), *Science and Golf III: Proceedings of the World Scientific Congress of Golf* (pp. 535–542). Champaign, IL: Human Kinetics.

Putting

[6]Hoadley, B. (1998). How to Lower Your Putting Score without Improving. In Farrally, M. and Cochran, A. (Ed.), *Science and Golf III: Proceedings of the World Scientific Congress of Golf* (pp. 186–192). Champaign, IL: Human Kinetics.

Holmes, Brian. (1991). Putting: How a Golf Ball and Hole Interact. *American Journal of Physics*, 59, 129–136.

[8]Karlsen, J. and Nilsson, J. (2008). A New Method to Record Aiming in Golf Putting—Applied to Elite Players. In D. Crews and R. Lutz (Eds.), *Science and Golf V: Proceedings of the World Scientific Congress of Golf* (pp. 395–407). Mesa, AZ: Energy in Motion, Inc.

[7]Karlsen, J., Smith, G., and Nilsson, J. (2008). The Stroke Has Only a Minor Influence on Direction Consistency in Golf Putting among Elite Players. *Journal of Sports Sciences*, 26, 243–250.

[5]Penner, A. (2002). The Physics of Putting. *Canadian Journal of Physics,* 80, 1–14.

Sources of Swing Power

[2]Hashimoto, H., Nozawa, M., Yoshioka, S., Otsuka, M., and Isaka, T. (2012). The Energy Conversion Efficiency of Drive Shot in Female Professional and Amateur Golfers. *Paper presented at the 30th Annual*

Conference of the International Society of Biomechanics in Sports, Melbourne, Australia.

Penner, R. (2003). The Physics of Golf. *Reports on Progress in Physics*, 66, 131–171.

[1]White, R. (2006). On the Efficiency of the Golf Swing. *American Journal of Physics*, 74, 1088–1094.

Sociology 101:
Crowd Behavior

Prerequisites: None

Golf is a social game, and I don't just mean beer buddies and side bets. I mean that the sport reflects society, and as the world changes, so does golf.

This influential role of golf dates back to the fifteenth century and King James II of England. At the time, the monarchy was especially weak, with threats of invasions bringing a constant need for archery practice. However, commoners and nobles alike were discovering this new sport called golf. The game was nothing like it is today, with caddies and clubhouses, but the distraction was enough for the king to take notice. He promptly made the sport illegal.

This didn't keep the nobility from playing themselves, of course. Mary Stewart, otherwise known as Queen of Scots, was well known for her golfing ability and even lived at a cottage near St. Andrews just to play. King James IV of Scotland was also known to swing a club on his frequent visits to Perth or Edinburgh. In short, while kings and clergy were busy telling everybody to avoid the game, especially on the Sabbath, they didn't have much problem partaking themselves.

Though this prohibition was eventually lifted, golf still evolved to become a game for the wealthy and privileged. One reason was money, as most people simply couldn't afford the equipment. Spare time was another factor, as was access to playing facilities, though commoners certainly enjoyed the game, too. They just didn't get much access.

Flash-forward several hundred years to the United States and what's called the "match of the century." When Bobby Jones and Walter Hagen squared off in the winter of 1926, golf couldn't have been more divided. Both players represented distinct populations: Jones was business royalty, the son of a wealthy lawyer from Atlanta who played only for love of the sport; by contrast, Hagen came from working-class German stock in Rochester, New York, with little money at all. Had the story been written by Hollywood, Hagen would have been the tough underdog, and Jones a snobby brat. Fortunately, this was not Hollywood.

It turned out that Jones was a rather likable fellow, and a decent golfer, too. In just a few years, he would even achieve a grand slam, winning all four major championships in a single season with style and class (more on this later). But at the time, Jones represented a dying breed—the gentleman golfer. Jones took no money from his victories, nor did he want it. As a true amateur, uninterested in the life of a touring professional, he played for the same reason kings and queens played before him—pure joy. Everybody saw that a change was coming, and soon professionals would compete for money and fame. The sport would become a business, and players like Jones would be left far behind. The question was how soon.

The match between Jones and Hagen was intended to be a friendly competition, but national attention quickly turned it into something more. Hagen already had seven major championships under his belt, yet socially he was an outcast. Not allowed to eat in clubhouse cafés, he was forced to bring his own food during tournaments, even the ones he won. In 1920, while competing in the British Open, he wasn't even allowed in the clubhouse locker room. Not afraid of conflict, he promptly had his chauffeur park his Austin-Daimler in front instead and used that as a changing space. Not surprisingly, this did not go over well with the establishment.

The competition, which consisted of 72 holes split between the two players' home courses, was supposed to be a close, hard-fought match. Instead, it wasn't even close. Hagen easily led by eight holes halfway through, and by the final round, the result of the match was a foregone conclusion. Hagen ended by sealing the win with 11 holes to spare, earning $10,000, with half going to charity and the rest spent on an expensive pair of cufflinks. He gave these to Jones as a gift. "Walter, you've ruined me twice!" exclaimed Jones. "First, there was the licking, and now I'll be busted the rest of my life trying to buy shirts to fit this jewelry."

Hagen had literally invented a new profession, career golfer, and the sport would never be the same. Removal of social barriers wasn't far behind. Soon after, Hagen would again be declined access to a clubhouse, except this time his playing partner was the Prince of Wales and future King of England. The club was welcome to dismiss Hagen, the prince claimed, but at the cost of his patronage. The Royal St. George's Golf Club was forced to recognize that their organization was nothing without that first word in its name, and Hagen was allowed inside. Discriminatory practices slowly eased, and Hagen was welcome to eat or change clothes at any clubhouse he liked.

Golf has always had an unusual place in society. It's a sport for both professionals and duffers, played in solitude and surrounded by coaches and spectators. Unlike with team sports, opponents are only so in terms of math, as number of strokes alone determines the winner. No matter your skill level or degree of competitiveness, there's always an option for you.

In this chapter, we'll review the social aspects of the game, from the role of spectators to the impact of betting. Although your ball is yours alone, we're never really alone on the course, and soon you'll see how the views and opinions of those around us affect the game.

Social sciences are termed *soft sciences* because they're abstract and difficult to measure. But this doesn't mean we can't take them seriously. Studying social interaction requires theory building and careful definition of terms. When we discuss golf, two terms are especially important, and we'll frame the rest of this chapter based on how they are constantly balanced. They are civility and discipline.

To see how civility and discipline define golf, let's take the obvious route and delve into Neo-Kantian twentieth-century European philosophy. I know, so predictable, but two philosophers in particular would have been great golfers if given the chance. Their names are Norbert Elias and Michael Foucault, and they have more to say about the sport than you'd expect.

Norbert Elias was a Prussian Jew best known for writing about the growth of civilized society. Though focused mostly on manners and etiquette, he had a lot to say about competitive sports, too. Sports like golf are important for society, he claimed, because they replace brutish or violent behavior with rule-based rivalry. Golf requires discipline, etiquette, and strict rules. Just as society's goal is to perfect civility, golf's goal is to develop the perfect swing, and by becoming better people (and better golfers), we develop a more enlightened society. By Elias's thinking, it was only a matter of time before the social barriers separating Jones and Hagen were broken. After all, men and women are measured by their character, and maybe golf score, not inherited sociocultural standing.

Michel Foucault, the French philosopher and notorious fan of turtleneck jumpsuits, cared less about civility than he did about discipline. When we play golf, we set goals and follow a specific learning pattern. This may include hiring instructors or reading books like this one. We also accept the basic rules of the game, like the fact that golf bags contain only 14 clubs and out of bounds markers indicate a return trip to the tee box. Players are expected to behave appropriately and wear the required clothing, not to mention pay generous greens fees to play. This makes golf like a test, one that is passed not by scoring a hole in one, but by showing up early for a tee time and dressing for play in something other than ratty jeans.

Civility and discipline are good ways of viewing golf because they show how the sport has grown under competing processes. On one hand, it's a demanding mental game that requires extreme self-control, not to mention confidence and a positive attitude. That's why millions flock to the sport, as a means to improve both physically and mentally. On the other hand, golf expects something from its participants too, like keeping proper score and respecting time-honored rules. In this manner, golf is appealing and demanding at the same time, a good way to test character.

Golf is popular largely because it's so steeped in rules and tradition, and that's why it's the official sport of business. As referenced by the *New York Times* in the 1990s, one private survey sponsored by the Hyatt Hotels Corporation found that 93 percent of business executives believe the golf course is an excellent place to network with clients. A third said they've made significant deals on the fairways, and 12 percent said that golf is more important than sex.

Still, we don't need to be a CEO to play. Many rounds are played casually or while alone, though even then there are usually bystanders present. This begs the question—do we play differently while being watched? The short answer is that for professionals, it doesn't matter. Jonathan Guryan of the University of Chicago Booth School of

Business took thousands of scorecards from professionals on the PGA Tour to find average scores.[1] Then he examined what happened when each player was paired with others of different skill levels, and it turned out that playing partners hardly matter at all. Regardless of who you play with, your driving distance, iron accuracy, and putting scores stay roughly the same. When issues like weather and course condition are factored in, the effect is practically nil.

This is surprising, since it makes golf one of the few activities that *aren't* affected by peers. Having a college roommate with a high GPA raises our own. Even grocery scanners and fruit pickers are more productive when surrounded by high-performing peers. What gives?

It's important to recognize that we don't always play the same with strangers. We may be fine when we play alongside another random player, but working closely with that partner changes things entirely. Take for example golf caddies at the Western Open and Augusta National tournaments.[2] For a long time, these events required players to use only local caddies, requiring normal partners to stay at home. As a result, competitors were forced to work with someone unfamiliar, and the cost was significant. When all other factors were teased out, having a new caddy cost an additional 0.6 to 0.8 strokes per round at Augusta. Not a huge impact, but enough to matter for people making a living. The effect was twice as large for the Western Open.

It's possible that professionals are especially immune to pressure, but I doubt it. Also skeptical was Yoshifumi Tanaka, an economics professor at Tezukayama University in Japan, who set up an experiment.[3] First, he built an artificial green with a target 13 feet away. Then, he asked a mix of amateurs and pros to putt as closely to the target as possible, sometimes in front of an audience and sometimes alone. Success was measured using average distance to the target, and player anxiety was monitored using attached heart rate monitors. Last, arm and club movements were recorded using reflective markers.

Tanaka found that both amateurs and professionals were affected by the spectators, even when their game didn't show it. Everybody showed an increased heart rate of about ten beats per minute in front of the spectators. Swing mechanics changed too, with decreased backswing and slowed motion of the forward stroke. Still, overall performance remained strong. Players of all skill levels putted just as well under pressure, something Tanaka attributed to another factor—money. Subjects were told that if they performed better in front of the audience, they could earn a significant reward, the equivalent of twenty dollars. Players of all levels more than compensated for the pressure.

Tanaka's study showed that being watched in and of itself doesn't have to hurt our game. But it also raised another issue—betting. His subjects had two reasons to feel pressure: the embarrassment of missing in front of others and the opportunity for reward. Nearly all of us have wagered something on the game. Surveys show that half of all golfers have bet $100 or more on a match. A third of us have bet so much we refuse to admit the actual amount. Yet, it's still not clear what impact this has on our play.

Overall, it appears that amateurs aren't helped by betting. In one study, groups of golfers bet five dollars on whether they could make challenging chip shots and putts, earning a reward when they shot well and losing money when they didn't.[4] When money was on the line, these players landed the ball over two feet farther from the target on the chip shots. They did only slightly better for the putts. By contrast, when a professional golfer was put through the same test, the money had no effect. (One would hope so! A professional who lets money influence his or her play isn't keeping a playing card for long.) By contrast, most amateurs better watch out for side bets.

So, pressure has its effects. Elias wouldn't have been surprised, since psychological and social pressures belong together like peanut butter and jelly (not his analogy . . . sorry, Norbert). Only when we work within these challenges do we grow into our own agency.

Turning next to Foucault and discipline, we see that one thing is never tolerated when it comes to betting on the course—cheating. Cheating in any form will lose you partners, and probably your club membership, too. Researchers have surveyed golfers and found that frequent betters have elaborate yet consistent rules about appropriate behavior.[5] Gamesmanship is not only tolerated, but encouraged. Betting of any amount, and in whatever form, is also accepted. However, failure to properly report your handicap will get you expelled from the group. So will stretching the rules of the sport, like taking a drop when not granted one by the rulebook. In one of golf's most famous stories, such devotion to honor and discipline cost one player the 1925 U.S. Open Championship. That player was none other than Bobby Jones, who was setting up to shoot for the green on the 11th hole. Nobody else was around to see, but as he addressed his ball, it moved slightly. Barely enough to notice, and certainly not enough to create an advantage. Still, the rulebook is clear—any ball movement during the address brings a one-stroke penalty. Jones assessed himself a stroke, despite several protestations, and promptly lost the tournament in overtime play. That single stroke had cost him the U.S. Open. When praised for the classy move, Jones's response would have made both Elias and Foucault proud—"You might as well praise me for not robbing banks!"

All this talk about civility and discipline might give the false impression that professional golfers are special. Not only do they keep calm under pressure, they don't care who is watching them, either. Except they do. It might not always be apparent in the lab, or when money is on the line, but they're not immune to social pressures. To show how, all you need to do is look at their scorecards.

The effect of social pressure on professional golf is best seen in terms of the home-court advantage. English soccer teams score one third of a goal more per game when playing at home compared to away. Teams in the NBA score three more points at home, and baseball teams earn a quarter of a run extra. Surely you'd expect golfers to have the same advantage. But they don't.

Before exploring why golfers get no such advantage, it's worth looking more closely at the home-field advantage. Yes, it's true that baseball teams play better at home, but the full story is complicated. Though home teams in the World Series win most of their opening games (60.2 percent), they also lose more often when there's pressure to finish off their opponent (40.8 percent). Home NBA teams win most of their opening games too (70.1 percent) but then lose the final home game (46.3 percent). Playing on a home field is helpful, but when thoughts turn to the goal of winning, the trend reverses and pressure overwhelms.

The same goes for golf. Though we'd expect golfers in their home countries to have an advantage for events like the U.S. or (British) Open, they don't. In fact, they have a disadvantage. Analysis of scores of local players during the British Open shows that they perform worse when playing at home, particularly in the fourth and final day of competition.[6] Like professional baseball and basketball players, when professional golfers need to finish off opponents at home, their scores falter, in their cases to the tune of about two strokes a match.

It's hard to say why golfers perform worse in front of home audiences. Maybe it's because attention turns to the competition itself, rather than to performance. Perhaps that's why players partnered with Tiger Woods score on average half a stroke worse per round than normal, because he's so intimidating.[7] That number is highest when the pairing is in the final round of a tournament, because then it's nearly impossible to avoid thinking of the end goal. Playing next to an elite competitor makes us forget that the goal is to achieve the lowest score, not to beat another person.

So, it turns out that competing for money, playing with Tiger Woods (arguably golf's most intimidating competitor), and performing for large audiences are all bad. This might seem discouraging, but it shouldn't be. Each has a common effect on the player—they distract him or her. When we think about outcomes, rather than the play itself, we falter.

Sport does not exist separate from its surroundings. When Jackie Robinson started at first base for the Brooklyn Dodgers in 1947, no black player had ever played Major League Baseball before. A few months later, military segregation ended, and not long after so did segregation in schools. When Katherine Switzer raced in the Boston Marathon under the gender-ambiguous name "K.V.," other racers actually tried to rip the number from her racer's bib. But she finished anyway, and soon after came Title IX, which promised equal federal money for women in college sports.

When Water Hagen won 11 majors despite being a working-class man, even kings took notice. Soon, the idea of golf being a "gentlemen's only" sport was history. Now clubs are open to everybody. When Bobby Jones called a foul on himself during the 1925 U.S. Open, players took the rules seriously but still considered the move exceptional. Who gives up the opportunity to win a major sports championship just for the sake of a silly rule?

The answer is that true golfers do. As the world changes, so does golf, and maybe it's good that these aren't independent things after all.

READING LIST

Civility and Discipline in Sport

Collinson, D. and Hoskin, K. (1994). Discipline and Flourish: Golf as a

Civilising Process? In A.J. Cochran and M. Farrally (Eds.), *Science and Golf II: Proceedings of the World Scientific Congress of Golf* (pp. 620–625). Grass Valley, CA: The Booklegger.

Effect of Partners, Spectators, and Betting

[4]Bordieri, J., Dixon, M., Loukus, A., and Bordieri, M. (2013). The Effect of Financial Contingencies on Golf Performance. *Journal of Applied Sport Psychology*, 25, 92–105.

Brown, J. (2011). Quitters Never Win: The (Adverse) Incentive Effects of Competing with Superstars. *Journal of Political Economy*, 119, 982–1013.

[2]Coate, D. and Toomey, M. (2012). Do Professional Golf Tour Caddies Improve Player Scoring? *Journal of Sport Economics*, 1, 1–10.

[7]Connolly, R. and Rendleman, R. (2009). Dominance, Intimidation, and Choking on the PGA Tour. *Journal of Quantitative Analysis in Sports*, 5, 1–5.

[1]Guryan, J., Kroft, K., and Notowidigdo, M. (2009). Peer Effects in the Workplace: Evidence from Random Groupings in Professional Golf Tournaments. *American Economic Journal: Applied Economics*, 1, 34–68.

[5]Smith, G. and Paley, R. (2001). Par for the Course: A Study of Gambling on the Links and a Commentary on Physical Skill-Based Gambling Formats. *International Gambling Studies*, 1, 102–131.

[3]Tanaka, Y. and Sekiya, H. (2010). The Influence of Audience and Monetary Reward on the Putting Kinematics of Expert and Novice Golfers. *Research Quarterly for Exercise and Sport*, 81, 416–424

Home Field Disadvantage

Baumeister, R. and Steinhilber, A. (1984). Paradoxical Effects of Supportive Audiences on Performance under Pressure: The Home Field Disadvantage in Sports Championships. *Journal of Personality and Social Psychology*, 47, 85–93.

[6]Wright, E. and Jackson, W. (1991). The Home-Course Disadvantage in Golf Championships: Further Evidence for the Undermining Effect of Supportive Audiences on Performance Under Pressure. *Journal of Sport Behavior*, 14, 1–10.

Earth Sciences 101: Geology, Weather, and Terrain

Prerequisites: None

Not many par threes measure over 300 yards. In fact, there's only one, and it's located in the Limpopo Province, South Africa.

About five hours from Johannesburg, the course is one of the most remote on the planet. To reach the tee box, first a player must navigate the resort's game reserve, staying clear of the many hippos, rhinos, and leopards that call it home. From there, it's a short helicopter ride to Hanglip Mountain at an elevation of 1,400 feet, where you'll find the Signature Course's famed "19th hole." At the tee box, the player takes aim at an Africa-shaped green a quarter mile below, hoping that the winds don't catch the ball during its twenty-second fall. Those who get a hole in one—and it hasn't happened yet—earn a million dollars and bragging rights as most extreme golfer on the planet.

One of the great things about golf is that every course is different, and every hole brings its own unique challenges. The seventh through tenth holes at the Brickyard Crossing Golf Course in Indiana are located inside the Indianapolis Motor Speedway. Players there have to skip these holes whenever there's a race, or else the term *golfing hazard* takes on a whole new meaning. The Prison View Golf Course in Angola, Louisiana, isn't just maintained by inmates at the local penitentiary, it's inside the maximum-security prison itself. Playing requires a full background check applied for at least 48 hours in advance. Then there's Nullarbor Links in Western Australia, which stretches between the towns of Kalgoorlie and

Ceduna, a distance of 848 miles, making it the longest in the world. Each hole is in a different town along the route, and though players are allowed to drive between holes, doing so on the fairways will earn immediate disqualification. You might also want to watch out for crows on the back nine; they'll steal your ball if you turn your back.

Golf is a great way to see new places. It's also a good excuse for being outdoors and experiencing nature. Anyone who has played the Old Course at St. Andrews knows it's completely different from Pebble Beach, which is completely different from Shinnecock Hills. Each of these locations is special because great courses don't just blend in with their landscapes, they become part of them. A well-designed course will always make you feel like you're part of the surroundings.

In this chapter, we'll explore how location always plays an integral part of the golfing experience. If helicopter rides and speeding race cars don't provide enough of a challenge, there are always unique weather conditions. In other words, no two games are alike, and in this class we'll see why.

Pebble Beach may be gorgeous, but it still has its share of nasty weather. The Pro-Am held annually in February is particularly notorious for hail, fog, and torrential rain. The Kapalua Plantation Golf Course in Maui, Hawaii, is known for wind, with gusts over 30 knots quite common. Still, these courses are nothing compared to the TPC Louisiana, home course of the Zurich Classic, played annually outside of New Orleans, thanks to a three-legged alligator named Tripod.

Nobody knows how poor Tripod lost her front right leg, or why she only shows up for crowds. But if there's a tournament to play, with lots of stray legs wandering near water hazards, you can be sure she'll make an appearance. In 2013, she even made a break across the 12th fairway during the first round of the tournament, approaching a rules official before returning to her home water hazard. One of the most fun aspects of golf is the unpredictability. Whether it's alligators or wind, steep cliffs or surprise water hazards, the future is never certain. And nothing is less certain than the weather. Though the TPC Classic is best known for Tripod the alligator, and perhaps the parties that follow on Bourbon Street, Louisiana's heat and humidity are probably more relevant to golf. All golfers know that weather has a huge impact on how a ball travels. Still, few recognize why.

Humidity is one of the most poorly understood influences because it's so complex. Most people think that damp, humid days mean shorter hits because the air is heavier with water, but not true. To be technical, the molecular weight of dry air is 29 grams per mole. That doesn't mean much to me either, except that an equivalent amount of water weights 18 grams. That's a third less than air's weight, meaning that balls actually travel farther on humid days, up to a yard or two. It just feels like they fly worse because we're so hot and sticky that everything feels like a chore.

Just because humidity means little in terms of driving distance, this doesn't mean we can ignore the air. As any golfer who has teed off in Denver knows, thin atmosphere helps. The longest NFL field goal in history belongs to Matt Prater, who knocked the ball 64 yards at Mile High Stadium. Not far behind him are Jason Elam (63 yards) and Sebastian Janikowski (63 yards), who also made their records in the Rocky Mountain State. So it shouldn't be surprising that golfers get an advantage, too. But how much?

In general, you can expect a good drive to travel ten yards farther in Denver than in New Orleans, simply because the Crescent City is located 5,000 feet closer to sea level. Greater elevation means less dense air, which is also why balls travel farther in warm air than cold. Cold air is thick, and as a result, balls carry less distance in the winter compared to summer, a difference of 1.3 yards for every 10 degrees.

Wind is another factor that changes day to day, and it's easy to see firsthand. Everybody has hit a great drive into a strong headwind, only to see it die prematurely. Though the effects of wind depend on everything from ball speed to club angle, in general you can probably expect 15 fewer yards on a decent drive for every five miles per hour of wind. So, if you normally strike the ball 300 yards off the tee, expect to come up short by about 10 percent against 10 mph gusts. Tailwinds are more complex. That's because two factors interact, the first being the extra push of the wind, urging the ball farther on. The second is loss of lift. This second issue isn't just a problem for golfers; it matters for airline pilots, too. When US Air Flight 1016 approached Charlotte, North Carolina, on July 2, 1994, everything appeared normal. Storm clouds around the airport had forced the pilots to make an instrument-based approach, though no one was worried—a much smaller Fokker

100 had just landed on the same runway moments before. But when the McDonnell Douglas DC-9 approached for landing, everything fell apart. Forward speed stalled. Pilots no longer were able to maintain direction. In the end, 37 people died because a severe tailwind had stalled the aircraft, crashing it into the ground.

Stalled drives are nothing compared to stalled airline disasters, but the physics behind them is the same. More wind behind our backs means less lift. One very complicated analysis of tailwind effects found that at winds of about 30 mph, we start losing driving distance, despite the extra push.[1] Granted, few of us are playing in hurricane winds, but now we have multiple reasons to stay inside. Odds are your drives will carry a dozen yards shorter or more, assuming you don't blow away first.

Yet, weather isn't the only thing making our golf days unpredictable, as course design matters, too. Prominent designers like Robert Trent Jones or Pete Dye are often treated like DaVinci and Michelangelo because their works are unlike any other. These courses take on personalities of their own by becoming one with their environments, which is why an inspired design for one location might be oddly mismatched for another. However, certain design elements are universal, and we can all appreciate the art when we see it.

The first type of course all players should recognize is a links course. This is the most misunderstood term in golf because so many locations use it incorrectly. By definition, a links course is one located at the sandy junction of earth and sea. It has undulating topography and few trees, and though wind isn't required, it's rare to play along the coast and not feel a stiff breeze. The term originated in Scotland, where heather and gorse are more plentiful than pines or maples and sand is a given. Playing on links courses requires a special set of skills, including an ability to hit the ball low. A high hit is sure to catch the wind, and that's seldom good. Being able to play difficult lies helps too, as uneven land and loosely maintained fairways are common. Links courses are seldom found anywhere but Great Britain, though some designs along the Great Lakes or Oregon dunes meet the criteria.

In the United States, parkland courses are far more common, which are defined by tree-lined fairways and frequent ponds and bunkers. These also lead to greater variety of design, with wide variations in aesthetics and strategy. Courses can emphasize costs for mishit shots, benefits for exceptional ones, or strategic play to avoid low-probability hits. They can also take on "freeway designs," which are long and straight with emphasis on distance. Many accentuate aesthetics, with waterfalls and perfectly manicured bunkers that look like they're never even seen an offshore wind.

Players who recognize what kind of course they're playing have an advantage because they don't fall for the design's traps. A course designed to penalize mistakes will call for conservative play, while one that favors risks can be played more aggressively. Freeway courses shouldn't be attempted without control of your slice, while one emphasizing aesthetics should encourage us all to stop and enjoy the scenery. Playing our best doesn't just require reading each lie. It requires reading the intention of the designer, because only then can you recognize the benefits and challenges of each type of play.

Recognizing the challenges imposed by the environment is important for course designers, too. You wouldn't try designing a parkland course along the beach, any more than you'd develop a links-style course in Oklahoma. When David McLay Kidd began walking the sandy dunes of Southwest Oregon, trying to decide where he'd place the greens for Bandon Dunes Resort, he didn't start with a design idea and then shape the environment around it. He worked the opposite way. First, he tore out the gorse, and then he walked the land. A lot. He studied and got to know each bump of the land personally, then went about designing his fairways around what was already there. The result was a true links course over five thousand miles from the British Isles. Several more courses would follow, along with an array of awards, all because he started with what the land gave him.

"I'd like to think that when someone plays a golf course that I've done, they have a sense of the golf course fitting into that natural landscape," said Kidd when interviewed afterward. "It doesn't feel like it was engineered into it. Bandon looks and feels like it belongs, that it fits into that landscape."

This variety of designs sometimes makes it difficult assessing a course's difficulty, but fortunately, the USGA has measurements for that. They're called course and slope ratings, and they represent relative difficulty for scratch and bogey golfers, respectively. Course ratings are straightforward and fall between 67 and 77. That's the average score a scratch golfer should expect to play given that course's challenges.

The slope rating is more difficult to interpret and represents the relative drop in performance for a bogey golfer. Higher slopes mean that the location has special difficulties not affecting most scratch golfers, but that can wreck an amateur's day (e.g., lots of bunkers or avoidable water hazards). The term "slope" represents slope of the line graphing the relative difficulty for these types of players, rather than physical slope of the course, though difficult courses can have slopes, too (and alligators, and cliffs, and anything else to make your day a challenge).

While the average slope of a course ranges from 55 to 155, players don't need to understand the math of how these numbers are calculated. However, they should be able to quickly look at a location's course and slope rating and know what to expect.

From Table 1, we see that a lot can be learned about a course without even seeing a fairway. Location A is probably of normal difficulty for all players, but Location B is particularly tough for those of normal skill levels. For that course, we might expect plenty of bunkers and water hazards close to the tee, no problem for scratch golfers but a terror for everybody else. Location C is difficult for everyone, so it's probably long and technical, which is why both scratch and bogey golfers find it difficult.

Another thing to recognize about course and slope ratings is that they affect everybody differently. There are almost as many playing styles as players themselves, though some variants are common. Take for example the "Steady Eddy." This represents about 12 percent of the golfing population, those players who consistently hit with fine

	Course Rating	Slope Rating
Location A Average difficulty for all players.	72	113
Location B Plenty of water hazards close to the tee, reachable by most players in regulation.	72	145
Location C Difficult for all players. Long and technical.	75	140

Table 1. Sample courses with different course and slope ratings

accuracy but never exceptionally far. If you're like me and play with an older parent, you know what I mean; twice a week, I walk nine holes with my 74-year-old father, who can land the ball on a dollar bill from a hundred yards but couldn't clear a water hazard to save his life (sorry, Dad, but you know it's true). He simply doesn't hit far, and as a result, slope ratings are his nemesis. He never gets the handicap strokes he deserves because his style of play is especially hurt by otherwise routine challenges. Which is good for me, because at a dollar a game, I've almost earned enough money so far to enjoy a Denny's breakfast.

In stark contrast to the Steady Eddy is someone called the "Wild Willy." This is me, because I can hit long, but I never know where the ball will actually land. This describes about 8 percent of golfers, and we get a benefit from slope ratings, because we play like scratch golfers in terms of distance and avoiding fairway traps. But in other ways we're far from scratch golfers, because with every tee shot there's no telling which fairway we'll hit.

So far, we've talked about wind and humidity. We've discussed weather and slope ratings. But we haven't discussed the most important environmental factor at all—the course itself. By that I mean the things we interact with directly, like grass and sand.

Players can benefit a lot from getting to know the materials used to construct the course. Mostly this means turfgrass, which does more than look pretty. The type of grass a course uses on its greens and fairways has an immense impact on the bounce and roll of the ball. One comparison of putting on five different types of turfgrass found variations of up to 25 percent in rolling distance. A putt that travels five feet on *Poa Annua* one day might travel over six on *Agrostis Capillaris* the next.

The average player isn't going to bother learning all kinds of turfgrass—indeed, the average course superintendent isn't, either—but we can all appreciate the variety. We can also recognize that subtle differences can lead to big effects. Over the course of a 14-foot putt, rolling friction will vary up to 10 percent between initial strike and the hole, due solely to differences in grass length and density. This means speed can be erratic, and a perfect putt in one direction might be disastrous in the other. A big part of this variation is due to natural fluctuations in the grass and the grain. This is the direction grass "leans" as a result of the most recent cut, with putts made against the grain rolling up to 15 percent shorter than in the opposite direction.

One solution is to ask your course superintendent which direction he or she mows on the green. And when the laughing stops, you can move on and remind yourself that it's just a game.

Still, there's something special about knowing that greens must be cut to an eighth of an inch to remove any effects of grain. Truly exceptional courses, the ones charging triple-digit greens fees, know this, and that's why they're so expensive. It's not easy maintaining greens that short. It's also not easy keeping fairways healthy enough to get you that extra bounce off the tee. Augusta National Course uses Bermuda grass on its fairways because it can be mowed very closely, almost like carpet, and it doesn't burn in the southern heat. Brandon Dunes uses a variety of western grasses, including fescue and bent, which lead to unpredictable bounces and rolls. This is exactly the kind of game you'd expect on the windy Oregon coast.

As if grain and turf type aren't enough, there's also the issue of time of day and traffic. Sun and trampling feet can take a toll on grass, particularly on the green. In one expansive study of golf greens conducted by researchers from James Madison University, rolling distances on the green were measured in the morning and afternoon over multiple days.[2] They wanted to know if time of day influences roll, and not surprisingly, they concluded that it does. Balls tended to roll fastest in the morning, right after the grass had been cut, which is why professionals like teeing off early. Once the days progressed, however, everything fell apart. A seven-foot putt one day became an eight-foot putt the next. One day the ball rolled seven inches farther in the afternoon compared to the morning, on another it rolled a full foot shorter. As the saying goes, grass hates both heat and feet, and it's nearly impossible to guess how the land will react.

Grass isn't the only surface on a course, either. Sand is the nemesis of many players, and it comes in almost as many varieties. The USGA states that sand should be between 0.25 and 1.0 millimeters (mm) in diameter, with most granules 0.5 mm or less. This size ensures proper cohesion and firmness, though don't bother bringing a ruler to the bunker—size is only part of the equation (insert your own joke here). Shape of the sand actually matters more, with coarse and angular particles providing firmer surfaces. This is the kind of sand on which you want your ball to land, because it's more likely to bounce or roll it away. By contrast, spherical particles tend to bury balls, leaving what are called *fried egg* lies. These are balls that dig below the surface, leaving only the top of the ball visible. Nobody wants that.

It's easy to talk about the course like it's some independent, separate entity. However, courses don't exist in isolation. They're like people, and how each behaves depends on how we treat it. Learning to read their challenges is part of the fun; after all, a missed putt is never the green's fault. It's our failure to judge that slope when we took aim. We don't play simple, uninteresting locations, because that defeats the purpose. Golf is such a mental game because we enjoy recognizing each designer's obstacles and then overcoming them.

This is the most important relationship you'll have on the course—with the land itself—and nowhere is this more apparent than green reading. Guessing the slope and roll of a putting surface is incredibly difficult, and good designers know this well. That's why they place challenging slopes exactly where the player wishes they weren't. This is especially cruel for amateurs, as they're the most foolishly optimistic about their reading abilities. Studies show that beginning golfers can't even accurately gauge the slope of the ground immediately below their feet; one study had novices stand upright while holding the putter vertically, as if using the plumb-bob technique to read a green.[3] Half weren't even able to stand vertically from the slope, much less read the angle of their putter. This error was enough to cause three inches of aiming error on a four-and-a-half-foot putt—enough to miss the hole completely.

The biggest problem most players have with reading greens is underestimating breaks. Dave Pelz, master of putting and the only person to get away with writing a book called *The Putting Bible*, found that players typically estimate breaks to be only 25 percent of their true value. This causes the ball to roll below the hole and catch any downhill slopes. The problem is so bad that amateurs continue to repeat the mistake even after making it on the same green moments before. For some reason, we hate aiming anywhere but the hole, and we pay the price.

One reason for this persistent error is how we use our eyes. When looking at downhill slopes, we tend to gaze at the top of the hole. This leads us to focus on the hole itself rather than the aim line and consequently underestimate the break. Players of all skill levels are guilty of this error, even professionals. To study these errors in judgment, Jon Karlsen and Johnny Nilsson of the Norwegian School of Sports Sciences took forty-three near-scratch golfers and measured these errors for themselves.[4] Each player attempted shots of between 7 and 63 feet while recording accuracy and consistency between shots. It turned out that green reading determined 60 percent of the players' success. That means nearly two-thirds of our struggles have nothing to do with the stroke itself, only our judgment. This was followed by technique, which determined 34 percent of our errors. That left only 6 percent due to green inconsistencies. Granted, a 6 percent error is enough to miss most putts, but it's just a drop in the bucket compared to our inability to judge a green's slope correctly. Reading greens is difficult, and most of our errors happen before we even strike the ball.

Playing golf is hard, but so is maintaining a course. Course superintendents work diligently to maintain their courses, and even then regular use takes its toll. From golf carts to spiked cleats, every time we play, we change our environment a little bit. Success means recognizing these effects and working with them. It also means studying the course's design and taking a moment to appreciate the unique challenges each hole presents. If every course were the same, the sport wouldn't be nearly as fun. Like making new friends, sometimes getting to know a course means building a relationship that lasts a lifetime. Because that's what playing a golf is, building a relationship with a course.

That relationship deserves respect. It's why we play the game.

READING LIST

Course Construction

Doak, T. (1992). *The Anatomy of a Golf Course*. New York: Lyons & Burford.

Hurdzan, M. (2005). *Golf Course Architecture: Evolutions in Design, Construction, and Restoration Technology*. New York: Wiley.

Knuth, D. (1990). A Two Parameter Golf Course Rating System. In A.J. Cochran (Ed.), *Science and Golf: Proceedings of the First World Scientific Congress of Golf* (pp. 121–134). New York: E&FN Spon.

Sheckelford, G. (2003). *Grounds for Golf: The History and Fundamentals of Golf Course Design*. New York: Thomas Dunne Books.

Strawn, J., Barger, J., and Rogers, J. (2011). Earth as a Medium: The Art and Engineering of Golf Course Construction. In S. Braun (Ed.), *Engineering Earth: The Impact of Mega-Engineering Projects* (pp. 1159–1190). New York: Springer, 2011.

Grass, Sand, Roll, and Bounce

Baker, S., Cole, A., and Thornton, S. (1990). The Effect of Sand Type on Ball Impacts, Angle of Repose and Stability of Footing in Golf Bunkers. In A.J. Cochran (Ed.), *Science and Golf: Proceedings of the First World Scientific Congress of Golf* (pp. 352–357). New York: E&FN Spon.

Baker, S. (1994). The Playing Quality of Greens. In A.J. Cochran and M. Farrally (Eds.), *Science and Golf II: Proceedings of the World Scientific Congress of Golf* (pp. 409–418). Grass Valley, CA: The Booklegger.

Canaway, P. and Baker, S. (1992). Ball Roll Characteristics of Five Turfgrasses Used for Golf and Bowling Greens. *Journal of Sports Turf Research Institute*, 68, 88–94.

Engel, R., Radko, A., and Trout, J. (1980). Influence of Mowing Procedures on Roll Speed of Putting Greens. *USGA Green Section Record*, 18, 7–9.

Foy, J. (2005). Grain on the Brain: Along with Putting Green Speeds, the Effects of Grain on Ball Roll Receive Too Much Television Air Time. *USGA Green Section Record*, 43, 36–37.

Hubbard, M. and Alaways, L. (1998). Mechanical Interaction of the Golf Ball With Putting Greens. In Farrally, M. and Cochran, A. (Ed.), *Science and Golf III: Proceedings of the World Scientific Congress of Golf* (pp. 429–439). Champaign, IL: Human Kinetics.

[2]Pelz, D. (2002). Diurnal and Temporal Variations of Green Speed. In Thain, E. (Ed.), *Science and Golf IV: Proceedings of the World Scientific Congress of Golf* (pp. 713–720). New York: Routledge.

Green Reading

[4]Karlsen, J. and Nilsson, J. (2008). Distance Variability in Golf Putting Among Highly Skilled Players: The Role of Green Reading. *Annual Review of Golf Coaching*, 1, 71–80.

Lier, W., Van der Kamp, J., and Savelbergh, G. (2010). Gaze in Golf Putting: Effects of Slope. *International Journal of Sport Psychology*, 41, 160–176.

[3]MacKenzie, S. and Springs, E. (2005). Evaluation of the Plumb-Bob Method for Reading Greens in Putting. *Journal of Sports Sciences*, 23, 81–87.

Pelz, D. (1994). A Study of Golfers' Abilities to Read Greens. In A.J. Cochran and M. Farrally (Eds.), *Science and Golf II: Proceedings of the World Scientific Congress of Golf* (pp. 180–185). Grass Valley, CA: The Booklegger.

Wind and Weather

Hunter, I. and Feland, B. (2003). Effect of wind resistance on the distance of a drive in golf. *Poster presented at the Southwest American College of Sports Medicine*, Las Vegas, NV.

[1]Stengel, R. (1992). On the Flight of a Golf Ball in the Vertical Plane. *Dynamics and Control*, 2, 147–159.

Premedicine: Fitness and Conditioning

Prerequisites: Premedicine: Kinematics and Human Anatomy

When Christopher Smith approached the 17th hole of the 2009 Arrowood Classic, played just north of San Diego, he didn't have time to mull over his tee shot. He had already been on the course for 49 minutes. Time was running out.

With the sky open and cloudless, and cool breezes rolling in from the Pacific, Christopher Smith should have spent the moment savoring the scenery and gorgeous weather. That's how most of us play, slowly and with frequent breaks to appreciate the time away from work. Smith plays a slightly different game, though. He still swings at little white balls with sticks, but for him it's a race, too. On this particular day, that race wasn't just against a clock, because Tim Scott, a former high school classmate and fellow speed golfer, waited ahead of Smith on the 18th hole. Scott had just birdied the seventeenth hole, and with the same amount of time on his clock. For Smith to catch up, he needed some good luck. Fast.

Speed golf is a growing phenomenon, now with national championships and regional clubs around the world. It follows the same rules as the regular version, with the goal of shooting the lowest score possible. The only difference is that playing time is added to score (one minute per stroke), and players don't have to remove flags during putts to conserve time. Players also carry fewer clubs, since they must sprint between holes with a modified bag in tow. This can present a problem, as Smith discovered while looking upon his 187-yard par three.

Normally he would use a 5-iron for this distance, but there wasn't one in his bag.

His only choices were a wood and a 6-iron. Wisely, he chose the 6-iron and came up slightly short.

Clearly, speed golf isn't for everyone. Few of us shoot par golf, and even fewer do so in under an hour. Which makes Smith's record of a 65-shot game in 44 minutes so amazing. For that game, he carried just six clubs—a driver, four wood, putter, wedge, and two irons. Not only do you need incredible endurance to play, but flexibility is important, too. The goal is to balance speed and accuracy, and now confronted with a bogey on hole 17, Smith was running out of both strokes and time.

One challenge of speed golf is that you never know whether you're in the lead or not. The pace is simply too fast. The best a player can do is keep swinging and running, and that's what Smith did. After retrieving his ball, he immediately sprinted ahead and teed up for his final drive. Then he was running again. Though he didn't know it, his opponent had just finished his round with a score of 69 in 52 minutes. This meant that Smith had to birdie to win and to do so at full sprint.

After his third shot, Smith found himself only a few feet from the hole, having made an amazing approach shot from a hundred yards. This left him 40 seconds to reach the ball and knock it in. There was no time to collect his breath or savor the moment. Before he knew it, Smith was knocking the ball in with several seconds to spare. He won the match with a score of five under par in 54 minutes, earning him a rather impressive trophy and the title of Speed Golf Champion.

Speed golf is a great option for those who want to get in better shape, though you don't need to be as dedicated as Scott to see benefits. He's golf's equivalent of Jack Nicklaus on steroids, a PGA golf instructor who runs marathons in less than three hours. For the rest of us, simply walking rather than riding the cart is a good alternative.

In either case, golf is a great way to stay fit and healthy, even if we don't do it at a full sprint. In this chapter, we'll see why.

Nongolfers are often surprised by how much exercise the sport provides. Even if you're not Christopher Smith, playing 18 holes can be a great workout. Golfing a full round without riding in a cart requires just over 10,000 steps, the minimum recommended daily number by most doctors. This translates to a distance of over five miles, burning up to 2,000 calories. Even playing while riding in a cart burns about 1,300.[1] That's not bad at all.

Still, burned calories are a poor way of measuring exercise, because our hearts need to be stressed to see benefits. That's why Timothy Sell and two other scientists from the University of Pittsburgh had a single average golfer play three games, each under different levels of exercise.[1] The first was while riding in a cart, the way most people play. The second was while walking but with a caddie carrying his clubs, and the third was carrying the bag himself. The bag was a normal weight, with 13 clubs, and the course was a standard 6,600 yards.

If finishing a round in under an hour sounds unusual, imagine doing so while attached to a portable telemetric metabolic system. That means wearing a face mask covering the mouth and nose (which allows for a full analysis of caloric expenditure and oxygen use), along with a heart rate monitor. From these instruments, the researchers were able to assess actual energy burned, along with changes in heart rate and oxygen use.

Doctors recommend moderate-intensity exercise three to five times a week. That corresponds to pushing our hearts to between 55 percent and 70 percent maximum capacity. For speed golfers like Smith, who compete at a near sprint, almost the entire match will be spent at the top of this range. However, Sell and his colleagues found that walking a course, even without racing, raises heart activity within this range two thirds of the time. That's 50 percent more oxygen consumption compared to riding a cart. Having a caddy leads to only a slight reduction in oxygen consumption.

If that's not enough reason to contemplate walking instead, consider another study of 30 golfers, all monitored by a similar apparatus.[2] It showed that most golfers can enjoy two hours of heart-beneficial exercise just by putting away the cart for a single match.

The type of course we play matters a lot, too. For example, golfers walking a flat course might get only minimal heart exercise, while those on hilly courses might spend the entire match enjoying beneficial cardio exercise. The same goes for playing in hot climates. Interestingly, in terms of playing ability, carts don't help our scores at all. In fact, there's some evidence that walking actually improves scores. So it might be worth parking the cart for a game just to see how it feels.

If you Google "Is golf a sport?" some pretty strange results come up. Most are blogs written by people with too much spare time and an unusual hatred for knickers and polyester pants, and not surprisingly they generally fall within the "No, it isn't" category. Still others offer thoughtful commentary. The current leading result is a list of reasonable arguments in both directions, and the primary reasons against are exactly what you'd expect—it doesn't involve running, so it can't be a sport. Even most dictionaries are against us, with the Macmillan, Oxford, and Merriam-Webster dictionaries all calling it a "game." When the Supreme Court ruled in *The PGA Tour vs. Martin* that walking is not an essential part of golf, claiming that disabled golfer Casey Martin could play with a cart (more on that later), golf's fate was sealed. If a game doesn't even require walking, how can we also call it a sport?

Don't ask this question to golfers, though. If golf isn't a sport, then how is Tiger Woods universally recognized as one of the richest athletes of all time? And how can the Associated Press have awarded female golfers "Athlete of the Year" honors 24 times, nearly a third of all awardees? Now that golf is part of the Olympics again, after a 112-year hiatus, isn't it hard to call golf *only a game*?

For me, the clearest evidence of golf being a sport is the impact it has on our bodies. Though there are exceptions, golfers are generally fit. Low-handicap players have greater hip and torso strength, as well as better flexibility in their hips, shoulders, and chest. They can bench press more than nongolfers and are stronger in their back, shoulders, and legs. They also have stronger arms, and apparently longer ones too, up to an additional 4 percent in length from shoulder to wrist. Except for arm length, these differences are most likely due to exercise and training, as extra strength and flexibility help us on the course. In fact, playing only a couple times a week can have a big impact on the body. When over 50 previously sedentary golfers were encouraged to increase their play to twice a week, their muscle and aerobic performance significantly improved, and so did their flexibility.[3] They lost on average three pounds and removed almost a full inch off their waist size. They even improved their HDL ("good cholesterol") levels, thus reducing risk of heart disease.

Though we don't always associate professional golfers with extraordinary fitness, being in shape has huge benefits for our game. Just look at Camilo Villegas. When Villegas was a freshman player at the University of Florida, he weighed only 138 pounds, and almost none of it was muscle. His body fat was at 12 percent and he found himself the shortest-hitting player on the team. Realizing he'd never make it in the PGA without some work, he started an exercise routine that would make the characters from *Rocky* proud. First came weights, then cardio, then yoga and pilates, and eventually he gained over twenty-five pounds of muscle and lost almost two-thirds of his body fat. His body wasn't the only thing to benefit either, because his golf game changed too, and soon he found himself with over ten million dollars in prize money from the professional tour. As icing on the cake, in the 1990s, he also won "player of the decade" honors in his home country of Colombia, and in 2006, *Golf Digest* named him sexiest player on the tour.

"Without fitness, I wouldn't be on Tour. No doubt about it," Villegas claimed later. "It's absolutely central to my success."

The important role of physical fitness has led many trainers to develop exercise programs to improve both health and golf score, and the results have been promising. Speed golf is always an option, of course, but I'm talking about more practical programs focusing on upper body and core strength. Strength exercises like bench presses, shoulder presses, and abdominal crunches have all been shown to increase clubhead speed, which leads to longer drives. When those exercises emphasize motions similar to those of the golf swing, for example plyometric exercises focusing on power (twisting the body while holding a medicine ball is a good example), benefits increase even more. One study found that an eight-week program led to an eleven-yard increase in driving distance.[4]

To see the benefits of a regular exercise routine firsthand, let's examine one training program in detail, as conducted by Brandon Doan.[5] As a doctoral student at Ball State University in Indiana, he took sixteen experienced golfers and administered an 11-week program emphasizing both strength and flexibility. Each performed 90 minutes of exercise three times a week, starting with trunk strengthening. Then came resistance training, followed by stretching exercises. After the training, subjects took a variety of tests to assess changes in their physical fitness ability, along with improvements in golfing skill.

Nearly every measure of strength, power, and flexibility improved after the training, generally between 10 and 20 percent. Subjects squatted 13 percent more weight, threw a medicine ball 20 percent faster, and rotated their bodies 15 percent farther than before. They also swung the club faster, enough to increase their driving distance over five yards. These results were impressive, as was the increase in club control, but what really impressed Doan was the subjects' improvement in putting ability. Before training, subjects missed 15-foot putts by an average of just under a foot. After the training, they were three inches closer.

This improvement in putting ability likely came about because exercises don't have to target specific swing motions; just being in better shape helps. That's why speed golfers like Christopher Smith spend so much time with cardiovascular training, in addition to their swing, because efficient bodies lead to better swings. It's also why stretching before taking to the course is so important, because it loosens our muscles and warms them up.

To understand the importance of warming up before exercise, perhaps it's best to start with a specific example—Rory McIlroy. Before he plays, he always starts with a specific routine designed to get his body ready for the test to come. First, he arrives to the course about an hour early and hits a few dozen chip and pitch shots. Then he moves to the bunker, where he hits a bag of balls from the sand before taking a stroll to the driving range. Once there, first come wedges, then short irons, then finally the driver, and with each swing, he slowly increases his power to constantly ask more of his body. Only at the end does he work on putting, and not for very long.

In case you're wondering, this is *exactly* the warmup you want to use, assuming that you have the time. As someone who plays for millions of dollars every week, McIlroy definitely has the time.

Fewer than half of all golfers use a warmup routine before play, and even that number may be optimistic. Though 30 percent of golfers claimed to stretch regularly before approaching the first tee, when scientists actually observed those same players, few actually did what they said.[6] Most just took a few air swings while at the first tee, usually two or fewer. When scientists secretly observed more than a thousand golfers for their warmup activities, fewer than a hundred stretched in a way that helped their game.[7]

Stretching doesn't just loosen us up; it prevents injury, too. We'll describe injuries in a future class, but for now it's worth knowing that golfers who don't warm up are three times more likely to get injured within the next year. The same goes for visiting the range, even if it's just light practice. If that isn't enough, know that warming up helps your swing, too. When golfers were trained to use a consistent warmup routine for five straight weeks, they showed a 24 percent increase in clubhead speed.[8] That's the difference between a swing of 80 miles per hour and one over a hundred.

The kind of stretching we use is key, and not just any form will do. In fact, some stretches will actually hurt your game, and sadly these are the common ones. They're called static stretches, and they involve doing things like touching your toes for 20 seconds. These don't extend muscles, but instead they have the opposite effect. Keeping muscles extended for long periods isn't good because the muscles get worked but without receiving any benefit. So they experience fatigue with nothing to show for it. There's also some evidence that static stretching introduces mild tissue damage and increases soreness after exercise.

Proper sports preparation does two things—loosen and warm. Loosening occurs in the muscles and tendons, stretching them and giving them oxygen. Warming allows muscles to use that oxygen more efficiently. Together, this helps us carry a load without any tearing, which is the goal of all exercise. Stimulating muscles with electrical current has the same effect, and so does a light jog, but for most of us, that's unrealistic. That's why dynamic stretching is the best alternative. Just five minutes of work is enough to prepare our bodies for the first tee.

Dynamic stretching involves engaging the same muscles used in full exercise, except with less intensity. This is what McIlroy's warmup routine does, and it works by increasing body temperature and improving flexibility at the same time. It starts with a few easy swings of the wedge, followed by a few harder ones with your irons. After that, take some full swings with the driver, exerting yourself a little bit more each time. The point is to work up slowly and gradually, allowing the movements to send oxygen to your muscles and prepare them for what's to come. When two groups of golfers applied different warmup regimens, the first a simple "touch your toes" routine and the second dynamic stretching just described, the differences were huge.[9] The static stretchers swung slower (4 percent) with shorter hits (6 percent) and also reduced accuracy (31 percent). They also made less consistent contact with the ball, meaning that lazy stretching doesn't just risk injury—it also leads to embarrassing misses.

But what about putting, you might wonder. McIlroy hits a dozen putts or so before heading to the first tee, so shouldn't you? Yes, but there's a catch. Hitting a few is good and important psychological preparation, but don't go overboard.

During warmups, it's important to practice the same movements you'll use on the course, but putting is special. Most players practice at least a few hits on the green beforehand because putting is so psychological, and sinking a ball or two sets a proper mindset and familiarizes us with the course conditions. Except there's a catch. The putting motion is very different from that of the full swing, and practicing one doesn't help the other. In fact, it may even hurt. Spending up to 40 minutes working on putting makes our full swings slower and also reduces rotation in the torso and pelvis.

The difference, due to fatigue, suggests that we're better limiting putting practice to a few strokes. Anything more doesn't help warm up the body and therefore should be saved for another day.

If you could shave strokes off your golf score by eating a nutritional bar, would you do it?

Probably so, which raises one last fitness issue—diet. Everybody knows that a balanced diet is important. As the cliché goes, we are what we eat, though sometimes foods affect our bodies in complex ways. Take for example Phosphatidylserine, which we'll call PS because, well, spelling is hard. It's an essential part of all cellular membranes and ensures proper health of all our cells. Increases in PS have been shown to improve cognitive functioning, reduce muscle soreness, and even combat stress. It's also a primary ingredient of the IQ Plus Brain Bar, otherwise known as the Choccotino Golf Bar, and when consumed once a day improves ball flight over 20 percent.[10]

The assertion may seem surprising, but it's supported by science. In the study just mentioned, ten subjects received IQ Brain Bars once a day for six weeks. Afterward, those subjects hit a series of golf shots at a target approximately 150 yards away. Since players of all handicap types were included, each was allowed to choose whatever club they liked, and professionals rated each hit for accuracy. Prior to taking the supplement, subjects hit straight shots about 40 percent of the time. That's not terrible, but not great, either. Afterward, their accuracy rose to greater than half. Subjects also reported reduced stress during the tee shots, while the placebo group showed no differences at all. So the benefits weren't just psychological, but rather they were due to stronger bodies and improved natural response to stress.

Phosphatidylserine isn't the only chemical to improve performance; so does caffeine. Most of us rely on coffee to kick-start us in the morning, and apparently it kick-starts our golf game, too. Just ask Kevin Streelman, PGA Tour professional and record holder for finishing with seven straight birdies to win the 2014 Travelers Championship in Cromwell, Connecticut. He doesn't just drink water when he plays, he drinks Avitae Water, a caffeinated version that shuns the sugar and artificial flavors common in most energy drinks. The company is also Streelman's sponsor, and apparently the relationship works, because he won his first tournament less than a year after entering the business relationship.

When one study gave golfers a sports drink spiked with caffeine, as compared to a normal version, some results were predictable.[11] Players reported greater alertness during play, an immediate result of caffeine's effect on brain metabolism. Caffeine is well known to increase the brain's access to chemicals like noradrenaline and dopamine, both key in maintaining vigilance and alertness. What was surprising was that putting performance improved, too. By the end of the match, they made roughly 30 percent more putts than controls, and when they missed, they were almost twice as close.

This doesn't mean that players should go out and load their golf cart up with coffee and nutrition bars. However, it does show the importance of diet on our game. Just as stretching warms up the body, feeding the mind has its benefits, too. It's possible to take golf too seriously, which might include leaving water at home and filling the thermos with coffee on a hot summer round instead. But we can all benefit from taking care of our bodies and making the most of our game. Sometimes that means improving our warmup routine, and sometimes it means skipping the cart and investing in a good carry bag.

We may not play just for our health, but it doesn't hurt that we get so much from the game. With a little knowledge about how our bodies operate, we can increase those benefits. As a result, we can play for a long, long time.

READING LIST

Caffeine and Candy Bars

[10]Jager, R., Purpura, M., Geiss, K., Weis, M., Baumeister, J., Amatulli, F., Schroder, L., and Herwegen, H. (2007). The Effect of Phosphatidylserine on Golf Performance. *Journal of the International Society of Sports Nutrition*, 4, 23–27.

[11]Stevenson, E., Hayes, P., and Allison, S. (2009). The Effect of a Carbohydrate-Caffeine Sports Drink on Simulated Golf Performance. *Applied Physiology: Nutrition and Metabolism*, 34, 681–688.

Exercise Value

Kobriger, S., Smith, J., Hollman, J., and Smith, A. (2006). The Contribution of Golf to Daily Physical Activity Recommendations: How Many Steps Does It Take to Complete a Round of Golf? *Mayo Clinic Proceedings*, 81, 1041–1043.

Peterson, M. (2008). Physical Activity Assessment and Cardiovascular Response During Golf Participation in Differing Ambient Temperatures: An Exploratory Analysis. In D. Crews and R. Lutz (Eds.), *Science and Golf V: Proceedings of the World Scientific Congress of Golf* (pp. 139–145). Mesa, AZ: Energy in Motion, Inc.

[1]Sell, T., Abt, J., and Lephart, S. (2008). Physical Activity-Related Benefits of Walking During Golf. In D. Crews and R. Lutz (Eds.), *Science and Golf V: Proceedings of the World Scientific Congress of Golf* (pp. 128–132). Mesa, AZ: Energy in Motion, Inc.

[2]Stauch, M., Liu, Y., Giesler, M., and Lehmann, M. (1999). Physical Activity Level during a Round of Golf on a Hilly Course. *The Journal of Sports Medicine and Physical Fitness*, 4, 321–327.

Strength and Flexibility

[5]Doan, B., Newton, R., Kwon, Y., and Kraemer, W. (2006). Effects of Physical Conditioning on Intercollegiate Golfer Performance. *Journal of Strength and Conditioning Research*, 20, 62–72.

Dorado, C., Moysi, J., Vicente, G., Serrano, J., Rodriguez, L., and Calbet, J. (2002). Bone Mass, Bone Mineral Density and Muscle Mass in Professional Golfers. *Journal of Sports Science*, 20, 591–597.

[4]Fletcher, I. and Hartwell, M. (2004). Effect of an 8-Week Combined Weights and Plyometrics Training Program on Golf Drive Performance. *Journal of Strength and Conditioning Research*, 18, 59–62.

Gergley, J. (2010). Latent Effect of Passive Static Stretching on Driver Clubhead Speed, Distance, Accuracy, and Consistent Ball Contact in Young Male Competitive Golfers. *Journal of Strength and Conditioning Research*, 12, 3326–3333.

Gordon, B., Moir, G., Davis, S., Witmer, C., and Cummings, D. (2009). An Investigation Into the Relationship of Flexibility, Power, and Strength to Club Head Speed in Male Golfers. *Journal of Strength and Conditioning Research*, 23, 1606–1610.

Hellstrom, J. (2009). Competitive Elite Golf: A Review of the Relationships Between Playing Results, Technique, and Physique. *Sports Medicine*, 39, 723–741.

Keogh, J., Marnewick, M., Maulder, P., Nortje, J., Hume, P., and Bradshaw, E. (2009). Are Anthropometric, Flexibility, Muscular Strength, and Endurance Variables Related to Clubhead Velocity in Low- and High-handicap Golfers? *Journal of Strength and Conditioning Research*, 23, 1841–1850.

[3]Parkkari, J., Natri, A., Kannus, P., Manttari, A., Laukkanen, R., Haapasalo, H., Nenonen, A., Pasanen, M., Oja, P., and Vuori, I. (2000). A Controlled Trial of the Health Benefits of Regular Walking on a Golf Course. *The American Journal of Medicine*, 109, 102–108.

Reyes, M., Munro, M., Held, B., and Gebhardt, W. (2002). Maximal Static Contraction Strengthening Exercises and Driving Distances. In Thain, E. (Ed.), *Science and Golf IV: Proceedings of the World Scientific Congress of Golf* (pp. 45–53). New York: Routledge.

Sell, T., Tsai, Y., Smoliga, J., Myers, J., and Lephart, S. (2007). Strength, Flexibility, and Balance Characteristics of Highly Proficient Golfers. *Journal of Strength and Conditioning Research*, 21, 1166–1171.

Wells, G., Elmi, M., and Thomas, S. (2009). Physiological Correlates of Golf Performance. *Journal of Strength and Conditioning Research*, 23, 741–750.

Warmup Routines

Evans, K., Refshauge, K., Adams, R., and Barrett, R. (2008). Swing

Kinematics in Skilled Male Golfers Following Putting Practice. *Journal of Orthopedic and Sports Physical Therapy*, 38, 425–433.

[7]Fradkin, A., Finch, C., and Sherman, C. (2001). Warm Up Practices of Golfers: Are They Adequate? *British Journal of Sports Medicine*, 35, 125–127.

Fradkin, A., Finch, C., and Sherman, C. (2003). Warm-Up Attitudes and Behaviors of Amateur Golfers. *Journal of Science and Medicine in Sport*, 6, 210–215.

[8]Fradkin, A., Sherman, C., and Finch, C. (2004). Improving Golf Performance with a Warm Up Conditioning Programme. *British Journal of Sports Medicine*, 38, 762–765.

Fradkin, A., Windley, T., Myers, J., Sell, T., and Lephart, S. (2008). Describing the Warm-Up Habits of Recreational Golfers and the Associated Injury Risk. In D. Crews and R. Lutz (Eds.), *Science and Golf V: Proceedings of the World Scientific Congress of Golf* (pp. 112–119). Mesa, AZ: Energy in Motion, Inc.

[9]Gergley, J. (2009). Acute Effects of Passive Static Stretching During Warm-Up on Driver Clubhead Speed, Distance, Accuracy, and Consistent Ball Contact in Young Male Competitive Golfers. *Journal of Strength and Conditioning Research*, 23, 863–867.

Gergley, J. (2010). Latent Effect of Passive Static Stretching on Driver Clubhead Speed, Distance, Accuracy, and Consistent Ball Contact in Young Male Competitive Golfers. *The Journal of Strength and Conditioning Research*, 24, 3326–3333.

Moran, K., McGrath, R., Marshall, B., and Wallace, E. (2009). Dynamic Stretching and Golf Swing Performance. *International Journal of Sports Medicine*, 30, 113–118.

[6]Smolinga, J. and Fradkin, A. (2008). Observed Warm-Up Behaviors Do Not Reflect Those Reported by Amateur Golfers. In D. Crews and R. Lutz (Eds.), *Science and Golf V: Proceedings of the World Scientific Congress of Golf* (pp. 97–104). Mesa, AZ: Energy in Motion, Inc.

Curriculum and Instruction

Prerequisites: Psychology 101: Putting and the Short Game

Day one: April 5, 2010. *Went out and putted for two hours. Don't have the "real" clubs yet, but it still counts as a start! So, down to 9,998 hours.*

This was Dan McLaughlin's first entry in his blog, posted soon after his visit to Broadmoor Golf Course in Portland, Oregon. It was 38 degrees outside and raining—typical for the Pacific Northwest that time of year—and McLaughlin had spent two hours practicing one-foot putts. As in, only one-foot putts. He didn't even own another club.

McLaughlin had just started what he called his "Dan Plan," a science-based strategy to become a professional golfer. Though he had no experience with the sport, he wanted to enter the PGA Tour, and that meant following a dedicated training regimen. First, he would work on putting, starting a few feet from the hole. Then he would work out to six feet, then 20, and by the end of the year, he would buy a wedge. The next summer he would be practicing with a partial set of irons, and in early fall, he'd be swinging a hybrid. He followed his plan religiously and didn't even get his first lesson with a driver until he'd been training for a year and a half. With the help of a local golf pro, two years after swinging a club for the first time, he was already breaking 80.

McLaughlin's plan may sound obsessive, and he acknowledges that it is, but it's rooted in science. The idea came to him after reading about the work of psychologist K. Anders Ericsson, who became somewhat of a celebrity after proposing what's popularly known as the 10,000-hour doctrine. It states that expertise isn't dependent on genes or luck. What really matters is practice, and lots of it. We're talking years of deliberate, motivated training, the kind that begins for most experts at an early age. For some of us, it starts later. The important thing isn't natural ability or when we start, it's that we spend at least ten years of concentrated work honing our craft. Spend that much time at anything, and you'll become an expert.

Ericsson's time requirement for expertise is often cited in terms of hours rather than years, because that's what actually matters: hours spent in training, not the amount of time that has passed since the commitment began. To reach 10,000 hours in ten years, you must work four hours a day, every day, without breaks except for weekends and holidays. McLaughlin's plan was more aggressive, because he figured that with 30 hours a week, he could reach his goal in just six-and-a-half years.

Sadly, McLaughlin never got his PGA card. Somewhere around hour 6,000, he suffered a back injury and had to move on from his quest. At the time, he was already shooting par.

"There were plenty of club pros that I would have played straight-up," Dan said afterward, still optimistic about returning to the quest one day. "At that level, on any day or any round you can beat anybody. But if they're having a good nine holes, they can do the same thing. I guess that's the nature of expertise."

Dan's plan was impressive, though most bodies are ill-equipped for such rigors. Fortunately, we don't need to be as dedicated as McLaughlin; we just want to play well enough to win a few dollars from our friends. This doesn't mean we can't be smart about how we practice. Despite massive improvements in equipment, golf scores have stayed relatively constant over the generations. The game should be getting easier to play, given our access to graphite shafts and multi-layered balls, but it isn't. One reason is that we don't take advantage of research into how people learn. McLaughlin didn't just go out and buy a set of clubs at a local store and start swinging. He developed a plan.

That plan had a certain brute-force component to it—his target was 10,000 hours, after all—but there was a methodology to it, too. Any player wanting to improve only needs to give the training some thought. This chapter will review what we can do to make the most of our time on the course.

Most of us would have a hard time spending two hours working on only one-foot putts. How much can we really improve from practicing such simple hits? Quite a bit, actually, because what matters is our focus. The primary finding of Ericsson's research wasn't the amount of time necessary to become an expert, it was the focus. Those 10,000 hours can't just be spent goofing around. If you want to make one-foot putts, then you need to practice them . . . repeatedly and with dedication. Just as long as your focus is there, improvement will follow.

The most important principle of golf training is implicit learning. When we work on our swing, we don't memorize facts; we give our muscles experience with specific motions. That enlists completely different parts of the brain from if you were, say, learning the rules of chess. Although we'll discuss those brain regions more senior year, let's say for now that muscle memory is what matters. When McLaughlin worked on one-foot putts, he familiarized his body with swinging a club. Most of us hate such simple practice because it's boring, but that's the point. No one said improvement would be easy.

Some may take this as an indication that we should overthink our practice, or that it must be boring in order to be successful. Not so. In fact, it's best to relax and not think too much. If you're making grocery lists in your head, you're probably not improving. If you're agonizing over every miss, you've got the same problem. The trick is to stay focused on the task without letting your conscious mind go into overdrive. Getting into a groove is the key.

To see why overthinking seldom helps, let's look at a study by Jonathan Maxwell at the University of Birmingham in England.[1] Maxwell is a psychologist who studies errors, particularly the kind that come while learning a new skill. His theory is that errors are more than just discouraging; they enlist our conscious minds when they don't belong. To test his theory, he had a group of golf novices make hundreds of putts ranging from one to seven feet. For the "short group," players started with the easiest putts first, then worked outward. The "long group" did the opposite, starting with the hardest. For the final "random group," distances varied without a pattern. Everybody hit the same number of putts, the only difference being the order in which they took them. Pretty simple, huh?

Maxwell suspected one group would have an advantage when tested after the training, and he was right. The short group made on average 41 out of 50 putts, five better than anybody else. This advantage persisted even for longer putts that nobody had rehearsed. So, starting with easy putts creates a persistent advantage.

The reason for such an advantage is implicit learning—our ability to hone skills without overthinking. As we discussed in Psychology 101, golf isn't a thoughtful sport. When we think about the putt or full swing, we engage the wrong parts of our brains. By starting with easy putts, we encourage our bodies to *just swing* and not overanalyze (in Psychology 101, we called this being overtaken by the Angel of the Odd). Long hits are notorious for leading to misses, and also for questioning what went wrong. That's a terrible way to learn. When McLaughlin started with one-foot putts, he did the best thing possible—he simply practiced and didn't allow his mind to get in the way.

Maxwell had another condition too, one I haven't told you about yet and that bolsters his "don't overthink" argument. After the training was over, he asked players to make extralong putts while being distracted by a separate task. The identity of the additional task doesn't really matter—it involved counting tones—the important point being that it got players' conscious minds working on something else. Those who started training with easier putts improved slightly, despite the distraction. The others, who trained with the long putts first—the kind that beg us to ask ourselves what went wrong following an error—missed 8 percent more.

So massive practice may be very important, but how we practice matters more. We must work on the right things, and for putting that means allowing our muscles to do the thinking.

Golf differs from football or soccer in countless ways, one being how players train. Not only is golf special in not being a contact sport, or team-based, there's also no strategic or tactical "rules" to learn that all players must assimilate. As a result, the paths to becoming a great player are almost as varied as the number of people who play professionally. Nick Lindheim didn't play junior golf, or college either, instead opting to train himself while pitching for his California high school. Tiger Woods did attend college and went to Stanford, as did Tom Watson and Patrick Rodgers, but they had the benefit of intensive training at home first. Larry Nelson didn't even take up golf until his twenties and still won three majors, and Keegan Bradley failed Q School and was forced to find another way into the big leagues. He played on the Nationwide Tour instead, until he got a late-season break and worked his way up from there. Less than a year later, he was rookie of the year with a major championship under his belt.

The pathway to becoming a great golfer is so varied because there is no fixed way to master sport, particularly golf. This means that variety and seeking out new challenges are more important than where you go to school, though certain tools for *how* we learn are universal.

One key ingredient for all golfers is the need for variable practice. In some ways, McLaughlin's plan wasn't ideal because even our muscles need some variety to learn. We progress best when we're challenged, and that means varying our conditions. Take for example practicing short putts. Although keeping things simple is key, we can still change the ball's location a little after every hit. Psychologists call this a variable-practice protocol, and it helps by encouraging a loose and open mindset. If we practice the exact shot over and over again, we'll probably improve, but the lack of variety will cost us. Studies show that engaging in variable practice not only improves accuracy, but also it makes backswings more fluid, more consistent, and leads to steadier contact.[2]

Feedback is another important thing to vary during practice. One nice thing about golf is that feedback is always immediate. After a good hit, we enjoy that wonderful sound of metal clubface striking squarely against ball. If we're lucky, we also see the ball land on our target, hopefully the green. But this feedback isn't always helpful. Sometimes we're better off not knowing where the ball goes, and this is especially true for putting. Studies show that we do best when we follow the ball's roll only a third of the time.[3] That benefit is long-lasting and leads to the ball stopping a foot closer to the pin on 12-foot putts, compared to looking after every putt. By looking away, we're discouraged from trying to fix errors after every swing. Again, the trick is to play and not overthink. I'm not saying that you should walk away from the green on your next hole, assuming that the ball went in without actually checking, only that you pause to allow the moment to sink in. It will help in the long run.

We must always remember that learning occurs in both our muscles and our brain, but only certain parts. The rest, the brain regions that do things like math and language, do little for our game. That's why playing golf-themed video games helps, too. I'm serious: sitting on the couch with a Playstation can improve your score, but only on one condition. Studies show that when our video game characters mimic actual putting, with body movements like in the real game, we get no benefit.[4] Yet, when we practice video golf using a symbolic power gauge, players leave the ball closer to the hole in real life. The reason is that the symbolic system doesn't encourage players to think in terms of real body movements. Instead it forces us to think abstractly, using concepts like *power*. Electronic and real-life versions have this in common, a focus on power, and so the correct brain regions are enlisted. Consciously paying attention to a virtual character's arm movements is just as bad as thinking about your own.

From these findings, it's easy to get the impression that learning to play golf is purely psychological. It isn't. Golf is a physical game, and improvement comes only when you tame mind and body together. This means developing a reliable rhythm.

Interestingly, even training on skills unrelated to golf can help when it coaxes the mind and body to work together. One tool is metronome training, which involves moving to a steady beat, like clapping with a tone or tapping our feet to a dancing rhythm. Just a dozen short sessions of such practice can improve our golf swing accuracy by about 20 percent. That improvement extends to different clubs and translates to the ball landing ten feet closer to the pin for most iron shots.

Teaching timing and fluid motion is difficult, which is why top golf instructors get paid so much. Beginning golfers are often overwhelmed, and a good instructor recognizes what to work on and when. You can't teach torso rotation, posture, and grip all at once. You can't teach rhythm either, only recognize when it's not there and respond accordingly, and that's what instructors are for.

The traditional learning model for sports trainers consists of four stages. The first is *explanation*, which means describing the desired skill. This might include addressing the proper grip, feet, or body position, or maybe even the full swing.

After explanation comes *demonstration*, where an expert illustrates the desired behavior. Before the birth of the Internet, the only way to see an expert swing was through television or personal lessons, but a lot has changed since the mid-20th century. Now you can study nearly any aspect of the game, and even read science books about the sport in your free time.

Next is *execution*, where the player tries the skill for herself. The first time I swung a club, I hit the ball almost a hundred yards. *That's amazing*, I told myself. *I thought this sport was difficult!* My instructor was less impressed and told me to try again. The next time the ball barely rolled five feet.

The reason my instructor was unimpressed had to do with the fourth stage, *feedback*. Not only was I holding the club's grip like a baseball bat, but my feet were completely together and I shifted my weight entirely wrong. He was right, of course, so we started again. "Let's revisit the grip first," he said, then he described again where my thumbs were supposed to go. He showed me his own grip, then had me try the swing again. This time the ball went twenty yards, slightly better than my last try, but nothing like my initial attempt. I probably swung a hundred more times before matching my beginner's luck.

My own instructor focused on the grip because that is literally the first thing you do before approaching the tee: you grip the club. Any aspect of our game can be revisited using this methodology, even after it has been supposedly learned. This is what Hank Haney did with Tiger Woods after becoming his personal trainer—he had Tiger rework his grip. The result was that Woods completely changed the way he held the club, and ultimately he placed six more majors in his victory column.

This isn't the only way we learn, however. In fact, there's good evidence that learning-centered approaches are better. These involve participation from students at every stage, making learning more about discovery than demonstration. Usually this starts with the most over-looked part of the sport—the short game. Students start with put-ting, usually with short putts like McLaughlin attempted on that cold Northwest morning. Then players move on to chipping, progressing up to the longer irons. The focus is on doing only what is immedi-ately achievable, which is why McLaughlin didn't even bother buying a driver for over a year.

The other important aspect of a learning-centered approach is focus on preswing posture and finish position. As we've addressed, thinking about the swing itself is never good. The process lasts less than a quarter of a second, too fast for the conscious brain to get mean-ingfully involved. We can, however, think about where we want to start and finish. By focusing on things like aim, preshot routine, and finish position, players get more from training time than focusing on the actual swing.

Although a learning-centered approach doesn't preclude following the traditional model, emphases are different. To benefit from learning, skills must be internalized, and this comes through practice, lots of it, especially when that practice is concrete. If your grip is causing you problems, rehearse it whenever you can, even away from the course. (I once found a broken club and cut away everything but the grip. It sat next to my desk for about a month for practice in my spare time until I got the grip right.) If reading breaks is your nemesis, go to the practice green and hit some balls. Studies show that hands-on practice using a learning-centered approach leads to more accurate putts and smoother swings than training with the traditional model.[5] We also gain more positive attitudes about what we've learned, making us more likely to continue practicing on our own.

Another issue to consider when training is to ensure that the skills you're working on transfer to the actual course. We've all visited a range and struck a few balls, thinking that this is how we're going to improve. But there's an old Chinese proverb that goes something like this: "We hear and we forget. We see and we remember. We do and we learn." To learn, we must mimic the motions and challenges involved in actual play, and this means leaving nothing out. Without feedback, practice is wasted. We can't work on skills without also placing them in the context of actual play, so if you visit the range and simply strike a bucket full of balls without any goals, you'll be unlikely to improve. However, imagining a fairway with bunkers, hazards, and greens in the distance takes you much closer to the real game. Scientists call this transfer training, and it's a key component of success, no matter which learning strategy you employ.

In addition to understanding different learning strategies, we must also be familiar with our own personality and the needs we bring to the instruction. Everybody learns differently, and student-teacher relationships do best when styles are matched. Though pedagogical approaches vary, three learning styles are key for golf, and it's worth familiarizing yourself with each before deciding on an instructor.

The first approach is Noetic, a term adopted from the Greek term for understanding. This is how 15 percent of beginners approach the sport, and it involves intuitive learning. Most Noetic learners can't say what happens when they swing, but they can describe it in broad concepts. They prefer to skip over details, at least initially, which lends itself nicely to not overthinking. Although most instructors can address details when necessary, over a third follow a Noetic teaching approach, which means that these learners generally have little problem finding an instructor matching their own personal style.

Over twice as common are the Rationalist learners, who analyze the sport at a deep, conceptual level. These are the thinkers, those who subscribe to magazines and visit websites and read books . . . anything to cut away a stroke or two. More instructors follow this pattern than any other, making this the default language of most golf teaching programs. At first glance, this seems like a bad thing, given how little our brains help us on the course, but it's not. Learning from outside materials is great, so long as the mind is shut off when it matters.

Last, we have the Empiricists. These are players who learn best through hands-on experience. They care less about abstract concepts and are more likely to buy a mirror than a book, because at least mirrors show you your forearm position during the backswing. They're the least fortunate learners of all, because only one in eight instructors prefers this style. In fact, nearly half of all instructors place this learning strategy last among their preferences, making empirical teachers rare indeed.

Recognizing your own learning approach is the first step when choosing an instructor. This doesn't mean all is lost if you're an intuitive learner and your instructor takes a rationalist approach; good teachers quickly recognize the needs of their students and adapt accordingly. It does mean, however, that everybody must speak a common language. Studies show that the primary aspect distinguishing expert instructors from beginning ones is their ability to listen.[6] Whereas novice instructors seek to convey information, experts seek to understand student questions and desires. Only when an instructor truly knows his or her student can a proper instructional style be identified. That's why instructors with more experience are able to teach more in a shorter amount of time. They know what their students need and get right to the point in addressing those needs.

Learning to play golf is hard, so there's no point in making it any harder. Some things we can easily control, like how we practice. Some things we can't, like what kind of learning style we prefer. When Dan McLaughlin set out to become a PGA Tour professional, he didn't just start his stopwatch and begin counting the hours. He developed a plan and stuck to it, and so can anyone else who desires to get the most out of their practice. It just takes recognizing that the brain isn't like a computer. We can't just memorize facts about the golf swing and consider the skill mastered. Instead, we must find ways to make play challenging and constructive, matching our instruction to our own personal styles.

Then, ten thousand hours later, we will accomplish our mission. It's as simple as that.

READING LIST

Deliberate Practice

Ericsson, K., Krampe, R., and Romer, C. (1993). The Role of Deliberate Practice in the Acquisition of Expert Performance. *Psychological Review*, 100, 363–406.

Implicit Learning

Chauvel, G., Maquestiaux, F., Ruthruff, E., Didierjean, A., and Hartley, A. (2013). Novice Motor Performance: Better not to Verbalize. *Psychonomics Bulletin Review*, 20, 177–183.

[4]Fery, Y. and Ponserre, S. (2001). Enhancing the Control of Force in Putting by Video Game Training. *Ergonomics*, 44, 1025–1037.

Hwang, G. (2003). *An Examination of the Impact of Introducing Greater Contextual Interference During Practice on Learning to Golf Putt* (PhD dissertation, Texas A&M University).

[3]Ishikura, T. (2008). Reduced Relative Frequency of Knowledge of Results Without Visual Feedback in Learning a Golf-Putting Task. *Perceptual and Motor Skills*, 106, 225–233.

[1]Maxwell, J., Masters, R., Kerr, E., and Weedon, E. (2001). The Implicit Benefit of Learning Without Errors. *The Quarterly Journal of Experimental Psychology*, 54, 1049–1068.

Poolton, J., Masters, R., and Maxwell, J. (2005). The Relationship Between Initial Errorless Learning Conditions and Subsequent Performance. *Human Movement Science*, 24, 362–378.

[2]Porter, J. and Magill, R. (2010). Systematically Increasing Contextual Interference is Beneficial for Learning Sport Skills. *Journal of Sports Sciences*, 28, 1277–1285.

Teaching and Learning Styles

Arnold, G. (1997). *Creating a Methodology for Teaching the Golf Swing* (MA thesis, Canadian Professional Golfers' Association).

Christina, R. and Alpenfels, E. (2002). Why Does Traditional Training Fail to Optimize Playing Performance? In Thain, E. (Ed.), *Science and Golf IV: Proceedings of the World Scientific Congress of Golf* (pp. 231–245). New York: Routledge.

[5]Lutz, R. (1998). The Effects of Traditional and Learning-Centered Golf Instruction on Skill Development and Attitudes Toward Golf. In Farrally, M. and Cochran, A. (Ed.), *Science and Golf III: Proceedings of the World Scientific Congress of Golf* (pp. 225–233). Champaign, IL: Human Kinetics.

Rancourt, R. and Searle, R. (1990). Golfers Do It with Style: Epistemic Orientations of Golf Instructors and Students. In A.J. Cochran (Ed.), *Science and Golf: Proceedings of the First World Scientific Congress of Golf* (pp. 105–110). New York: E&FN Spon.

[6]Webster, C. (2006). *A Comparison of Expert and Novice Golf Instructors from a Communication Perspective* (PhD dissertation, University of Georgia).

Timing Training

Chan, C., Tzu-Ling, Y., and Wen-Tzu, T (2010). Temporal Pattern of Distance Control in Golf Putting after Rhythm Training. *Paper presented at the 6th Annual World Congress on Biomechanics, Singapore.*

Libkuman, T., Otani, H., and Steger, N. (2002). Training in Timing Improves Accuracy in Golf. *The Journal of General Psychology*, 129, 77–96.

Sommer, M. and Ronnqvist, L. (2009). Improved Motor-Timing: Effects of Synchronized Metronome Training on Golf Shot Accuracy. *Journal of Sports Science and Medicine*, 8, 648–656.

Junior Year

The transition to junior year is the biggest in college. It's when we stop being underclass students and start being curious explorers in a new, intellectual world. Classes become more advanced, and we start asking the questions that concern experts, too.

Golf University believes that junior year is the time to explore topics we've already seen, but now even deeper. We'll see how courses interact with their environments, making them healthier in some cases and not in others. We'll see how anxiety and emotion play important roles in our game, and how to achieve a mental state that the psychologist Mihaly Csikszentmihalyi calls *Flow*. That's the ability to focus so completely that our entire being is fully engaged. We'll learn how engineers are developing equipment to improve our play and how doctors are helping athletes avoid injury. In short, we'll take what so far has been a good start and go even further.

Junior year is also a time when we start taking electives on topics outside our major. Rarely in life do we get to take intentional detours, but college electives enable us to do just that. In junior year, that means taking a step back from the math and science classes and delving into the history of sport. Most people know that golf was born in Scotland, and that the first players were from St. Andrews, but don't tell the Chinese that. They were hitting balls with sticks just as early as the Scots, and maybe even before, making the sport's parentage less like a straight line and more like an episode of Jerry Springer.

So let's get back to classes and take a field trip to New Jersey, just a short 3-wood from downtown Manhattan. It's not the kind of location you think of when it comes to golf, but that's the point. And so begins our exploration of the ecological impact of the sport we all love.

Earth Sciences 201: Environmental Issues

Prerequisites: Earth Sciences 101: Geology, Weather, and Terrain

Let's face it: New York City and golf go together like Houston and hockey. Or maybe Vancouver and baseball.

Sure, there are still some people who swing clubs in the greater metro area. Staten Island has quite a few courses, as does Brooklyn and Queens. It's just that with ten million people crammed inside 500 square miles, there's not much room for bunkers or tee boxes. That's precisely what makes Liberty National Golf Club so impressive. Even if the course hadn't once been a superfund site and toxic waste dump, it would be worth visiting.

Located in Jersey City just a couple of miles from the southern tip of Manhattan, Liberty National has one of the most scenic views in the country. Look to your left from the first tee, and you'll see the Statue of Liberty. Peek over the fourth green, and you'll see the Manhattan skyline, and the same goes for the 18th, though be careful with your slice. Spend too much time admiring the view, and your final tee shot will land in the Hudson River.

Not long ago, things weren't so positive for this Jersey landmark. Before the turn of the century, the site was more like someplace Tony Soprano might take a disloyal subordinate to, not somewhere you'd expect to find a high-end sports facility. In addition to once being an Italian internment camp, it had a long history as a Standard Oil refinement site and World War II munitions storage facility. Time and abuse left the land covered with corroded oil tanks and contaminated soil, not to mention a designation by the EPA as one of the most toxic sites in the country. In other words, not the kind of place where you'd expect to play golf.

"It was an eyesore," claimed Paul Fireman, the multimillionaire who now owns the site. "But it had a major attitude about it. The location was iconic. How could you not want to do something with this property?"

And so he did, starting with the soil. Because the ground was so toxic, the entire site had to be capped using six million cubic feet of dirt. This required covering the worst parts with a half-inch-thick polyethylene blanket, followed by trucks and trucks of soil, up to 200 loads per day for two years. Once the ground was raised, over 50 feet in some places, then came actual fairways and greens. But even that didn't go smoothly, and several players remarked that the course lacked charm. "They took a perfectly good landfill," one visitor exclaimed. "And then they ruined it."

Back to the drawing board. Fireman had designer Tom Kite try again, this time with even greater environmental improvements. A buffer was built along one of the course's creeks, a wetland area that's now home to a large population of black-crowned night herons. Three acres of salt marsh were expanded to accommodate a local species of terrapin. Fireman even deepened the man-made lakes and added an elaborate pumping system to control contaminants seeping in from the ground.

Two hundred and fifty million dollars later, Liberty National is now one of the safest and most sought-after tee times in the country. With initiation fees over half a million dollars, the course will make its money back one day, I'm sure. Just not soon. Don't worry too much about Fireman, though. As founder of Reebok, he's not running out of money anytime in the near future.

Golf has a mixed history when it comes to environmental issues. Though Liberty National is a great success story, at least for those rich enough to enjoy it, other locations haven't been so kind to their surroundings. Pesticide runoff, intense watering, and reduction of wildlife habitat can all make a course unappealing. Yet, this doesn't have to be the case. The sport grows every time we discover new ways to make it greener, and by learning about these efforts, we can ensure a healthy sport for years to come. In this chapter, we'll explore the environmental impacts of golf, showing how courses delicately balance ecological responsibility with the need for fun and recreation.

The first thing all golfers should recognize is that the global antigolf movement is real, and not without justification. Golf courses consume over two billion gallons of water per day, roughly half a percent of all water used in United States. Pesticides seep into local streams, and nitrates alter nutrient transport through the entire eco-system. And let's not forget the issue of space, with American golf courses covering more acreage than Rhode Island and Delaware com-bined. This makes the sport's footprint far from subtle.

Yet, this doesn't mean the sport's impact has to be negative. One way golf courses increase environmental responsibility is by reduc-ing water use, primarily through recycling. Sometimes this is accom-plished by building retention ponds to collect rainwater, for example at Groesbeck Municipal Golf Course in Lansing, Michigan. This course was recently rebuilt to minimize water use, and now it contains seven acres of storage ponds and 30 acres of wetlands. From these improve-ments, the course can now store and reuse up to ten million gallons of water a day.

Though most golfers seldom think about drainage while on the course, we can all help by patronizing courses that reduce water use and also ones supporting local wildlife. That second issue is especially sig-nificant, since the average course consumes plenty of land—up to 150 acres by most estimates. Fortunately, most courses set aside land just for preservation, but even when they don't, there's plenty to share. Only 30 percent of most golf course land is maintained, which includes fairways, greens, and tee boxes, meaning over two-thirds can remain undevel-oped. This leaves valuable woodland or lake area for wildlife that might otherwise be forced to compete with condos and strip malls instead.

Johan Colding and Carl Folke at the Royal Swedish Academy of Sciences in Stockholm conducted probably the most thorough exami-nation of golfing ecosystems.[1] They performed a meta-analysis of 17 separate studies, each examining the effects of golf on birds, amphib-ians, and even insects. The goal was to determine if golfing facilities reduced the number of local species, and if so, which ones were most threatened. They also wanted to see if the type of course mattered for the ecosystem—for example, hilly, flat, or forested.

Overall, results were promising, with two-thirds of the courses providing greater ecological value than nearby, nonsporting areas. This extended to birds, insects, and even local fauna. Courses located in urban areas fared best by providing the wildlife a hidden home among buildings and traffic, though even nature-protected sites were comparable to their surroundings. Ironically, a little development improves biodiversity because so many species have become dependent on humans. This doesn't mean we should start paving all the forests, only that mixed-space use isn't so bad. It turns out that lots of animals are used to having us around.

Related to both wildlife and water use is the complicated issue of runoff. Anytime fertilizers or pesticides are applied to the land, these materials threaten to make their way to the groundwater. From there, they may get ingested, sometimes by wildlife and sometimes by us. Golf courses are no exception, and managers must be responsible in how they treat their land. Courses with poor grading or inadequate containment may lose most of their pesticides and fertilizer to local lakes and rivers, while those with good soil and containment may not have any impact at all.

Runoff is so hard to predict because so many factors influence where the chemicals go. Greens produce almost no runoff contamination because they're well drained and the grass is always dense, while fairways contribute significantly more. Weather matters too, as humid locations like Atlanta and Houston experience much larger runoffs, while drier climates like Fresno experience up to 16 times less. That's because more rain means more chemicals being washed away, and major rain events can take a huge toll. One study estimates that at least once a decade, most sites will experience a storm large enough to match runoff experienced over the entire rest of the year.[2]

To some extent, runoff is beyond a course manager's control, but designers can still minimize its impact. Take for example Braeburn Golf Course in Wichita, Kansas. As part of a study with Wichita State University and Southern Illinois University, this course developed a wide-ranging program to reduce contamination from fertilizer and pest control.[3] Nitrogen fertilizers were replaced with slow-releasing organic alternatives, and buffer zones were placed around ponds with drainage outlets feeding into a nearby filtration area. Even basic processes like pesticide application were improved by spraying only when environmental conditions allowed for safe and concentrated application.

Now, chemical contamination is nearly eliminated. Nitrate and phosphorous runoff, the primary ingredients in fertilizers, decreased between 40 percent and 80 percent. Whereas nearby lakes accommodated only snails and leeches before the renovation (eww!), now, a variety of simple organisms provide ample food for larger animals looking to call the improved location home.

Another thing course managers can do is implement BioBanking offsets. These are areas set aside to foster biological diversity, often with big impacts. The movement is especially big in Australia, where Camden Lakeside Golf Course once initiated a massive project to improve its own biodiversity.[4] Before the course was built, local water systems were eroded, grasslands were overgrazed by cattle, and animal populations were dwindling. To remedy this, the course planted native trees and shrubs, while also developing fringes around water hazards. This allowed local species to grow and develop, with grass away from the fairways allowed to grow so that weeds and plants not native to the area could be removed. As a result, the land now houses over a hundred local species of frogs, birds, and even bats, compared to only thirty before the renovation began.

The biggest challenge for course owners is finding ways to protect the environment while also saving money. A solution may be effective, but if it's too expensive, then there's little point. Fortunately, composting systems are both cheap and effective. Golf courses require extensive maintenance to keep grass green and free of disease, and chemicals help control these dangers. But they also deplete microorganisms, which prevent turf disease. With composting, which takes existing organic material and uses that instead, such chemicals can be eliminated altogether. This saves money too, especially when the composting material is taken from the land itself.

As one example, Clear Lake Golf Course in Manitoba now uses mown grass from its putting greens and kitchen waste from its clubhouse and applies it to tee boxes and greens. The cost of implementing this composting system was minimal, and now fewer artificial chemicals are released into the environment. When a similar composting system was applied to a single fairway at the North Shore Country Club in Glenview, Illinois, the grass became measurably greener and denser and contracted 80 percent fewer turf-grass infections. Not bad.

One reason so few courses use composting systems is practicality—how do you apply it? Fertilizing a course is difficult enough, especially in summer months when traffic is high, so how could you spread organic waste without offending too many noses? Fortunately, scientists have developed a unique solution—compost tea. It's an unusual name but apt, as it involves dipping a bag filled with solid compost into a huge vat of water. That water is then aerated, and after a week, the bag is removed. The result is a tea that can be spread over turf like regular water, except the tea both feeds the grass and keeps it healthy. Such solutions, once considered extraordinary, are now common ways courses keep their environments protected and safe.

As a player, it's hard to tell if a course is being managed properly. We could ask the course superintendent which fertilizers they use and whether they compost, but that will probably get you funny looks. Fortunately, there are simpler solutions, for example, asking if the course belongs to the Audubon Sanctuary Program. That's the joint effort by the USGA and Audubon International to certify courses in six areas of environmental health—planning, wildlife management, education, chemical reduction, water conservation, and water quality management. Over two thousand courses are currently enrolled, each receiving the latest developments in course ecology and maintenance. Research shows that membership costs are fully recovered by participating courses due to increased traffic, offering little justification for a course to avoid joining. So next time you hit the links, ask your local municipal if they've heard of the program, and if not, say that you'd love it if they considered it. Change may come slowly, but even slow change is better than none at all.

Few topics are more controversial than global warming, our final health topic. One problem is politics, since sometimes opinions are easier to accept than science. But let there be no mistake, the science exists and is real. The research concerning climate change may be complex, but it's also unwavering—our planet's temperature is rising due to increased consumption, and that increase isn't slowing down.

Atmospheric carbon dioxide is rising at a rate never before seen. Whereas atmospheric concentrations of the gas were barely three hundred parts per million 50 years ago, now they are closer to four hundred. That means more ultraviolet light is being absorbed in the atmosphere, thus causing the air to be warmer. This has led to a degree and a half of warming so far this century, and scientists expect an even greater increase in the coming decades.

Since golf courses cover so much land, it's natural to wonder if they're part of the problem. Maintenance and construction certainly require burning of fossil fuels, and that's never good. Liberty National discovered this firsthand when they moved two hundred trucks of soil a day for over two years. Golf courses contain extensive trees and grassland, which is great for the environment, but is that enough to compensate for all the gas used to produce them? One of the clearest examinations of how golf courses affect greenhouse gases like carbon dioxide comes from a study by environmental scientists Adam Selhorst and Rattan Lal of The Ohio State University.[5] They took soil samples from 11 private and public courses ranging from two to 97 years old, all built on previously agricultural farmland in the Midwest. Then they measured capacity of the soil to sequester carbon dioxide from the atmosphere.

From their measurements, they estimated that the courses produced on average fifteen tons of carbon dioxide a year. That's a lot, with the biggest source being fuel burned for mowing and other maintenance (72 percent). However, turfgrasses and other carbon-dependent plants more than compensated, sequestering over 2,400 tons over a course's lifetime. Other studies have shown that golf courses can take in almost two hundred tons of carbon a year when you also consider the benefit of trees soaking up greenhouse gases.[6] So, apparently golf courses can be effective carbon sinks, so long as they're not built by an army of trucks trying to remediate an EPA superfund site.

Golf isn't as harmful to the environment as many people think it is. The sport takes a lot of space, but that isn't always bad. Sometimes the courses are the only green space hidden within wide swaths of urban sprawl. That land also helps tie up atmospheric gases that would otherwise keep raising our temperatures. Though Canadians are now seeing longer golf seasons due to global warming, up to seven additional weeks according to one study,[7] most would agree that the extra days on the links aren't worth it.

For as long as there's urban development and fossil fuels, there will be concern for the planet's well-being. At least golfers can sleep well knowing their sport is relatively green.

READING LIST

Biodiversity

Block, D. (1997). Disease Suppression on the Links. *Biocycle*, 38, 8–13.

[4]Burgin, S. and Wotherspoon, D. (2009). The Potential for Golf Courses to Support Restoration of Biodiversity for BioBanking Offsets. *Urban Ecosystems*, 12, 145–155.

[1]Colding, J. and Folke, C. (2009). The Role of Golf Courses in Biodiversity Conservation and Ecosystem Management. *Ecosystems*, 12, 191–206.

Global Warming

[6]Bartlett, M. and James, I. (2011) Are Golf Courses a Source or Sink of Atmospheric Carbon Dioxide? A Modeling Approach. *Proceedings of the Institution of Mechanical Engineers*, 225, 75–83.

[7]Scott, D. and Jones, B. (2006). The Impact of Climate Change on Golf Participation in the Greater Toronto Area: A Case Study. *Journal of Leisure Research*, 38, 363–380.

[5]Selhorst, A. and Lal, R. (2011). Carbon Budgeting in Golf Course Soils in Central Ohio. *Urban Ecosystems*, 14, 771–781.

Pesticides, watering, and runoff

Audubon International. (2000). *Certification Handbook: Audubon Cooperative Sanctuary program for Golf Courses*. New York: Selkirk.

Beard, J. (1994). Environmental Protection and Beneficial Contributions of Golf Course Turfs. In A.J. Cochran and M. Farrally (Eds.), *Science and Golf II: Proceedings of the World Scientific Congress of Golf* (pp. 399–408). Grass Valley, CA: The Booklegger.

[3]Davis, N. and Lydy, M. (2002). Evaluating Best Management Practices at an Urban Golf Course. *Environmental Toxicology and Chemistry*, 21, 1076–1084.

Dinelli, Dan. (2004). Compost Scores High on Golf Course. *BioCycle*, 45, 52–54.

Environmental Institute for Golf. (2007). *Golf Course Environmental Profile: Property Profile and Environmental Stewardship of Golf Courses* (EIFG Report).

Grobe, K. (2003). Golf Courses Find Value in Compost Tea Programs. *BioCycle*, 44, 22–23.

[2]Haith, D. and Duffany, M. (2007). Pesticide Runoff Loads from Lawns and Golf Courses. *Journal of Environmental Engineering*, 133, 435–446.

Limehouse, F., Melvin, P., and McCormick, R. (2010). The Demand for Environmental Quality: An Application of Hedonic Pricing in Golf. *Journal of Sports Economics*, 11, 261–266.

Lyman, G. (2012). How Much Water Does Golf Use and Where Does It Come From? *USGA Summit on Golf Course Water Use*: United States Golf Association (TGIF Record 214418).

McCartney, Daryl. (2001). Organics Recycling at Golf Course in Canadian National Park. *BioCycle*, 42, 27–30.

Whitney, M. (2001). Golf Courses More Than a Walk in the Park. *Parks and Recreation*, 46, 75–78.

Seminar on Golf History (Elective)

Prerequisites: None

Everybody knows that golf was born in Scotland. Specifically, high-land farmers and shepherds once got the idea to hit small balls with sticks from one location to another (sometimes even between villages), and a whole new sport was born.

There are several reasons to believe this likely oversimplified story. As we've learned, Scottish kings made the sport illegal as early as the fifteenth century, claiming it distracted soldiers from archery practice. A few hundred years later, the first rules of the game were published in Leith, a small village near Edinburgh, where you'll also find the first courses. Today you can still play at Musselburgh Links or the Old Course at St. Andrews, both located along the North Sea and shared claimants for oldest course in the world (Musselburgh Links only has nine holes and so is frequently forgotten by the record books).

But, perhaps the history of golf is more complicated. Could the sport have evolved elsewhere, or originated in multiple places at once?

One mystery regarding the origins of golf is its name. The simplest answer is that the Scots borrowed the term from the Dutch *kolve* or *kolf*. It too is a sport involving little balls and sticks, the name taken from the crook of a shepherd's staff. This would connect the sport's history with continental Europe, and the relationship only deepens from there. We know that people in Brussels were already playing *soule à la crosse*, which like *kolve* used shepherds' crooks, except with running mixed in and also swinging at opposing players. In one Flemish version of *King Arthur's Tales*, the evil sorcerer Merlin meets up with British soldiers and joins them in a game, only to strike one of his opponents in the shin. The story ends with the player calling Merlin a bastard for the affront, which is ironic, since Merlin was supposedly the illegitimate son of the devil. So he *was* a bastard, technically speaking. But I digress.

All this suggests that the sport prohibited by King James II wasn't the innocent game we think of today. In actuality, we have no idea what they played back then. The Irish have long engaged in hurling, a sport where balls are struck with sticks between goalposts. The French played *jeu de mail*, a curious mix of croquet and billiards. It's undeniable that stick and ball sports have existed for centuries, making it possible that golf evolved like eyes and wings—more than once, and in multiple locations. Trade was extensive between the British Isles and continental Europe far earlier than the 15th century, and travelers almost surely swung the occasional club during their travels. Why shouldn't the sport be a shared invention among European brethren?

A more complicated challenge to golf's Scottish origins comes from the Chinese game *Chuiwan*, which existed hundreds of years before any kilt-wearer even thought about inventing a cleek. We know that *Chuiwan* involved hitting balls into holes, like golf, because earliest references mention digging into the ground so a daughter could practice her game. Ancient murals show players swinging clubs similar to those of the modern sport, and they even held them in a manner similar to that of today, though with one hand instead of two. Players waited their turns to swing and had caddies carrying their clubs.

The Chinese version also used equipment remarkably similar to the European version, with *Chuiwan* relying on the *Cuanbang* (driver), *Pubang* (wood, also called a brassie), and *Shabang* (wedge). Anyone curious about the game's equipment or rules only needs to read the 13th-century manuscript *Wan Jing* for inspiration, which discusses several key rules of the sport, along with equipment descriptions and tips on betting. These similarities raise the question of whether news of *Chuiwan* ever reached Europe. And if it did, did it influence the sport we know today? We'll probably never know.

Regardless of its earliest origins, golf quickly became uniquely a game of the Scots, who were also responsible for giving us the rules we enjoy today. The first official list of articles governing play—a total of 13 in all, many of which remain today—was published in 1744 for an event held by the Gentlemen Golfers of Edinburgh. You're still not allowed to change balls midhole, and shots landing in the water still incur a one-shot penalty. Time has changed some things, though. Players no longer tee off next to the hole they just finished or earn a free drop if their ball lands inside a soldier's trench. That second rule doesn't come up often today, mostly because warfare is uncommon on most courses, as are stray horses taking your ball (rule #10). Still, it's good to know history is on your side for a free drop, should luck turn against you.

Even with these rules, however, there was a lot variation between different clubs. Locations like Aberdeen, Perth, and Blackheath all had their different means for dealing with problems like hazards and lost balls; for example, a ball landing in a water hazard at St. Andrews could be dropped six yards behind the hazard, but one at Bruntsfield Links had to be thrown over the head, though the player was free to toss it as far as he or she liked. Fifty years later at St. Andrews, it became acceptable to tee up next to the drop instead. If a player accidentally played his opponent's ball at Blackheath, there was no penalty at all, but at other locations it meant a lost hole or the opponent claiming a free stroke. As travel increased and rules started to conflict, madness ensued.

Eventually, The Royal and Ancient Golf Club of St. Andrews became the official governing body, leading to the first-ever consolidated code in 1899. Finally, there were universal rules for problems like balls landing out of bounds and what happens when you putt into the flagstick. However, the good feeling didn't last long, as the Americans decided to create their own governing body at about the same time. Fortunately, most of the major rules and topics were uniform.

Changes in the rules continued for many years, and the rules continue to change today. Twice during the 1948 PGA Championship, Ben Hogan faced an unusual challenge. Though his ball was only a couple of feet away from the cup, his opponent's ball was in the way. Today, the solution would be simple, as standard rules allow the opposing player to mark and lift his or her ball, but not so in Hogan's time. Called a stymie, the situation gave Hogan only two choices—chip over his opponent, despite still being on the green, or go around. And this is what he did, the first time successfully lifting his ball over his opponent with a wedge and landing it next to the hole. The second time, he hugged his opponent's ball, seemingly curving it toward the cup and dropping it in for the victory.

Scoring has its own history too, and it's almost as complicated as the rules. When players first started swinging clubs, calculating scores was a complicated process, and sometimes players didn't even bother keeping track. They just kept tally of how they were playing compared to one another, making score a relativistic affair. Not surprisingly, this didn't last long, and by the late 19th century, golf clubs were standardizing expected scores. The term "bogey" was likely created first, with each hole having something called a "ground score" or "bogey." That's equivalent to what we call par today, and though nobody knows for sure where the term "bogey" came from, it's probably not a coincidence that a common song at the time in local music halls was, "Hush! Hush! Hush! Here Comes the Bogey Man." According to one story, the term began when a player remarked about another at the Great Yarmouth Club just east of Norwich that he was he was a "regular bogey man." The compliment, which meant his opponent was playing a solid game, was akin to saying that he was playing like a bogey man or devil might play—without error. The Brits being a superstitious bunch, the name stuck.

Not surprisingly, the idea of envisioning yourself playing an imaginary devil or goblin who always shoots the standard score wasn't a good, long-term solution. That's why the Americans developed their own system, which they called "par" and was defined by distance from the tee box to the hole. A hole up to 225 yards was a par three, up to 425 a par four, and up to 600 yards a par five. Everything else was a par six. Fortunately, the par six concept was eventually dropped, though some courses still flaunt these conventions today. At the moment, the longest hole in the world is in Ulaanbaatar, Mongolia, and it's 1,250 miles long. The current record holder for the hole, Adam Rolston, a twenty-eight-year-old former rugby player from Northern Ireland, swung 20,093 times to get the ball in the hole, which I'm guessing means this is the hole's par. Just bring your jacket if you try to beat this score, because Ulaanbaatar rests almost a full mile above sea level, at roughly the same latitude as Montreal, making it also the coldest national capital in the world.

The term *birdie* is another American term that the English were forced to accept, and according to one story it can be traced to a specific moment. Though the Yanks had been using "bird" for a long while to mean anything excellent, in a 1962 interview for a groundskeeping magazine, someone remarked about one player's incredible approach shot being a true "bird of a shot." Then came a bet about the player finishing the hole under par, with the final bet-winning score being a "birdie."

For beginners, these terms can seem confusing, I know, but just be thankful we don't still use "whaup" or "curlew." There was a time when these terms were used to describe holes in one, and not surprisingly, the names didn't stick.

One final question remains about the origins of another important golf standard—why do courses have 18 holes? One story is that it takes 18 shots to finish a fifth of whisky, making it a perfect number for a sport involving walking and drinking, though it's almost surely apocryphal. The math simply doesn't agree, since by standard measurements, there are only 16 shots in a fifth, unless your bartender is shortchanging you. The real story is probably more complicated and involves everybody following the lead of the Old Course at St. Andrews. It used to have 22 holes, which was close to becoming a standard, but then came some rearranging of greens to match the available landscape, with several holes being collapsed into one. Then came the 18 holes, which are standard today.

Still, feel free to share the whisky story instead. It's definitely more fun.

Another reason to call golf a Scottish invention is because of the people involved. Just as with other sports, it's easy to think of golf in terms of the people who shaped it, both historically and in modern forms. It would be hard to talk about golf today without mentioning names like Jack Nicklaus, Tiger Woods, and Phil Mickelson, because these players, along with numerous others, haven't just been great athletes. They changed the sport itself. Nicklaus showed that the sport is as much about grit as it is about technique, and Woods showed how power and psychology can make competitors cower, even though the sport isn't about head-on competition. Odds are that in a hundred years, these players will be seen as institutions in the same way Aberdeen and St. Andrews are seen today.

Yet, who were the figures that most shaped golf in its infancy?

Certainly, any talk about great golfers and golf advocates must start with Old Tom Morris. Though St. Andrews has a huge personality of its own, it's still nothing compared to this man whom we call "Old" simply because he would raise a son with the same name who was nearly as influential. Old Tom Morris, a four-time winner of the Open Championship, isn't known for his swing, though his playing résumé is impressive. He did win three Open Championships at the same time the Americans were fighting their Civil War across the pond. Another victory, his fourth, came even later. But more important was his role as course designer; as the father of modern groundskeeping, Morris revolutionized many aspects of the modern game that we take for granted today—yardage markers, tee boxes, and even manicured bunkers. Before Morris, grass was often cut by cattle, not machines, but he got the idea to treat greens and hazards differently. Thanks to pioneers like Morris, we now have manicured putting surfaces and strategically placed sand traps, as well as courses designed by experts rather than the whims of nature. You can even see Morris's gravesite at the St. Andrews Cathedral, just a short distance from where he died still working to make the Old Course the modern work of art that it has become today.

Although it would be impossible to address all of history's golfing greats, a few players took key roles in seeing the sport grow to its current fame, including the incomparable Harry Vardon. Born in Jersey between the English mainland and Normandy, he won six Open Championships at the turn of the 20th century. He also invented the modern grip, which involves overlapping fingers like we know of today. Not only that, he helped bring the sport to the United States through a series of playing exhibitions, which led to a whole new generation of athletes. Winning the U.S. Open during his first visit to the States didn't hurt his future reputation, either.

One player who certainly benefited from Vardon's influence was Francis Ouimet, who attended one of those clinics and used it as motivation to compete himself. In one of the greatest matches in golf history, at age twenty, Ouimet took on Vardon and British long-hitter Ted Ray at the U.S. Open, and he actually won. Not only did this signal the start of American prominence on the international golf scene, it drew great attention to the sport along the mainland; and for the next 30 years Vardon, Ouimet, and a new generation of golfers would develop the sport into the international phenomenon that we know of today.

The parade of great golfers that came next each could deserve his or her own book. Arnold Palmer revolutionized the concept of charismatic golfer, as at home in rural Texas as he was at his hometown of Latrobe, PA. Jack Nicklaus made his name in the era of televised play not through charisma, though he had that too, but through dominant and intimidating performances, earning him the name "The Golden Bear" and 18 major championships. That's a record unlikely to be broken anytime soon. Yet, some names stand out for revolutionizing the game in different ways.

Take Ben Hogan, for example. He didn't win the most championships, not even close—his nine major victories constitute half that of Nicklaus. His putting was below average too, so bad that when he wrote an entire book about golf technique, putting didn't get a single sentence. No, Hogan's contribution was to the swing itself. At a time when everybody was learning how to swing a club in his or her own way, Hogan developed his "Five Lessons" for mastering the stroke, and it worked perfectly. He was one of the first players to assign individual clubs to specific distances, and when he aimed for a spot, he almost always hit it, despite once nearly dying in a head-on collision with a Greyhound bus. The accident, which fractured his pelvis, collar bone, and ankle, not to mention giving him a severe blood clot, led to circulation problems that would plague him for life. Yet, largely due to his steady work ethic and severe determination, he still earned 64 wins on the PGA Tour, fourth most all time, and when later greats like Jack Nicklaus are asked who had the best swing in history, their answer is almost always Hogan.

Some golfers aren't well known, but their impact has still been just as great. John Shippen, the son of a Presbyterian minister at the Shinnecock Indian Reservation, was one of the first African Americans to play the sport professionally, though his road to acceptance wasn't easy. A caddy at Shinnecock Hills, he was encouraged by its members to give play a try when the U.S. Open came to the course in 1896, many even offering to cover his entry fee. However, other more traditional players complained, saying that someone of his skin color didn't belong on the course. The opinion that blacks should stay away from golf, which wasn't uncommon at the time, was met with resistance from the USGA, which replied that the other players were welcome to boycott. In fact, if nobody else showed up, they would be happy to give

Shippen the victory outright, which silenced many complaints. In the end, Shippen took sixth place, earning him ten dollars and recognition as a pioneer in the area of African American rights. Much later, he also earned a posthumous membership to the PGA.

The history of women's golf is also filled with numerous great names, and their battle for equality on the links was no easier. In 1893, amateur golfer Horace Hutchinson had this to say about the future of women's golf, immediately before the first ladies' championship:

> *Constitutionally and physically women are unfitted for golf. They will never last through two rounds of a long course in a day. Nor can they ever hope to defy the wind and weather encountered on our best links even in spring and summer. Temperamentally, the strain will be too great for them.*

Next came other ridiculous restrictions, for example Lord Moncrieff's restriction that women not hit the ball farther than 70 yards. Why? Because "that cannot well be done without raising the club above the shoulder . . . now we do not presume to dictate, but we must observe that the posture and gestures requisite for a full swing are not particularly graceful when the player is clad in female dress."

In case it wasn't clear, that last statement claimed that women shouldn't play golf because then everybody could see under their skirts. Because what else could women possibly wear?

One could spend 20 pages repeating all the crazy things that have been said over the ages about the rise of women's golf, but rather than that, I'd like to introduce one woman who showed the world that female golfers were in every way a man's equal, not just on the course, but on the professional teaching circuit, too. Her name was Helen Hicks.

When Helen Hicks entered the golf scene, a few women were already calling themselves professionals of the sport, but Hicks invented her own term—a businesswoman golfer. With Gene Sarazen and Babe Zaharias, another female entering the male ranks, she went on tour representing Wilson Sporting Goods, where she wowed fans with playing demonstrations and positive, upbeat lessons. She must have done well, because soon, Wilson gave her a tour on her own, which also allowed her to sell her own signature brand clubs. With few opportunities to play for money, Hicks jumped at the chance to compete in the Women's Western Open, which she won handily, becoming the first professional to win the title. Then came more play, and more wins, and soon women got their first professional organization, earning Hicks a role as founding member of the LPGA. Others would soon follow, like Lady Margaret Scott, Joyce Wethered, and Glenna Collett, all of whom regularly struck the ball hundreds of yards, despite Moncrieff's warnings. The sport would never be the same, and we're stronger for it.

When discussing the history of golf, one can't escape a discussion of the equipment itself, because it has evolved just as much as the people and courses. Take for example golf balls, or, as they were once called, "featheries." Before modern technology took hold, balls were larger than they are today and made of leather, stitched together from three separate pieces and filled with boiled feathers. Those feathers were stuffed inside the ball through a small hole and left to expand once the water dried. The application of a quick layer of paint enabled the ball to develop a resilience that allowed for hits almost as long as today's version. Still, the technology wasn't perfect. As feathers were repeatedly hit, they tended to move, allowing the ball to take unusual shapes. And the materials weren't cheap either, costing more than five dollars per ball by today's standards. Still, they can't have been too bad, because according to one legend, Frenchman Samuel Messieux once hit a feathery over 350 yards. Wow!

After featheries came gutties, which were made from the coagulated juice of the gutta-percha tree, a common material at the time for insulation. It had the benefit of remaining round and consistent in shape, along with being much cheaper, and soon a technology boom was born. Not long after, Coburn Haskell and an employee from B.F. Goodrich got the idea of winding rubber bands around a solid core. This gave the ball great potential energy, and an arms race was born. Next came research with different kinds of cores, and rubber windings, and eventually we got the ball everybody knows of today. Even now, more than a hundred years after the arrival of the first "nonfeatherie," many balls still have cores surrounded by rubber thread, much like Haskell's design.

Golf clubs went through a significant evolution too, in tandem with the ball. Back when players still used featheries, clubs had to be forgiving because balls were so expensive and fragile. Wood clubfaces were common, with forged metal faces being saved for getting out of holes or ruts left from wagon wheels. As ball technology developed, so did clubs, which more frequently included forged iron faces, though with flat and smooth surfaces. That changed at the turn of the century too, when players realized that grooves enabled them to use spin. This allowed for more control, especially around the green, a major priority, since balls were now becoming less likely to fly sideways because of unwanted lumps from irregular feather insides.

The next major development came after World War I, when improved technology and greater access to resources allowed for use of steel shafts. Before this, most clubs were made from hickory, often by hand, and they were assigned funny names rather than the familiar numbers we know of today. A long wood was called a brassie. A short wood was a spoon, and a long iron was a cleek. Middle irons were mashies, short irons were niblicks, and lofted putters were called jiggers. Yup, you read that right, many players at the time used modified putters around the green with very low lofts, usually less than 10 percent, just for hitting around the fringe. Today the jigger lives on as a chipper, which some people still use today but is rarely found in most bags.

The problem with hickory clubs was that they were both expensive and unwieldy, so it's not surprising that changes were to come, and the answer was steel. Steel allowed for longer and more reliable hits, and a swing revolution was born. It wouldn't take long for steel to be replaced by graphite, and wood clubfaces to be replaced by titanium. In other words, if a club could be made lighter or stronger, somebody was willing to give the manufacturing a try.

So, where did golf come from, and how did it get where it is today? The easy answer is that the sport was born in Scotland, but ignoring China or the Netherlands is like ignoring the Greeks or the French Revolution when talking about democracy. Yes, the Americans have their Constitution, but sometimes movements occur through shared inspiration and a common, great idea. History cares little for political or geographic boundaries.

So, golf almost surely is Scottish, at least in terms of soul, but there's certainly some Dutch blood in there. And French. And Chinese, too. If nature loves flying animals so much as to evolve them multiple times and in countless different species, why can't multiple societies invent a sport where balls are hit long distances by sticks?

It's a good way to spend an afternoon. Just don't let your archery skills falter too much. And don't play any pickup games with sorcerers. They're a nasty sort.

READING LIST

General History

Browning, R. (1985). *History of Golf: Classics of Golf Series*. New York: Classics of Golf.

Bulter, A., Hamilton, D., and Zhou, W. (2017). *Chiu Wan: An Ancient Chinese Golf-like Game*. Partick Press: St. Andrews, Scotland.

Ceron-Anaya, H. (2010). An Approach to the History of Golf: Business, Symbolic Capital, and Technologies of the Self. *Journal of Sport and Social Issues*, 34, 339–358.

Gillmeister, H. (2002). Golf on the Rhine: On the Origins of Golf, with Sidelights on Polo. *The International Journal on the History of Sport*, 19, 1–30.

Hongling, L. (1991). Verification of the Fact that Golf Originated from Chuiwan. *Australian Society for Sports History Bulletin*, 14, 12–23.

Price, C. (1962). *The World of Golf*. New York: Random House, Inc.

Psychology 201: Control and Flow

Prerequisites: Psychology 101: The Angel of the Odd and the Imp of the Perverse

Tiger Woods wears only red shirts on Sunday, the final day of most tournaments, because his mother told him it's his power color. He hasn't broken the pattern since college. Paul Azinger only marks his ball with pennies, Lincoln looking to the hole, because it helps guide the ball. Ben Crenshaw never uses balls numbered higher than four, because, well, to do otherwise would be crazy.

Such superstitions are rife in golf, and sports in general, because they help us feel like we're in control. There's nothing worse than missing a short putt, or sending an errant drive out of bounds, for no apparent reason. But illusions of control can cause problems too, especially when we forget that they're just tricks.

Doug Sanders never uses white tees because they're bad luck. He also tosses finished cigarettes between his legs, never to the side, because it's good luck and he was born before tossing cigarettes as litter was recognized as a jerk move. These are the superstitions elite golfers maintain to keep their sanity, though the 1970 British Open challenged all that. As Sanders approached the final hole of golf's most historic contest, all he needed was par to ensure a victory. Normally, this would be the time for sticking with routine, but then his partner's caddy handed him a very special white tee. This exact tee had been used by a close friend of Sanders several years before to win the same tournament. Sadly, his friend had died shortly after the win, making this particular tee special.

Sanders had planned on taking the same flight that killed his friend, but circumstances had saved his life, and now this white tee was asking him to forget his superstitions and pay tribute to his lost comrade.

Sanders had no choice but to tee off and risk his fate. You can't blame the caddy for not knowing about Sanders's "no white tees" rule, or for being sentimental, but sadly it cost Sanders dearly.

So begins professional golfing's most tragic collapse, and on its biggest stage. With only an easy par four remaining, he quickly found the green and left himself a three-foot putt to seal the victory. All he needed was this gimme shot. He took his time and lined up, but thoughts of that white tee wouldn't escape his mind. Then . . . he missed. Next came a playoff with Jack Nicklaus and a loss by a single stroke.

"Something negative had been triggered," Doug later claimed. "I knew by using that tee I had broken my own trend."

If only life were as simple as always using the right color tees. But it's not, and that's why simple solutions are so tempting. This chapter explores the many ways players deal with this lack of control, and we start with superstition because it's so common. Why has no winner of Augusta's Par-3 contest ever won the full tournament? One answer is dumb luck, but players have also recognized the pattern, and now some reportedly have thrown the contest for fear of ruining their chances the next day.

In this class, we'll see why some players are willing to do so much just for the perception of control. In freshman year, we learned about the Angel of the Odd and the Imp of the Perverse, but now it's time to take these beasts to another level. It's time to explore a concept called *Flow*.

Superstitions give the impression that life is under our control, and that's not necessarily bad. Sometimes it even helps, but we better use them right. When avid golfers are asked to putt with a club formerly owned by a prominent professional, they sink significantly more hits.[1] It doesn't even matter if the background is fabricated—believing that a club is good luck helps, and being told that one is cursed can be just as bad.

One way scientists measure superstitious behavior on the course is the Four-Ball test. Players are asked to make a series of putts using balls of different colors, all stored in a large bucket. Some are red, others blue, and others pink, the important point being that the player chooses his or her own. The goal is to sink as many putts as possible, with a small reward if the player does well.

Not surprisingly, nearly everybody develops a superstition eventually, choosing one color over the others. Some are quick to develop a "favorite ball," others take more time, but what really matters is which kind of shots bring about the preference. Studies show that amateurs are likely to adopt a "lucky ball" under one circumstance in particular—short putts.[2] These are the kinds that give beginners the most trouble, and so they beg for additional help. Did you just miss a two-foot tap-in with a blue ball? Better not try that again. Never missed from within a foot using red? If so, then that's your color.

By contrast, a different pattern emerges for skilled players. For them, long hits demand the most control, and these are the most likely to develop lucky favorites. Experts couldn't care less about that short putt, because extra luck in these cases is just wasted. Best to save that red ball for the twenty-foot downhill screamer, because you'll need all the luck you can get.

Such superstitions may seem silly, and they are, but they're also part of a much larger psychological phenomenon. I'm talking about our need to establish control over our own mental state. When we believe that our game depends on chance, we lose motivation. It's like giving up, except we're not ceding to anyone or anything in particular, just randomness and life itself. Although things like shirt or ball color don't actually affect play, these choices show that we're still trying.

Fortunately, there are other things we can do to control our psychological game, things that are scientifically proven. Take for example preshot routine. Instruction books emphasize checking stance, posture, and grip before every swing because it ensures consistency, but there are psychological benefits, too. These steps provide a mental structure for the entire swing, a feeling that every shot is the same. Improvement comes with practice, and there's no better way to improve than to make each swing like the thousands that came before it. If that means ensuring a proper wardrobe and tee color too, then so be it.

We see the importance of preshot routines every time professionals play on television. From the way they step to the ball—first the left foot, then the right—to the way they waggle the club before drawback, these players prove that consistency is key. And preshot routines are a big part of that consistency.

Studies show that skilled players spend more time setting up their shot than amateurs do, and this time is well spent.[3] It even predicts who will have a better shot. When 12 professional players were monitored during competition, one thing differentiated successful hitters from unsuccessful ones—time spent before swinging.[4] Those who took longer to set up their shots landed the ball closer to the hole and achieved lower scores than those around them, simply by taking the time to visualize success.

Sometimes the need to maintain a brisk pace keeps us from developing a reliable preshot routine. Sometimes we're just lazy. That's a shame, because these routines don't just help consistency, they overcome biases that might otherwise hijack our game.

One such bias is called undeserved optimism. That's our tendency to overestimate chances of success, and it's killer. In Psychology 101, we learned that imagining ourselves hitting into a bunker is the best way to do just that, but teeing up with delusions of grandeur is just as bad. If you've never hit a ball over two hundred yards, what are the chances of doing so today? Optimism is great for avoiding bad thoughts, but when it coaxes us toward bad decisions, it becomes the enemy.

Establishing a consistent preshot routine is one way to avoid such biases, which means paying close attention to shot selection. Following the underserved optimism bias, players frequently choose low percentage shots because they imagine only positive consequences. Take for example the study by two psychologists from the Center for Behavioral Medicine in Chicago, Daniel Kirschebaum and Edmund O'Connor.[5] They set up an observation station at the fourteenth hole at Winnetka Golf Club in Illinois with one goal in mind. They wanted to see under what circumstances players made risky shots, and what prompted them to be so foolish.

The par-four hole they chose had recently been changed so even regular members were unaccustomed to the design, and it was filled with danger. The green was over 250 yards from the tee, beyond most players' reach. A small lake stood in between, the kind begging for optimistic play. There were also extensive trees lining the fairway, ensuring that mishits would land in the woods. The choice should have been easy—lay up short of the lake and save thoughts of birdies for another hole.

Alternatively, players could take a big risk and shoot for the hole. Though the risky shot wasn't impossible, the local club pro made it clear—hitting long wasn't worth it. The smart play for almost everybody was to aim shy of the water. Kirschebaum and O'Connor stationed themselves at the tee boxes and took notes about each player's shot before receiving any advice, recording the ball's landing location each time. They also noted which clubs were used.

Then, some players were given a second ball. This ball, the experimenters requested, should be hit following the local pro's recommendation, aiming short of the water. Even if the player thought he or she could hit the ball farther, that player should save his or her energy for the next shot. The researchers recommended that players imagine a green at the target location, then aim as if the hole were in the center.

Usually, we assume that having more choice is best. For their first shot, players had two options—lay up or be aggressive—and they supposedly chose based on their own skills. However, this is not what the experimenters saw.

More than half of the players used a driver on their first shot, with almost 90 percent of people leaving themselves in a bad position. This led to an average score of just over bogey for the hole, 5.34 strokes. For those asked to take the second shot, the vast majority choose between a 6-iron and a wedge. Nearly half the shots were excellent, with one in ten players improving by a full stroke when their final score was recorded.

Sometimes choice doesn't help, especially when it tempts us to make bad decisions. To overcome this bias, we must think in the long term. Like a superstitious belief causing you to miss a gimme putt, unchecked optimism can kill your score, especially if it coaxes you to try the impossible.

Take Phil Mickelson's breakdown at the 2006 U.S. Open, a collapse nearly as tragic as the one Sanders had experienced decades before. As he approached the 18th hole on the final day, with a one-stroke lead and ready to earn his third major victory of the year, everybody supposedly knew what was about to happen—Mickelson was finally about to surpass Tiger Woods. All he needed was to play conservatively and the win was his. However, what followed was a case study in bad judgment. First, he got aggressive off the tee and sliced his ball into the course's hospitality tent, leaving it well left of the fairway. Then he had a choice—either play it safe and knock it back onto the fairway, or skirt a tree and aim for the green. Mickelson chose to be aggressive, as he'd done most of his career, and hit the tree instead. Then he overhit his next shot too, landing the ball buried in a bunker.

With an up-and-down shot still promising victory, he aimed for the hole and the win and trickled his shot off the green instead. What resulted was a bogey and a very disappointing second place.

"I still am in shock that I did that," he shared with the media afterward. "I just can't believe that I did that. I am such an idiot. I can't believe I couldn't par the last hole. It really stings."

So many decisions go into every shot, most beyond our conscious awareness. Every time we step up to the ball, we prepare both our minds and bodies for what is to come. Ideally, this includes an honest assessment of risks, though optimism isn't always the rule. Sometimes we find ourselves so afraid of screwing up that cautiousness dooms us instead.

The discovery of another kind of bias—loss aversion—was so important, it even won its discoverers the Nobel Prize. The psychologists Daniel Kahneman and Amos Tversky won their prize in the field of economics because it's best understood in terms of gains and benefits. Have you ever found a twenty-dollar bill in a forgotten drawer or pair of pants? If so, you were probably pleased. Now think back—have you ever lost the same amount through a hole in your pocket?

Odds are that the losing experience was even more frustrating than the find was pleasant. As Kahneman and Tversky found, people hate losing even more than they like winning. We assess risk in terms of vulnerability and disappointment, and this can hold us back from otherwise great opportunities.

We see this especially in putting, where professionals are significantly less accurate when shooting for a birdie, compared to par.[6] This finding is surprising, since birdies are like bread and butter on the professional tour—they're what keeps families fed. Yet, even pros worry more about difficult follow-up shots than circles on their scorecard. Putts are left short when they really matter, simply because of caution and fear, and this trend remains even after controlling for other factors like average distance to the hole. We're more afraid of shooting bogey than we're excited about accomplishing something special.

The amazing thing about this loss aversion is that it depends so much on stakes. Early in tournaments when everything is still up for grabs, the effect is greatest. These are the holes where putting accuracy differs the most between attempting birdie and par, and so this is when we're the most afraid. Earning a great score on the first day of a tournament won't ensure a win, but shooting bogey golf promises an early trip home. Later on, when winning requires shooting better than par, and birdies start being the key to a potential win, the effect subsides. Players unconsciously accept the risk of losing, and they drop their conservative play.

Though such biases won't ruin your game, they will cause you to adopt strategies that hurt in the long run. They're not rational, but neither is sport. This can be frustrating and emotional, yet sometimes our unconscious desire to avoid that terrible shot is too powerful to overcome.

Part of making good decisions is controlling our emotions, specifically anxiety. We play cautiously, or attempt foolish shots, when the wrong parts of our brain take control. This isn't easy to avoid, but recognizing the problem is a good first step. So is knowing how anxiety affects our bodies, and how to work with it to improve our game.

The first thing to recognize about anxiety is that golfers are an uptight bunch. When anxious thoughts are counted over the course of days, called trait anxiety, golfers prove themselves truly exceptional. In fact, golfers tend to be more anxious than athletes in the worlds of soccer, baseball, rugby, swimming, and long-distance running. One reason golfers are so uptight is that arousal is part of play, as sport is a unique blend of physical and psychological challenges. Without anxiety, it wouldn't be as fun to play.

Unfortunately, anxiety also hurts our scores. People who score high on tests of competitive anxiety play worse than more relaxed individuals, as observed by numerous controlled studies. This doesn't mean all anxiety is bad, or that we're necessarily doomed by our emotional responses. The secret is to harness that anxiety, and skilled athletes know how to do just that. Though skilled athletes report comparable anxiety levels to amateurs, they're more likely to interpret those feelings in a positive way.

To see how professionals manage that anxiety, we only need to look at the heartbeat. The heart is a great tool for measuring arousal because it's so straightforward—faster heartbeats mean more arousal.

This arousal has a big effect on our mental focus, because swinging a club requires intense concentration. All swings start with preparation, when we choose both our shots and our clubs. Heart rate increases during this phase by up to 30 percent, and that's unavoidable. This is when we must convince ourselves not to attempt that driver shot over the water hazard, and it's not easy. A single bad decision can cost several strokes or more, and our hearts know it.

Also unavoidable is stress during the swing itself, known as the moment of truth. If we didn't feel at least a little arousal during the swing, we wouldn't be playing. The remaining component, of course, is a middle phase between preparation and execution, when the player sets up for the shot to come. This is the moment where anxiety truly kills us, and the heart becomes the surest indicator of future success or failure.

When professional and amateur golfers were connected to heart rate monitors, one thing was obvious for both groups—lower heart rates while setting up meant better shots.[7] Some players even reported "being in rhythm" at this moment, like the concept of "Flow" that we'll discuss very soon. It's okay to be nervous as you approach the ball, and a little anxiety during the swing itself is okay, too. But you're doomed if you let your mind race when it should be focused on the hole. There's a time for concentration and a time for being relaxed.

The same goes for putting, where skilled players know how to calm themselves immediately before striking the ball. The effect is greatest for longer putts, and also when players are given pressure in the form of extra noises. These are the most difficult shots and require the greatest levels of concentration. The more relaxed our heart rates, the more likely we are to succeed. There's a term for this moment of intense concentration, and it's called *Flow*. Psychologist Mihaly Csikszentmihalyi coined the term, which he used to describe the psychological state of being fully engrossed in action. It's the confidence we feel in being able to meet whatever challenges are to come, also known as being "in the moment." Though we often think of flow in terms of reaction-based sports, like tennis or basketball, concentration is just as important for mental games like golf. Establishing proper mindset prior to the shot matters just as much as—or more than—having fast reflexes. When competitive golfers are asked what best characterizes their peak performance, focus and immersion win easily. Professionals forget about everything else but the game, and even then, attention is directed only toward factors within control. This means considering shot selection and overall strategy, but forgetting about the consequences. One survey of 23 playing and teaching professionals found that concentration is the key to better play. Another survey of European female golfers found that attitude and focus were the most important factors in meeting self-directed goals. One series of interviews with PGA Tour golfers found that successful play occurred only when mental focus was integrated into their preshot routines. We play better when we introduce flow into our game.

Take for example this quote from Tiger Woods, shortly after he won the 1997 Masters by 12 strokes, one of the most lopsided victories in the history of sport:

> *There comes a point in time when you feel tranquil, when you feel calm; you feel at ease with yourself. And those two weeks, I felt that way. I felt very at ease with myself. And for some reason, things just flowed. And no matter what you do, good or bad, it really doesn't get to you. Even the days when you wake up on the wrong side of the bed, for some reason, it doesn't feel too bad; it's just all right.*

It's not easy improving our mental game, but it's not impossible, either. Just as physical training programs improve strength and flexibility, mental programs can improve psychological outlook. For most players, the best interventions are cognitive-behavioral, which uses thoughts to encourage stable emotions and behavior. We do this by taking a rational assessment of our strengths and weaknesses. As you might expect, this isn't simple, but the benefits can be significant. When 17 beginning golf students were given cognitive-behavioral training before putting, they shot more accurately and left the ball closer to the hole.[8] They also had more consistent preputt routines and a greater positive outlook.

Another option is hypnosis. This might seem surprising, but hypnosis has a long history of improving flow in sports. The sport psychologists John Pates and Ian Maynard saw this when they had three experienced golfers undergo hypnosis to improve their chipping performance.[9] Each player established baseline skill before the experiment by attempting nearly a hundred chip shots onto a green 20 yards away. After this came multistage hypnosis training, which involved vivid imagery practice and introduction of a special trigger. The trigger was a song chosen by each player due to its special, positive associations. This song was played while the subject visualized his or her best performance on the course, the goal being to associate it with feelings of success.

The test came when players were asked to attempt the same chip shots as practiced earlier, but now with the trigger to help them. All three subjects shot significantly better while playing their chosen song in their head, landing the ball on average three and a half feet closer to the hole. They also reported higher levels of flow, as measured by a Flow State Scale. When asked to attempt the same chip shots without the songs, all three players performed worse again. It was as if the training hadn't happened at all. The difference hadn't just been the practice, it had been their ability to remember what it was like being in a flow state, as prompted by the song.

These results make flow seem like some mysterious entity conjured only by hypnosis and magical songs, but it's more than that. It's what happens when we take control of our own mental processes. In Psychology 101, we personified intrusion of conscious awareness using the Angel of the Odd. Now we're talking about replacing anxiety and unconscious biases with feelings of being in the moment. Establishing clear preshot routines is one way to encourage this state, and so is mental training and hypnosis. But the outcome is always the same.

What's key is the belief that even luck and chance are within our control. Those lucky shirts or pennies might not have magical powers, but they don't need to. They just need to convince us that we're in charge.

READING LIST

Anxiety and the mental game

Beauchamp, P. (1998). Peak Putting Performance: Psychological Skills and Strategies Utilized by PGA Tour Golfers. In Farrally, M. and Cochran, A. (Ed.), *Science and Golf III: Proceedings of the World Scientific Congress of Golf* (pp. 181–189). Champaign, IL: Human Kinetics.

Cook, D., Gansneder, B., Rotella, R., Malone, C., Bunker, L., and Owens, D. (1983). Relationship Among Competitive State Anxiety, Ability, and Golf Performance. *Journal of Sport Psychology*, 5, 460–465.

[4]Crews, D. and Boutcher, S. (1986). An Exploratory Observational Behavior Analysis of Professional Golfers During Competition. *Journal of Sport Behavior*, 92, 51–58.

Cunningham, G. and Ashley, F. (2002). Debilitative and Facilitative Perceptions of Trait Anxiety Among Students in a College Golf Class. *Perceptual and Motor Skills*, 94, 739–742.

Douglas, K. and Fox, K. (2002). Practice for Competition in Women Professional Golfers. In Thain, E. (Ed.), *Science and Golf IV: Proceedings of the World Scientific Congress of Golf* (pp. 257–263). New York: Routledge.

Han, D., Kim, J., Lee, Y., Bae, S., Kim, H., Sim, M., Sung, Y., and Lyoo, I. (2006). Influence of Temperament and Anxiety on Athletic Performance. *Journal of Sports Science and Medicine*, 5, 381–389.

Hellstrom, J. (2009). Psychological Hallmarks of Skilled Golfers. *Sports Medicine*, 39, 845–855.

Ismail, M. (2016). Effectiveness of "PIM" Training on Putting Performance and Pre-Competitive Anxiety of the Golfers. *International Journal of Golf Science*, 5, 26–37.

Jones, G. and Swain, A. (1995). Predispositions to Experience Debilitative and Facilitative Anxiety in Elite and Nonelite Performers. *The Sport Psychologist*, 9, 201–211.

[3]Koyoma, S., Tsuruhara, K., and Yamamoto, Y. (2009). Duration of Mentally Simulated Movement Before and After a Golf Shot. *Perceptual and Motor Skills*, 108, 327–338.

McCaffrey, N. and Orlick, T. (1989). Mental Factors Related to Excellence Among Top Professional Golfers. *International Journal of Sport Psychology*, 20, 256–278.

Thomas, P. and Over, R. (1994). Psychological and Psychomotor Skills Associated with Performance in Golf. *The Sport Psychologist*, 8, 73–86.

Weinberg, R. and Genuchi, M. (1980). Relationship Between Competitive Trait Anxiety, State Anxiety, and Golf Performance: A Field Study. *Journal of Sport Psychology*, 2, 148–154.

Flow and cognitive-behavioral training

[8]Beauchamp, P., Halliwell, W., Fournier, J., and Koestner, R. (1996). Effects of Cognitive-Behavioral Psychological Skills Training on the Motivation, Preparation, and Putting Performance of Novice Golfers. *The Sport Psychologist,* 10, 157–170.

Csikszentmihalyi, M. (1990). *Flow: The Psychology of Optimal Experience.* New York: Harper & Row.

Nicholls, A. and Polman, R. (2005). The Effects of Individualized Imagery Interventions on Golf Performance and Flow States. *Athletic Insight,* 7, 43–65.

Stein, G., Kimiecik, J., Daniels, J., and Jackson, S. (1995). Psychological Antecedents of Flow in Recreational Sport. *Personality and Social Psychology Bulletin,* 21, 125–135.

Heart rate

Boutcher, S. and Zinsser, N. (1990). Cardiac Deceleration of Elite and Beginning Golfers During Putting. *Journal of Sport and Exercise Psychology,* 12, 37–47.

Hassmen, P. and Koivula, N. (2001). Cardiac Deceleration in Elite Golfers as Modified by Noise and Anxiety During Putting. *Perceptual and Motor Skills,* 92, 947–957.

[7]Lonetto, R. (1990). The Coordination of Heart Rate, Personality and Effective Shot Making. In A.J. Cochran (Ed.), *Science and Golf: Proceedings of the First World Scientific Congress of Golf* (pp. 116–120). New York: E&FN Spon.

Neumann, D. and Thomas, P. (2011). Cardiac and Respiratory Activity and Golf Putting Performance Under Attentional Focus Instructions. *Psychology of Sport and Exercise,* 12, 451–459.

Hypnosis

[9]Pates, J. and Maynard, I. (2000). Effects of Hypnosis on Flow States and Golf Performance. *Perceptual and Motor Skills,* 91, 1057–1075.

Pates, J., Oliver, R., and Maynard, I. (2001). The Effects of Hypnosis on Flow States and Golf-Putting Performance. *Journal of Applied Sport Psychology,* 13, 341–354.

Superstitions and biases

[5]Kirschenbaum, D. and O'Connor, E. (1999). Positive Illusions in Golf: Empirical and Conceptual Analysis. *Journal of Applied Sport Psychology*, 11, 1–27.

[1]Lee, C., Linkenauger, S., Bakdash, J., Joy-Gaba, J., and Profitt, D. (2011). Putting Like a Pro: The Role of Positive Contagion in Golf Performance and Perception. *PLoS One*, 6, 1–4.

[6]Pope, D. and Schweitzer, M. (2011). Is Tiger Woods Loss Averse? Persistent Bias in the Face of Experience, Competition, and High Stakes. *American Economics Review*, 101, 129–157.

Van Raalte, J. and Brewer, B. (1991). Chance Orientation and Superstitious Behavior on the Putting Green. *Journal of Sport Behavior*, 14, 41–50.

[2]Wright, P. and Erdal, K. (2008). Sport Superstition as a Function of Skill Level and Task Difficulty. *Journal of Sport Behavior*, 31, 187–199.

Physics 201: Engineering and Technology

Prerequisites: Physics 101: Forces and Inertia

The golf ball may not weigh more than 1.62 ounces. It must also be no smaller than 1.68 inches in diameter and, when struck by a mechanical swing robot, cannot have an initial velocity faster than 250 feet per second (170 mph) or travel more than 280 yards.

Golf is a game of rules, though sometimes those rules are complicated. If your ball lands on a snake, you better hope that it's dead. That would make it a loose impediment and removable, though if it's alive, it becomes an outside agency. Then you better get your first aid kit. If your ball lands inside the clubhouse, the rules allow you to open a window and hit it back on the course. Except of course if it's lodged in an orange. In that case, you have to either hit the orange too, or cut your losses and be thankful you're not paying for a second broken window.

These rules sometimes seem silly, but all stem from specific instances where clarification became necessary. Which makes it so surprising that until the 1970s, there were no rules about golf balls and dimples. Balls could be covered with dimples, grooves, or nothing at all, so long as they didn't fly too fast or too far. This gave Fred Holmstrom, a physicist from San Jose State University, an idea. He and Daniel Nepela, a chemist at IBM, didn't play golf, but they knew that the game was incredibly hard, especially for beginners. The biggest problem for most of these players is their slice. Maybe dimples were the key.

Holmstrom and Nepela started by sanding down a sample ball to reduce its weight. This gave them a few fractions of an ounce to play with, which they used by inserting glue in the dimples along the poles. By creating an asymmetry, they hoped to minimize horizontal spin, and by only filling some of the holes, they allowed the ball to adjust itself naturally in flight while maintaining lift. The solution worked, because when the ball hit the course, slices were reduced by 75 percent. Distance decreased by only a few yards.

Naturally, Holmstrom and Nepela were thrilled. On June 25, 1974, they received a patent, and soon the "happy non-hooker" specialty golf ball swept the country. Fortunately, they used the name *Polara* for commercial purposes.

Many claimed the ball would ruin golf, removing the challenge separating duffers from professionals. Others viewed it as a needed solution for players struggling to enjoy the game. Nearly everybody had an opinion, including the USGA, which outlawed the ball in 1981, along with any other asymmetrical designs:

> *USGA Rules of Golf, Appendix Three, Paragraph Four: The ball must not be designed, manufactured or intentionally modified to have flight properties which differ from those of a spherically symmetrical ball.*

With a single rule change, the Polara ball became illegal, and so were any others using asymmetrical physics to their advantage. You can still buy Polara balls, of course, now produced by Aero-X Golf, Inc., and with even better curve correction. You just can't use them on the PGA Tour. Even in amateur play, if your partner learns you're using a USGA nonapproved ball you'll probably find yourself apologizing and paying off any bets, regardless of score. You might be invited back to the club one day, but I doubt it.

Golf equipment has changed drastically over the last hundred years, and in this chapter we'll see how technology makes such improvements possible. We'll also see what the constant stream of innovations means for the average player. Some of these benefits are real, while others just take money from your wallet, and a little physics can help you tell the difference.

The Polara golf ball works by harnessing a mechanism discussed in Physics 101—rotational kinetic energy. Horizontal rotation is bad, at least for most players, while vertical rotation is good. By limiting dimples to the equator, only good spin is encouraged.

Other aspects of dimple designs, like width, number, and depth, have sought to improve performance, too. Research has shown that increasing dimple depth increases lift, though the benefit peaks around .008 inches.[1] Beyond that, the lift-to-drag ratio drops and the benefit subsides. By contrast, dimple width—as well as overall number of dimples—seems to have little impact on flight.

Except with extreme cases like the Polara, it doesn't even matter how the dimples are arranged. It's nearly impossible to make a perfectly symmetrical ball due to the problem of dimple arrangement, though the most common number of dimples is 336. One unintended consequence of this number is a "row effect," in which several groups of dimples fall into a straight line. Such rows reduce the protective turbulent layer, and so drag increases. Even seams along the ball's outer coating can have the same effect, which is why manufacturers like Titleist now stagger their seam design. However, seams are not really necessary, as studies show that row effects don't influence ball flight that much, only a yard or two at most.[2]

The biggest variety in golf ball design is with interior construction, which can also have a big impact on cost. Prices range from less than a dollar to several dollars a ball, based on material and number of layers. This adds up fast, since the average ball lasts only 23 shots before being damaged or lost. A player with a 20 handicap has a 5 percent chance of losing a ball after every hit, though we do occasionally find one that somebody else has abandoned. This raises the average life expectancy to about 60 shots, which isn't bad but still translates to over one lost ball per match, on average.

Frequent losses make golf balls the largest repeating cost to the golfer after greens fees, so it's worth knowing which type works best for you. Unfortunately, there are so many choices with so many factors to take into consideration that it can be difficult knowing where to start. There's hardness, number of layers, and type of material, to name just a few qualities. The most familiar distinction for the average player is number of layers, with all commercial balls having two or more. More layers generally means higher cost, but that doesn't mean they're always better. What really matters is hardness, which is measured by how much the ball compresses after being struck by the club.

All balls have a core and an outer cover, while only multilayered balls have an additional mantle in between. This mantle provides additional compression, which *usually* means softer hits. It depends on the material, which varies widely. The softer the ball, the more "feel" it has due to its spending more time on the face of the club. The result is more feedback for the player, but at the cost of less power. Hard balls are generally preferred by low handicappers for this reason, because they're willing to sacrifice touch for distance. Less club contact time can also mean less rotation, but the type of outer coating matters, too. The key is how well the club's grooves grip the ball, leading many manufacturers to pair harder interiors with softer covers. Of course, that doesn't necessarily guarantee that any single design is best, and one should always be wary of manufacturers who promise everything.

To see what this means in practical terms, three scientists from Spalding developed a computer model of golf ball impacts under different launch conditions, looking at things like spin, launch angle, and speed.[3] Several balls were tested, each with the same core but with a different mantle or cover. For example, one ball had two layers and a relatively soft cover, while another had three layers with a hard cover and soft mantle. All balls were hit with simulated drivers, irons, and wedges, each using a medium-handicap swing, and the scientists assessed which ones performed best.

Results were clear—balls with soft outers cover had the most spin, and thus best performance around the green. But they also had over 50 percent more spin when hit by the driver, reducing distance off the tee by a dozen yards or more. When these balls included a hard mantle, however, results changed. Softer chip shots had plenty of spin to stop after landing, but drives kept their forward momentum. Contrast this with three-layer balls with the opposite construction—a hard cover and soft mantle. They had little spin, regardless of the shot, making them fine off the tee but dangerous for everything else.

All these differences can seem dizzying, and that's the point. Most manufacturers don't advertise detailed specifications of their products, because ambiguity helps when you want to promise everything. Right now, the most popular ball on the professional circuit is the Titleist Pro V1, winning over four times more tournaments than its nearest competitor. It has a hard core and soft cover, not unlike the best performers in the scientific study. It also costs slightly more than similar alternatives due to its urethane cover, versus the more common surlyn, which adds more spin at the minor cost of durability.

Fortunately, despite all the science, it doesn't matter much what you choose if you're not a professional. Studies show that even the best technology can't replace skill, and a good player will succeed no matter how his or her ball is constructed. When researchers from the Centre for Sports Science in Chichester, England, gave players of all handicaps an assortment of balls, they saw that neither distance nor accuracy varied much based on ball alone.[4] Low handicappers hit farther and more accurately regardless of what they used, and high handicappers consistently struggled, with only one exception. Balls that have spent time in water hazards, regardless of player skill, are sure to cost both distance and accuracy. It doesn't matter what a ball once cost: once it swims with the fishes, it deserves to be retired.

If you've never swung a hickory golf club, you're missing something. Back in the 1950s, before manufacturers began experimenting with steel, that's what nearly all clubs were made of—hickory shafts with either forged steel iron faces or persimmon for the woods. Though heavy, these clubs were great for keeping the player honest, because there was no leniency for mishits. Today, most clubs have weight on the faces distributed along the perimeter, allowing for relatively straight shots even when the ball is hit off-center, but not so a few decades ago. Hitting on the toe with a hickory club meant a ball traveling almost sideways, and often a sore wrist, too.

Club design has changed drastically over the past fifty years, though not always for the better. One would expect that any high-end golf set would help your game, though this isn't always the case. When Tiger Woods became the global spokesperson for Nike golf, many people were skeptical. The clubs weren't just hard to hit, they were downright evil. Phil Mickelson openly praised Woods for playing so well, despite his bag, and a running joke on the tour was that the devil probably doesn't play golf, but if he did, he'd surely use a set of

Nike irons. Nike eventually folded their club manufacturing, deciding to focus on clothing and shoes instead, but the damage had been done. Who knows how many tournaments Tiger might have won, or Rory McIlroy, Nike's other prime representative, if they'd had different clubs in their bag.

Improved technology has allowed manufacturers to innovate with longer shafts and larger faces, though this brings challenges, too. Longer clubs are harder to hit, no matter how technologically advanced they are. That's why most players make more consistent contact with their pitching wedges than their drivers, because farther hits always come with a cost.

The biggest decision a player has to make when choosing clubs is material. Almost all shafts are made of either carbon composite or steel, with steel shafts being heavier and less flexible. Flex is how we measure the amount the shaft bends during the swing, and it's also one of the least understood concepts in golf. The general rule is that players with slower swings should choose flexible shafts because they need the extra speed. When swing power is combined with the whipping action of a flexible shaft, you're sure to get greater distance. It's a well-known fact, and it's also wrong.

The problem is that bending occurs in more than one direction. There are actually three directions the shaft can flex, and each does more than just add velocity to the ball. First there's flexing in the direction of the swing. This alters both speed and loft, depending on the direction of the bend. There's also flexing up and down, which either raises or lowers the toe of the clubface. This will determine where impact occurs on the clubface. Last, there's movement in the direction of the shaft itself, which fortunately is so small that we can ignore it for now.

However, the amount of flex in the other two directions can be significant, up to five inches or more. This influences the speed and direction of the hit, but we can't simply assume that more flex means faster swings. Because so many things change at once, translating flex to forward velocity requires something called "maximizing the kick." Maximizing kick means timing the club's flex just right so that everything converges at once. Early in the downward swing, clubs bend up toward the toe, with the club head lagging behind the wrist. As the downward swing accelerates, the head continues lagging while radial force pulls it away from the body. By the time impact occurs, the head will whip to almost two inches ahead of the grip, and if everything goes right, both speed and loft will be greater than had there been no flex at all. However, idiosyncrasies in the player's swing can change a lot. The kick can come early, or late, and in those cases, it's hard to say what will happen.

This leads to both good news and bad news. The good news is that although flexibility can be unpredictable, the actual consequences are minor. Though exact numbers vary based on which study you believe, loft and speed will probably only vary by 5 percent, depending on your club construction. Sasho Mackenzie, now a professor of Human Kinetics at St. Francis Xavier University in Nova Scotia, has studied shaft flexibility extensively using a detailed computer model and shown that loft varies very little, depending on shaft flexibility.[5] It's not that players get nothing from the kick, because it can add an additional 15 mph to the swing. It just doesn't matter how much flex the club has. You'll get enough "kick" from most clubs, regardless of how they're made.

The bad news is that even if you do choose to optimize your clubs, you'll probably be guessing. When researchers from the University of Calgary took 22 golfers and tested them with a variety of drivers, they found that most hit the same regardless of club. For the rest, there did indeed exist an "optimum shaft flexibility," but there was no telling which one club worked best without testing them all. Manufacturer recommendations were correct only a third of the time, roughly as frequently were you to guess.

So, if you want new clubs, the best thing you can do is to find a patient club fitter. The cost will be an entire afternoon, but there are worse ways to spend a weekend.

This isn't to say that club fitting is an exact science. In fact, there's no surer proof that the player is what matters, not the equipment, than U.S. Amateur champion Bryson DeChambeau. When he won the Memorial Tournament in June 2018, he had only one length of iron. That is, all his irons were 37.5 inches, about the same as a normal seven iron. Though different clubface angles allowed him to vary the distance of his hits, the constant length ensured that DeChambeau always swung with the same arc, and along the same plane, one swing after the next.

The idea of a one-length iron set was patented in the 1970s, though it has yet to catch on. The idea is that constant length clubs are easier to hit, especially for beginners. It reduces variability, so if you master one club, you should master them all. The idea works, at least in theory, and at least until you get to the lower lofts, where distances become a bit compressed. Regardless, don't expect to buy the same clubs DeChambeau uses, because Cobra custom-makes those just for him.

DeChambeau's experiment with single-length clubs shows how no rule about golf equipment applies to everybody. If the club works for you, use it. This is certainly what Patrick Reed does, winner of the 82nd Masters Tournament and one of the few golf professionals who doesn't have equipment sponsors. This isn't due to their lack of trying—Ping, Titleist, and Callaway have all tried wooing him in one way or another. But since he likes them all, that's what he uses. As in, when we won the Masters he had a Ping driver, Callaway irons, a putter by Odyssey, and balls by Titleist.

"On the equipment side, I'm just out there doing my thing. I'm using whatever I want to use," he said after his win, explaining that committing exclusively to one manufacturer might limit his game. "It's hard to believe that there is one company that makes 14 perfect golf clubs and a perfect golf ball for every player."

Another part of the club that has changed significantly over time is the clubface. Cavity-back irons and titanium driver heads now make the game far easier than a decade ago, again through physics. Mishits happen when the center of gravity of the club doesn't lie behind the ball, usually with negative consequences on our aim. Now, irons are built with weight distributed around the perimeter of the clubface, rather than concentrated in the center, thus distributing center of mass more evenly and compensating for any error.

Drivers also include a trick for correcting mishits, and it has to do with the shape of the clubface. Many players are surprised to see that their driver's face is convex, with a noticeable bulge in the center. At first, this might give the impression that mishits should be pushed even farther to the side, but this ignores rotation. Convex driver faces introduce spin in the direction of the aim, enough to compensate for most off-center hits. Studies show that the optimal driver design includes curvature with a radius of about 8.5 inches, translating to a bulge of about a quarter of an inch for most clubs.[7] This can cause hits that would ordinarily travel 25 yards to the side to stay within ten yards of the target, even as part of what appears to be the worst mishits.

Although this is a physics class, it's worth taking a moment to recognize that psychology matters, too. Advanced technology can bring benefits, for example correcting spin, but it also improves subjective feel. That second factor—feel—can't be ignored, because perceptions matter as much as anything. When scientists from Cleveland Golf had players swing a set of high-end clubs (e.g., Callaway, TaylorMade, Cobra), compared to a set from Walmart (*gasp!*), the differences were hardly noticeable.[8] Most outcomes, like distance, accuracy, and spin, hardly varied at all. In fact, the budget clubs outperformed the high-end ones in several categories, including durability. Apparently, Walmart does not think you will treat your future clubs with diligent care.

Yet, when players rated their impressions of the clubs, the high-end models won hands down. Of all subjective judgments, 91 favored the more expensive options. Only 14 favored the cheaper alternatives.

This issue of perception is complicated, though two factors are particularly important. The first is sound, because we all love the *click* you hear after a well-hit shot. In general, the louder the impact, the more satisfying the hit, which is why manufacturers cater to customers' ears as well as their scores. The second issue is vibration, with all players preferring smoother hits. Though most buyers claim that vibration and feel matter most, this isn't actually true. Studies show they judge their satisfaction mostly by the sound of the ball coming off the club, then use price tags to determine the rest.[9]

Perceptions can trick us in other ways too, as with putters. No aspect of the game is more personal than putter choice, which is why no book, video, or instructor can say which one is right for you. However, you can make yourself aware of certain biases. For example, studies show that players prefer to hit with mallet putters but aim better with blade designs. This was shown by scientists from the Norwegian School of Sports Scientists, who had dozens of players practice with six different blade designs and six mallets.[10] Aim was measured using ultrasonic devices, and preferences were rated by subjective judgment.

Overall, mallet designs were rated easier to use, with two-thirds of the subjects preferring this design. However, they also led to the worst aim, roughly 6 percent worse compared to blades. The effect was highest for short putts, meaning that you're far more likely to miss that gimme shot when it matters the most. Ugh!

There's one last kind of technology to consider, and it does not pertain to ball or club. It regards all the extra equipment that fills our bags. Visit any store or online retailer, and you'll find thousands of swing aids, training tools, and GPS devices. Nearly all of us have tried at least one, though it's tough knowing which of these devices actually helps. There's no way to examine them all, but let's look at a few to make you more efficient in how you spend your money.

The first is the Medicus Dual-Hinged Club, one of the most popular swing aids on the market. This club includes a hinge partway down the shaft that "breaks" every time the player strays outside the optimal swing plane. Though feedback is always good and the physics behind the idea is sound, it's unclear how this actually helps learning. That's why researchers from the University of Alabama trained golf students for ten weeks with the equipment, then compared them with others who were given standard clubs.[11] Both groups were trained the same and tested using targets just over a hundred yards away, and when their results were compared, the researchers found that everybody improved by about 20 percent after the training. It didn't matter which club they trained with, so the Medicus Club didn't hurt, but it didn't help much, either.

The second tool involves an entirely different kind of technology. We've all stood far away from a green and wondered what the distance actually was. On the professional tour, you must rely on a caddy for help, but the rest of us have alternatives. We could use our own subjective judgment, or maybe a marker on the fairway. But far more fun is breaking out that range finder or GPS. Which raises the question—are they worth the money?

That's a difficult question, and it depends a lot on the brand. Scientists from the University of Wales in Cardiff once conducted a test using several available commercial alternatives and found that laser rangefinders are best, in general.[12] They produce about half the variation in distance measures compared to GPS, although this is slightly misleading. Both actually perform quite well, generally within a few yards at worst, and even if you choose a cheap GPS, you're probably receiving accurate enough information. This makes either a solid choice if you've got the money.

Golf has changed drastically over the past several decades, mostly due to rapid advancements in technology. Some improvements are worth notice, but many aren't, and a little knowledge of physics helps tell the difference. Though technology is an important part of the game, our equipment will always matter less than how we use it (insert your own inappropriate joke here).

As long as there are different kinds of clubs and balls, there will be companies looking to help you spend your money. Choose wisely and play often.

READING LIST

Clubface

[7]Penner, A. (2001). The Physics of Golf: The Convex Face of a Driver. *American Journal of Physics*, 69, 1073–1081.

Winfield, D. and Tan, T. (1996). Optimization of the Clubface Shape of a Golf Driver to Minimize Dispersion of Off-Center Shots. *Computers and Structures*, 58, 1217–1224.

Club shaft

MacMenzie, S. (2011). How Does Shaft Flexibility Affect the Delivery of the Clubhead to the Ball? *The Journal of Applied Golf Research*, 3, 891-899.

MacKenzie, S. and Sprigings, E. (2010). Understanding the Mechanisms of Shaft Deflection in the Golf Swing. *Sports Engineering*, 12, 69–75.

[5]MacKenzie, S. and Springings, E. (2009). Understanding the Role of Shaft Stiffness in the Golf Swing. *Sports Engineering*, 12, 13–19.

Milne, R. and Davis, J. (1992). The Role of the Shaft in the Golf Swing. *Journal of Biomechanics*, 25, 975–983.

[6]Worobets, J. and Stefanyshyn, D. (2008). Shaft Stiffness: Implications for Club Fitting. In D. Crews and R. Lutz (Eds.), *Science and Golf V: Proceedings of the World Scientific Congress of Golf* (pp. 431–437). Mesa, AZ: Energy in Motion, Inc.

Worobets, J. and Stefanyshyn, D. (2012). The Influence of Golf Club Shaft Stiffness on Clubhead Kinematics at Ball Impact. *Sports Biomechanics*, 11, 239–248.

Feel

Roberts, J., Jones, R., Mansfield, N., and Rothberg, S. (2005). Evaluation of Impact Sound on the "Feel" of a Golf Shot. *Journal of Sound and Vibration*, 287, 651–666.

[9]Roberts, J., Jones, R., Mansfield, N., and Rothberg, S. (2005). Evaluation of Vibrotactile Sensations in the Feel of a Golf Shot. *Journal of Sound and Vibration*, 285, 303–319.

Roberts, J., Jones, R., Rothberg, S., Mansfield, N., and Meyer, C. (2006). Influence of Sound and Vibration from Sports Impacts on Players' Perceptions of Equipment Quality. *Journal of Materials: Design and Application*, 220, 215–227.

Golf balls

[2]Aoyama, S. (1998). The Row Effect Anomaly in the 336 Octahedron Dimple Pattern. In Farrally, M. and Cochran, A. (Ed.), *Science and Golf III: Proceedings of the World Scientific Congress of Golf* (pp. 457–463). Champaign, IL: Human Kinetics.

Barro, Robert. (2000). Economics of Golf Balls. *Journal of Sports Economics*, 1, 86–89.

[1]Beasley, D. and Camp, T. (2002). Effects of Dimple Design on the Aerodynamic Performance of a Golf Ball. In Thain, E. (Ed.), *Science and Golf IV: Proceedings of the World Scientific Congress of Golf* (pp. 328–340). New York: Routledge.

Gelberg, J. (1996). The Rise and Fall of the Polara Asymmetric Golf Ball: No Hook, No Slice, No Dice. *Technology in Society*, 18, 93–110.

[4]Hale, T., Bunyan, P., and Sewell, I. (1994). Does it Matter What Ball You Play? In Farrally, M. and Cochran, A. (Ed.), *Science and Golf III: Proceedings of the World Scientific Congress of Golf* (pp. 362–368). Champaign, IL: Human Kinetics.

Monk, S., Davis, C., Otto, S., and Strangwood, M. (2005). Material and Surface Effects on the Spin and Launch Angle Generated from a Wedge/Ball Interaction in Golf. *Sports Engineering*, 8, 3–11.

Smith, D. (2008). A Method for Creating Symmetric Golf Ball Dimple Patterns Utilizing Conway Notation. In D. Crews and R. Lutz (Eds.), *Science and Golf V: Proceedings of the World Scientific Congress of Golf* (pp. 408–414). Mesa, AZ: Energy in Motion, Inc.

Strangwood, M., Johnson, A., and Otto, S. (2006). Energy Losses in Viscoelastic Golf Balls. *Journal of Materials: Design and Application*, 220, 23–30.

Sullivan, M. and Melvin, T. (1994). The Relationship Between Golf Ball Construction and Performance. In A.J. Cochran and M. Farrally (Eds.), *Science and Golf II: Proceedings of the World Scientific Congress of Golf* (pp. 334–339). Grass Valley, CA: The Booklegger.

[2]Tavares, G., Sullivan, M., and Nesbitt, D. (1998). Use of Finite Element Analysis in Design of Multilayer Golf Balls. In Farrally, M. and Cochran, A. (Ed.), *Science and Golf III: Proceedings of the World Scientific Congress of Golf* (pp. 473–480). Champaign, IL: Human Kinetics.

Other topics

[8]Brunski, J. (2008). An Objective Performance and Quality Comparison of Professional Line, Premium Golf Clubs to Value Sets Sold Through Mass Merchants. In D. Crews and R. Lutz (Eds.), *Science and Golf V: Proceedings of the World Scientific Congress of Golf* (pp. 445–454). Mesa, AZ: Energy in Motion, Inc.

[11]Hall, M., Colclough, S., MacBeth, J., and Currie, S. (2008). The Effectiveness of Two Commercial Golf Swing Training Aids in Teaching Beginning Golf. In D. Crews and R. Lutz (Eds.), *Science and Golf V: Proceedings of the World Scientific Congress of Golf* (pp. 286–292). Mesa, AZ: Energy in Motion, Inc.

[12]James, N., Rees, G., Noble, G., and Kingslet, M. (2007). The Agreement Between GPS, Laser, and Walking Assessments of Approach Shot Distances in Golf. *Paper presented at the International Academic Conference on Social Sciences, Calgary, Alberta, Canada.*

[10]Karlsen, J. and Nilsson, J. (2008). Golf Players Prefer Mallet Putters for Aiming, but Aim More Consistently With Blade Putters. In D. Crews and R. Lutz (Eds.), *Science and Golf V: Proceedings of the World Scientific Congress of Golf* (pp. 402–407). Mesa, AZ: Energy in Motion, Inc.

Fundamentals of Public Safety

Prerequisites: None

Navy Lieutenant George Prior might be the unluckiest guy on Earth. He got to play three days of golf, and had a good time too, but it also cost him his life.

Prior's unfortunate story started on a Sunday in August, when he enjoyed a lazy eighteen holes at the Army Navy Country Club in Arlington, Virginia. He had so much fun that he went the next day, and then again the day after that, enjoying what would be a dream vacation for most players. But then something strange happened.

When he left the course, he didn't feel well but thought little of it. Then he developed a splitting headache and severe nausea, and the feeling worsened. After checking into a local hospital, he developed a rash and severe blisters. Then came a fever of over 104 degrees. The more doctors tried to help, the worse his condition became, and only a week later, he was dead.

Doctors were stumped. Only after he died did they realize that Prior had experienced a severe allergic response to the chemical Daconil 2787. That's a common fungicide found on golf courses, one that had been used by the Army Navy Club twice weekly. Later, it was discovered that Prior had been chewing on his golf tees between holes and after three days had ingested enough chemical to shut down most of his major organs.

Though most players aren't as unlucky as Prior, injuries and other unfortunate accidents do happen, and this class explores the major safety issues associated with the sport. Few of us chew on our golf tees, so we probably don't have to worry about toxic poisoning, but there are plenty of other risks to health and well-being. This chapter will help you manage those risks to avoid serious injury . . . or worse!

In general, there are three ways to hurt yourself on a golf course—strains, strikes, and loss of judgment. Strains occur when we pull muscles or overextend joints, and they're the most common. Less common are strikes with clubs, balls, or carts, but they present more serious danger, causing injury or even death. Finally, you have lapses in judgment like Prior's, which are the most odd but also the most educational. No one expects to die from toxic poisoning on a golf course. However, if you habitually chew on tees between holes, and those tees taste a little funny . . . well, you've got to expect *something*.

Starting with strains, lower back injuries are the most common muscle ailments, usually due to overaggressive swings. Half of these injuries come when body rotation reaches maximum power, typically just after impact. Studies of lumbar loads show that the spine experiences compression between two and seven times our normal body weight during the golf swing.[1] This pressure acts along the axis of the spine itself, pushing the discs closer together, while at the same time the spine is warped in the direction of the swing, introducing a sheer load of roughly 120 percent of our body weight. That's asking a lot of a spine, or any body part, for that matter.

Still, most of us are flexible enough and can take the exertion. This means our greatest threat is repetitive strain. Torque your body once, and it will probably be fine. Do it over and over, and eventually something will fail.

One contributing factor to back injuries is the modern swing. In our previous classes, we learned that swing power comes from something known as the X-factor, the difference in rotation between the hips and shoulders. This difference leads to torque, which is then transferred to the ball. However, the back wasn't meant to bend this way, at least not often. Before the advent of the modern swing, golfers didn't rely on the X-factor and turned both their hips and shoulders together. They didn't hit as far, but they also broke down in pain and injury much less frequently.

To see the strain put on our bodies from the modern swing, just view videos of Walter Hagen or Bobby Jones, then compare them with

Tiger Woods or Dustin Johnson. The ending swing positions for these players are completely different, with Hagen and Jones standing almost upright at follow through. By comparison, modern players bend their backs to extremes, with hips unnaturally leading the way. It should come as no surprise that Hagen and Jones experienced no serious injuries during their playing careers. Woods, on the other hand, has had four back surgeries and counting.

One option for casual players is to minimize the X-factor. This can still lead to a reliable swing so long as hips and shoulders rotate together, something physical therapists call the stabilized-spine swing. We achieve this by initiating the backswing with both hips and shoulders, keeping the spine angle constant throughout the takeaway. The swing ends with a transfer of weight to the forward foot, leading to a 13 percent reduction in compressive forces on the spine. Sheer forces should be reduced by almost half.

When twenty beginning golfers were trained to use the stabilized-spine swing, they were still able to maintain roughly the same clubhead speed with much less strain on the back, compared to the modern version.[2] In other words, just by treating their backs with caution, they mitigated their pain.

Another option is to adopt a modified version of the modern swing, reducing X-factor but not eliminating it altogether. Since the swing depends less on rotation than on smooth coordination of body movements, lowering rotation has only a small effect on ball speed. When beginning golfers learned the regular swing, then asked to try again while reducing their backswing, they decreased total body turn by 46 percent. Yet, their club speed remained the same. So did their accuracy.[3]

Other bodily injuries are slightly less common, such as injuries to the elbow, shoulder, and wrist. These are usually minor and treatable, though their effect can be significant. Such injuries can cost the player on average five weeks of playing time a year, and since most injuries occur early in the year (maybe because we're not in playing shape yet? Who knows?), this means a severely shortened season. Roughly 80 percent of these injuries are due to overuse, rather than a single incident, but surprises do occur. In one case, a player broke his patella during an aggressive follow-through with the driver. Another player broke a rib during a fairway hit with his wood. One 58-year-old woman severed an artery in her hand while playing in her first golf tournament, an injury that almost cost her life.

Nearly everybody has heard about Tiger Woods's fourteenth major championship, but few appreciate just how much pain he was in at the time. Having undergone knee surgery just two months before, normally Woods would have sat out the competition, but this was his home course. Played at Torrey Pines near San Diego, California, the U.S. Open's long and challenging course was exactly what his body didn't need—doctors had already informed him that his knee was a mess, with shredded ligaments everywhere, and that he'd suffered a double stress fracture in his lower leg. He'd need surgery again, soon, and even standing upright might eventually not be an option. His body was broken.

The rest, as they say, is history. Even when Woods needed to make a twelve-foot putt on the final hole to force an 18-hole playoff, everybody knew he'd put the pain aside. When he needed to birdie the eighteenth hole again, this time to force sudden-death, he sank the putt once more. Grimacing and limping every time he moved, Woods looked like a man possessed, and in the end, he won in sudden-death, having played 91 holes without both working legs. Nobody seemed to remember that he'd shot a 53 just a week before—on the front nine. At the time, he was still wearing a knee brace, though now he'd won his fourteenth major. Yet, at what cost? As of this writing, he hasn't won another one.

So treat your body with care, because it's the only one you have. Everybody likes an extra ten yards off the tee, but not at the cost of a back, wrist, or shoulder. It's not worth it.

Have you ever stood near a tee box, safely away from your partner's drive, only to see an errant slice fly by your head? Ever wondered what would have happened had the ball struck your noggin instead?

Universities are generally cautious about the experiments their researchers perform, and as a result, remarkably few controlled studies exist involving players being hit by projectiles at close distances. Nevertheless, *Golf Digest* did conduct one such study, and it was as violent as you'd think.[4]

The experiment started with a mechanical driver being set up in Rancho Santa Fe, California, just north of San Diego. It was programmed to strike a shot at 135 miles per hour, translating to the ball accelerating at 40,000g's, the same as one hit by a low-handicap player. Then a crash test dummy was placed 35 yards in front and to the side, roughly where a bystander might wait patiently for his partner to tee off. It was the kind of position spectators might often take, assuming the chance of a slice to be minimal. No big deal, right?

It was a big deal. The researchers had set the machine up to hit just that kind of shot, and as you'd expect, the result was cringeworthy. The first ball struck the dummy in the crotch. Next came two more crushing blows to the body until finally the machine struck the dummy square in the forehead.

Sensors showed that the blow was one tenth the impact of being in a head-on car crash. That's not enough to kill you unless you're unlucky, but if you were lucky, you wouldn't have been hit in the first place. The same kind of strike hit Thomas Grennan at Blackwolf Run Golf Club in Kohler, Wisconsin. He remained conscious after the strike and remained optimistic about his recovery for several days. Still, brains are notoriously sensitive to such trauma, and he eventually died from a cerebral hemorrhage.

Injuries involving being struck by a golf ball or club are common, but seldom deadly. Surveys show that half of all casual players have been hit by a ball at least once, with one in four strikes being to the head or neck.[5] That makes head injuries the most common reason golfers visit emergency rooms each year. Most of the time, the consequences are minor and don't lead to serious damage. However, trauma to the head or neck is never good. Collisions have led to brain damage and aphasia, epilepsy, and even extreme hemorrhaging and death. One analysis of traumatic brain injury by the Centers for Disease Control and Prevention found that more golfers than horseback riders require hospitalization for head injuries. About the same number of golfers require hospitalization for head injuries as those riding bicycles or mopeds.[6]

Because they are so easily damaged, the eyes are our most vulnerable areas to injury. One five-year analysis found that over half of such injuries were caused by being hit by a ball, with the rest involving a strike by the club.[7] Though most incidents don't lead to blindness, golf is notorious for having high rates of enucleation, a fancy term for full removal of the eye, something many viewers learned about following Brooks Koepka's sixth tee shot on the opening day of the 2018 Ryder Cup. The fluke drive missed the fairway and entered a crowd of spectators, striking Corine Remande's right eye and destroying it completely. Unlucky, to be sure, but not unheard of. In fact, golf ranks just behind air hockey and air guns as the most dangerous sports in this arena. Nobody likes getting hit by golf balls, clubs, or anything else for that matter, but no matter how bad your day is, you can at least take comfort in that fact that you're not Bobby Cruickshank. As a former war hero and one of the most popular players during the 1934 PGA season, Cruickshank was in a great place to win the U.S. Open. On the final day of play, with a two-stroke lead, all he had to do was play conservatively to win. His ball was lying safely on the fairway not far from the eleventh green, and all Cruickshank had to do was swing back and aim for the pin. That's when things got strange.

First, after the hit, his ball didn't make the green. Instead, it rolled into the creek guarding the green's front, called Baffling Brook, a tragic turn indeed. Seeing his chances to earn his first major win disappear, Cruickshank was so frustrated that he tossed his club in the air. It was a normal act of frustration that most all of us have indulged in at least once, a way of dealing with stress. This is when things turned strange, because quickly it became apparent that the hit wasn't as unlucky as he thought. After entering the brook, rather than sinking, the ball bounced squarely off a rock and rolled back up to the green. Thanks to some extraordinary luck, he was only a simple putt away from extending his lead.

Too bad that his wedge was still in midflight. Predictably, when it eventually fell back to Earth, it struck him squarely on the head.

Bloodied and dizzy, Cruickshank took a long moment to collect his thoughts, because his were surely scattered about the fairway. In one brief moment, he was both spared a bogey (at least) and suffered a possible concussion. Sadly, although Cruickshank eventually did two-putt to finish the hole, he didn't play the same again. After stumbling his way through the final holes, he ended up finishing two strokes back, all because he took his frustrations out on a wedge that had actually brought him some incredible luck.

Injuries involving lapses in judgment are often hard to analyze because they're so strange. Yet, they show what happens when we stop paying attention. George Prior was unlucky and didn't deserve to die, but chewing on golf tees is a terrible habit, especially if your course uses fertilizer or pesticide. And nearly all do.

Chemical treatments are generally applied with caution and pose no danger to health. Studies show that even if you played every day, you'd still receive only a third of the maximum herbicide exposure dose recommended by the EPA.[8] Unless you hit the course immediately after it has been treated, or habitually lick the ground between holes, any residue will be harmless by the time you tee off.

This makes playing on treated courses safe, so long as you don't put equipment in your mouth or start eating the grass.

Though chemical poisoning shouldn't top your list of worries unless you work at a course, carts can pose a significant danger, especially when used improperly. Sometimes injuries are beyond our control—I'm thinking of one particular cart battery spontaneously catching fire in New Jersey—and most involve excessive speed. After all, carts don't have seat belts or exterior protection. This isn't negligence on the part of manufacturers, since even if carts did have restraints, nobody would use them. If you're the kind of guy to race your cart between trees away from the fairway, seatbelts probably aren't going to help you anyway.

In general, the golf cart design is terrible in terms of stability, including cases in which they are used properly. Even at speeds of 11 mph—less than half the maximum speed set by manufacturers—slippage of the front wheels during turning can eject most occupants. Testing with dummies shows that acceleration during rapid turns exceeds 0.7g's. That's near the lower end of acceleration on the Shock Wave ride at Six Flags, Texas—not huge, but still enough to ruin your day if you're not careful.

Most cart-related injuries occur when someone is ejected after a sharp turn or flip. Over half involve children, and most involve alcohol consumption, which isn't surprising. One option is to keep the beer at home and maybe the kids, too (though the latter seems extreme). Alternatively, you could ask your local club to install front brakes on their carts, if they haven't already. The reason carts tip, especially on downhill slopes, is that their breaking efficiency drops to zero on inclines greater than 20 degrees. To give a frame of reference, that's only two-thirds the incline on Filbert Street in San Francisco, site of Steve McQueen's famous car chase in the movie *Bullitt*. (Those old enough to remember the movie are puckering up a little right now. For the rest of you, go check it out. Seriously, it's a classic.) This makes golf carts a little unstable, no matter how good the driver is. Brakes controlling the rear wheels don't help, which is a shame, because that's where they are for most carts. Brakes in the front nearly eliminate the risk.

Like injuries from carts, injuries that result from being in the wrong place at the wrong time usually start with bad judgment. For example, dozens of people are bitten by alligators each year, though deaths are uncommon. Fewer than 20 have been reported in the United States, with most incidents occurring in Florida. Nearly a third, 29 percent, occurred while golfers were trying to recover lost balls near water hazards. That makes this the second most common cause of alligator attacks, after swimming. (Except, of course, if you count people approaching alligators intentionally. That happens a lot too, though when stupidity becomes assumed, there's no telling what will happen.) By comparison, between 1999 and 2014, more than nine hundred people died from provoking bees, hornets, or wasps. Compare that with nine deaths from alligator attacks, and 78 from other reptiles. More than a thousand were killed by cows, horses, or other mammals (not even counting dogs). A good rule of thumb is that if it has legs, teeth, or a tail, give it the respect it deserves.

Lightning is also generally avoidable, though storms can form quickly. Studies show that golfing is the third most common activity in the event of a lightning injury, after hiking and camping, and even this might be an underestimation.[9] Not all strikes are reported, especially close calls that happen when there are still a few holes left to play. One reason golfers are susceptible is that games last several hours, sometimes making weather prediction difficult. Courses are also notorious for having few shelters.

Fortunately, most strikes aren't fatal, as Lee Trevino found when he was struck during the 1975 U.S. Open near Chicago. Trevino's case is unusual, because he wasn't the only one who found himself in danger, as several players that day received shocks. The problem started when storm clouds started rolling in on the second day of play at Butler National Golf Club, and officials decided to halt play. But it was too late, because Tony Jacklin was already midswing when the strikes started coming. When he was struck, he tasted a burning in his mouth, and his eight iron was ejected 30 feet from his hands. His partner, Bobby Nichols, was also knocked to the ground, and when officials smelled the odor of burned wire coming from his breath, he was immediately rushed to the hospital.

However, the worst was saved for Trevino. He and his partner, Jerry Heard, were huddled under an umbrella on the thirteenth green, under a tree and next to a full bag of irons—not the place you normally want to be during a lightning strike, which they found out the hard way. Though the strike didn't hit them directly, instead making contact with a nearby lake, the shock still stunned everybody nearby. Both suffered serious burns, and Trevino would experience chronic back problems for the rest of his life. Somehow, Heard managed to return from the hospital in time to finish his round, though he also suffered lifelong back injuries and never returned to his full playing ability.

"Evidently, I was gone," Trevino claimed afterward in his normal loquacious style. "The electricity stopped my heart. When I woke up, I was in pain. The doctor said if I hadn't had such a strong heart I would be dead."

These stories may make golf sound dangerous, but it's not if we're cautious. We play because it's fun, and any time we engage in sport, we assume some risk. Often injuries are a direct result of our love for the game, making them part of the action, and I doubt many of us will give up our play just because watching television is safer.

Take, for example, the case of one forty-six-year-old man who presented to the Royal Victoria Hospital in Belfast, Ireland, with reports of pain traveling down his groin. Soon the throbbing became overwhelming, and that's when the doctors discovered that he'd severed his femoral artery (actually, the upper portion of the artery as it passed through the pelvis). Apparently, he had been hitting so many golf balls that the stress literally tore the artery apart. Striking hundreds of balls a day without a break will do that to you, and for this person, it almost meant death. Fortunately, the doctors caught the injury in time, and he made a full recovery.

It's hard to question dedication like that, or to convince ourselves that the sport isn't worth it. It's not wise to chew on tees or to play so often that we rip our bodies apart, but otherwise the gains outweigh the risks.

Just stay away from the alligators. That should be common sense.

Reading List

Acute Injuries

[9]Cherington, M. (2001). Lightning Injuries in Sports: Situations to Avoid. *Sports Medicine*, 31, 301–308.

[7]Jayasundera, T., Vote, B., and Joondeph, B. (2003). Golf-Related Ocular Injuries. *Clinical and Experimental Ophthalmology*, 31, 110–113.

Langley, R. (2005). Alligator Attacks on Humans in the United States. *Wilderness and Environmental Medicine*, 16, 119–124.

[5]Nicholas, J., Reidy, M., and Oleske, D. (1998). An Epidemiologic Survey of Injury in Golfers. *Journal of Sport Rehabilitation*, 7, 112–121.

Yoong, S., Davison, G., and O'Donnell, M. (2012). Spontaneous Dissection of the External Iliac Artery Secondary to Golf Club Manufacturing. *Vascular and Endovascular Surgery*, 47, 73–75.

Back Injuries

[2]Archambault, M., Ling, W., Chen, B., and Gatt, C. (2008). A Kinematic and Kinetic Analysis of the Modern and Stabilized-Spine Golf Swings. In D. Crews and R. Lutz (Eds.), *Science and Golf V: Proceedings of the World Scientific Congress of Golf* (pp. 3–12). Mesa, AZ: Energy in Motion, Inc.

[3]Bulbalian, R., Ball, K., and Seaman, D. (2001). The Short Golf Backswing: Effects on Performance and Spinal Health Implications. *Journal of Manipulative and Physiological Therapeutics*, 24, 569–575.

Cole, M. and Grimshaw, P. (2009). Low back pain in golf: Does the crunch factor contribute to low back injuries in golfers? *Proceedings of the International Conference on Biomechanics in Golf, Limerick, Ireland.*

Gluck, G., Bendo, J., and Spivak, J. (2008). The Lumbar Spine and Low Back Pain in Golf: A Literature Review of Swing Biomechanics and Injury Prevention. *The Spine Journal*, 8, 778–788.

[1]Lim, Y. and Chow, J. (2002). Estimating Lumbar Spinal Loads During a Golf Swing Using an EMG-Assisted Optimization Model Approach. In Y. Hong (Ed.), *International Research in Sports Biomechanics* (pp. 189–200). New York: Routledge.

Seaman, D. and Bulbulian, R. (2000). A review of back pain in golfers:

Etiology and Prevention. *Sports Medicine, Training and Rehab*, 9, 169–187.

[4]Smith, S. (2010). Duck! You Dummy. *Golf Magazine*, June 21.

Sugaya, H., Tsuchiya, A., Moriya, H., Morgan, D., and Banks, S. (1998). Low Back Injury in Elite and Professional Golfers: An Epidemiologic and Radiologic Study. In Farrally, M. and Cochran, A. (Ed.), *Science and Golf III: Proceedings of the World Scientific Congress of Golf* (pp. 83–91). Champaign, IL: Human Kinetics.

Chemical Exposure

[8]Kenna, M. (1998). Preliminary Assessment of the Effects of Golf Course Pesticides on Golfers. In Farrally, M. and Cochran, A. (Ed.), *Science and Golf III: Proceedings of the World Scientific Congress of Golf* (pp. 694–703). Champaign, IL: Human Kinetics.

[8]Knopper, L. and Lean, D. (2004). Carcinogenic and genotoxic potential of turf pesticides commonly used on golf courses. *Journal of Toxicology and Environmental Health*, 7, 267–279.

Kross, B., Burmeister, L., Ogilvie, L., Fuortes, L., and Fu, C. (1996). Proportionate Mortality Study of Golf Course Superintendents. *American Journal of Medicine*, 29, 501–506.

[8]Murphy, K., Cooper, R., and Clark, J. (1994). Dislodgeable and Volatile Residues from Insecticide-Treated Turfgrass. In A.J. Cochran and M. Farrally (Eds.), *Science and Golf II: Proceedings of the World Scientific Congress of Golf* (pp. 505–510). Grass Valley, CA: The Booklegger.

General Injury Types and Rates

Batt, M. (1992). A Survey of Golf Injuries in Amateur Golfers. *British Journal of Sports Medicine*, 26, 62–65.

Fradkin, A., Cameron, P., and Gabbe, B. (2005). Golf Injuries - Common and Potentially Avoidable. *Journal of Science and Medicine in Sport*, 8, 163–170.

Fradkin, A., Cameron, P., and Gabbe, B. (2006). Opportunities for Prevention of Golfing Injuries. *International Journal of Injury Control and Safety Promotion*, 13, 46–48.

[6]Gilchrist, J., Thomas, K., Wald, M., and Langlois, J. (2007). Nonfatal

Traumatic Brain Injuries from Sports and Recreation Activities. *Morbidity and Mortality Weekly Report*, 56, 733–737.

Gosheger, G., Liem, D., Ludwig, K., Greshake, O., and Winkelmann, W. (2003). Injuries and Overuse Syndromes in Golf. *The American Journal of Sports Medicine*, 31, 438–443.

McHardy, A., Pollard, H., and Luo, K. (2006). Golf Injuries: A Review of the Literature. *Sports Medicine*, 36, 171–187.

Theriault, G. and Lachance, P. (1998). Golf Injuries: An Overview. *Sports Medicine*, 26, 43–57.

Golf Carts

Long, T., Fugger, T., and Randles, B. (2005). Vehicle Performance Characteristics and Seat Belt Effectiveness in Low Speed Vehicles and Golf Cars. *Technical Report of the National Highway Traffic Safety Administration*, Washington, D.C.

McGwin, G., Zoghby, J., Griffin, R., and Rue, L. (2007). Incidence of golf-cart related injury in the United States. *The Journal of Trauma Injury, Infection, and Critical Care*, 64, 1562–1566.

Miller, B., Waller, J., and McKinnon, B. (2011). Craniofacial Injuries Due to Golf Cart Trauma. *Otolaryngology-Head and Neck Injury*, 144, 883–887.

Seluga, K., Baker, L., and Ojalvo, I. (2009). A Parametric Study of Golf Cart and Personal Transport Vehicle Braking Stability and Their Deficiencies. *Accident Analysis and Prevention*, 41, 839–848.

Seluga, K. and Ojalvo, I. (2006). Braking Hazards of Golf Cars and Low Speed Vehicles. *Accident Analysis and Prevention*, 38, 1151–1156.

Watson, D., Mehan, T., Smith, G., and McKenzie, L. (2008). Golf cart-related injuries in the U.S. *American Journal of Preventative Medicine*, 35, 55–59.

Senior Theses

Ask any senior, and he or she will say that the final year of college is when things finally come together. We've already taken most of our classes, and what's left are the specialized topics. These are also the most fun because they're the most diverse, on subjects seldom receiving the attention they deserve.

In *Golf University*, senior year is saved for advanced theses. We'll explore how our brains allow us to benefit from practice even without a club in our hands. We'll see how the game has changed in terms of age, gender, and race. We'll even address the most practical lesson of all—how to keep from being sued. Our bodies don't respond well to being hit by golf balls, and neither do houses, cars, or neighbors. Knowing your legal responsibilities can mean the difference between a bad day and a lawsuit.

And it starts with, of all things, a Vietnamese POW camp.

Behavioral Neuroscience: The Brain on Golf

Prerequisites: Psychology 101: The Angel of the Odd and the Imp of the Perverse

Psychology 201: Control and Flow

Before the Vietnam War, James Nesmeth was an average golfer. He usually scored in the middle 90s, and though he didn't play often, he loved the game. Like most of us, for Nesmeth the course was a refuge, a place for fun and relaxation.

Then came the war, capture, and a cramped prison cell.

As a combat pilot, Nesmeth had already flown many dangerous missions over North Vietnam, but eventually his luck ran out and he was shot down and captured. Stuck in a tiny POW cell and removed from human contact, he had nothing to do but watch the days go by. Days turned to weeks, and weeks to years. What had started as a positive outlook slowly turned dire.

Then Nesmeth got an idea—he would work on his golf game! His cell was only five feet wide, the same as its depth, so there wasn't room for swinging a club. But when you have an active imagination and plenty of time, who needs clubs? Nesmeth started by constructing an eighteen-hole course in his mind, with tee boxes and greens and even a clubhouse. He imagined water hazards and sand bunkers. The smell of freshly cut grass filled the air, along with the feel of the warm sun bathing his skin. If it was a nice day, he added squirrels and birds, and since the world was his own creation, they were always nice days.

For seven years, Nesmeth played that eighteen-hole course, imagining swing after swing. Every step, from gripping the club to returning flags to their holes, received its proper attention. There wasn't a part of the course that Nesmeth hadn't explored, and by the time the war ended and he returned home, that place was as familiar as any he'd seen in real life.

Then came his actual return to the sport he loved.

Despite seven years of abuse and psychological toil, Nesmeth returned to his home course excited to play but expecting to struggle. He'd not exercised in years, and shooting par in your head is one thing, but doing so in real life is another. Then he shot a 74! This was over twenty strokes better than any game he'd ever played before, an improvement unheard of without serious training. His body might not have been actually holding clubs, but his brain had, and the effort had made him a par golfer.

I wish I could tell you that Nesmeth's story is true. It has been shared by motivational speakers for decades, starting with Zig Ziglar in the 1970s and continuing today. I personally believe it, because the parts that matter are always the same. In one version, he hits a hole in one off his first tee, and in another, he wins a small tournament. Still, in every version, he doesn't just rehearse his swing, he lives it. Nesmeth's course was as real as any in the world, at least to him, and that's what made the difference.

In this class, we'll explore the important role of the brain on the golf course. We've already had two psychology courses, so we know the impact anxiety and stress can have on our game. Now it's time to talk about the good things our brains do for us. For Nesmeth, that brain kept him sane and stole a dozen strokes off his handicap.

Maybe it can do the same thing for you, and you don't even need to lock yourself up in a cell to find out.

At first glance, basketball has little in common with golf. It's usually played indoors, it's a team sport, and there's no special equipment required, except a ball and hoop. Yet, these sports do share one thing, and that's reliance on a very complicated brain.

To see how important mental rehearsal is for sports in general, let's take a trip to Detroit, where researchers decided to explore rehearsal scientifically.[1] Their project started when they identified a hundred high school students and asked them to attempt a series of basketball free throws. Some belonged to the local varsity team, some played junior varsity, and the rest were novices, though all were told they would be shooting for science. The researchers wanted to make them expert players.

Not surprisingly, the varsity players shot best when they started, but the real manipulation came next. Everybody was split into two groups, with the first group spending the next two weeks engaged in regular practice. Players started with five practice throws each day, followed by another twenty-five to improve their score. They were called the physical practice group, and when the training concluded, they repeated their assessment. Each tried another twenty-five free throws to see how many they could make.

The second group had a very different experience. They also practiced every day for the next two weeks, but they didn't use a ball or basket. Instead, they were asked to imagine stepping onto the court and engaging in the same routine. The only difference was that they weren't even given a ball, hoop, or anything else except their imagination.

In our earlier psychology classes, we learned that positive visualization helps our golf game while negative visualization hurts it, but this was something different entirely. It wasn't even practice in the traditional sense. It was mental rehearsal in lieu of contact with real equipment, and it led to nearly as much benefit as playing with an actual ball.

At the end of training, those practicing with actual balls significantly improved, as you'd expect. Varsity players made 16 percent more shots, junior varsity 24 percent, and novices 44 percent. Not bad. Yet, those who just imagined practicing did just about the same. They improved by 15 percent, 23 percent, and 26 percent, respectively, almost identical to those engaged in actual practice, except for the novices.

Apparently, just thinking about free throws is enough to improve your skill, so long as you have a little experience under your belt. The phenomenon is called mental rehearsal, and it works because learning doesn't just happen in the muscles. It happens in the brain.

Mental rehearsal is useful for all sorts of sports, not just basketball. One metastudy involving over a thousand subjects found that mental rehearsal improves performance on nearly any task involving both cognitive and physical components—swinging a tennis racket, serving a volleyball, and even playing the trombone.[2] Those with some experience improve whether the rehearsal is physical or not, with novices being the only exception because they need actual hands-on training to start. Once they get going, however, thinking about getting better is enough.

Benefits aren't limited to sports, as surgeons improve from mental rehearsal, too. When doctors are given either textbook learning or time spent mentally rehearsing surgery, those engaged in visualization complete their procedures more effectively. They not only handle tissue more cleanly, but also their incisions are more precise—simply because that's how their mind imagined it.

We see benefits from such rehearsal because sports require the complex coordination of muscles, and all muscles are controlled by the brain. That control must be practiced to be mastered, and the brain doesn't care if the situation is real or not. The same regions that once kept us from tumbling off cliffs now help us hit little golf balls over a hundred miles an hour. We just need our brains to get the particulars right.

The most important thing to know about the brain is that it doesn't work like a computer. We often think of the brain as taking input, processing information, and making decisions, like a machine. But in reality, life is more complicated. The brain doesn't have a single, central processor. Instead, it has between ten and a hundred billion neurons, all connected and sharing information in the form of chemicals and electrical pulses. No single neuron is in charge, and no neuron stays silent for long.

In fact, most neurons fire at least six to ten times per second, and that's when we're not doing anything at all. Even when we're asleep, our neurons are still firing. We have very busy brains.

From this, you might get the idea that brains are not efficient machines. They aren't. In fact, they're like teenagers—they're loud and messy and spend way more energy on simple tasks than is conceivably necessary. This complexity has helped us to invent democracy and build advanced societies, but it leads to complications, too. It means that learning new skills isn't a matter of increasing brain activity. Instead, it decreases it.

This seems like a paradox, I know, because the more we exercise our brain, the more connections it makes. But this doesn't increase the volume, it decreases it, because the talk becomes more coordinated. The effect is like cheering in a stadium after a big football play. After a touchdown or interception, crowds erupt in massive noise, but that noise doesn't send any information, only enthusiasm. Compare that with what happens when mascots coordinate the audience in a cheer like "De-fense!" Even if only a tenth of the people in the stands join in, the message will be loud and clear and more powerful than if everybody just drunkenly yelled.

Following mental rehearsal, important messages have a better chance of getting through all the background noise, and so we become better players. Even then, however, it matters which brain regions are active. As we learned in previous classes, our brains do plenty of things that *don't* help our golf game. There's language, and problem solving, and math, to name just a few. When you rehearse, either mentally or in real life, only regions involving motor action should be enlisted. Take for example a study by researchers from the Radiology Department of the Cleveland Clinic Foundation.[3] Six golfers were placed in a magnetic resonance imaging (MRI) scanner, revealing which brain regions were most active when those players rehearsed their swings in their head. When they did, two regions lit up—the motor cortex and the cerebellum.

It's worth taking a moment to discuss what these regions do. The motor cortex manages intentional action, like controlling our arms and legs, so it's obviously important for golf. So is the cerebellum, which does fine-tuning work and error correction. Which brings us to another finding regarding those six golfers who were monitored by the MRI—lower-handicap players had quieter brains. For them, the only region that increased its activation level during the imaginary swing was their motor cortex. High handicappers had motor cortices that were active too, but so were sensory regions and abstract processing areas. They gave the swing lots of thought, and more voices were enlisted than was necessary.

This coordination of neurons for mental rehearsal leads to some interesting consequences, like heavier brains. Granted, all brains are about three pounds give or take, no matter how you use them, but some are denser than others. Frequent play increases connectivity so much, we can see it on a physical level. When the brains of skilled golfers with low handicaps were compared with those of novices, MRI analysis showed that the skilled players had bigger motor cortices.[4] Specifically, they had more gray matter, which is composed of cell bodies inhabiting the outer layer of the brain.

This doesn't necessarily prove that playing golf makes your brain bigger, of course. It's possible that people with bigger motor cortices play golf because of natural aptitude. To see which direction the causal arrow points, the psychologist Ladina Bezzola of the University of Zurich gave eleven golf novices 40 hours of training over the course of several months.[5] She had their brains imaged by an MRI scanner before the training began, and also when they were done, intending to examine any changes.

Scans showed that motor areas grew roughly 3 percent as a result of the training, an impressive gain by neuroscientific standards. Those who finished the fastest also had the biggest gains. What's even more interesting is that those same subjects showed a 1 to 2 percent *decrease* in activity in their motor areas, despite the increased volume.

It's worth remembering here the analogy of the audience in the stadium. Quieter brains don't imply inactivity, only more coordination. The same thing happens when we learn any motor skill—we start with lots of activity because our neurons have nothing meaningful to say. They're like an annoying coworker talking on and on about his weekend . . . on a Tuesday. There are plenty of words, but no substance. But give the neurons a story to tell, and things finally come together. The practice allowed the golfers' brains to develop the regions that matter while filtering all the garbage away.

Looking at the brain this way shows why it's so important to have a quiet mind on the course—active brains aren't effective, just loud. When brains are examined during rehearsal of preshot routines, those belonging to skilled players are more silent. By contrast, novice brains have visual, motor, and even emotional centers yelling like mad. Effective minds work by silencing unneeded noise, and sometimes that's accomplished by actual practice. Sometimes you can close your eyes and get the same benefits.

If you have any question about the future merging of technology and sports training, look no further than Halo Neuroscience. That's the company based out of San Francisco, founded by doctors, neuroscientists, and athletes, with the goal of using brain science to improve sports performance. Their device is called the Halo Sport, a device worn on the head like a ball cap while engaged in sports practice, like swinging a golf club. It sends quick electrical pulses to the brain as you learn, which the developers claim induces something called "hyperplasticity." That's a state of rapid learning, and the company claims you can add at least five miles per hour to your swing, simply by giving their device a shot.

Nevertheless, research on the long-term effects of such stimulation is mixed, and most evidence supporting the benefits of such electrical pulses has been with small studies. For example, when a dozen bicyclists were given such a device and asked to use it while engaged in intense training, most reported reduced levels of fatigue and peddled slightly longer before requiring rest. Yet, their bodies responded the same. Heart rate didn't change, and neither did lactate accumulation in the muscles. The brain felt less tired, but the body still called the shots.

Another issue with using extreme measures like shocking our brains is the difficult decision of where to zap. Halo Neuroscience recommends focusing on the motor control centers of the brain, at least when training for golf, but we've already learned that the entire brain matters, not just the part that moves our arms and legs. Unless you've mastered your calm mind, you're probably not looking for *more* activity in your brain on the course. Actually, you want less. One study even used electrical stimulation on the temporal lobe, which has little to do with motor activity at all, and saw similar benefits for endurance cyclists. Who knows what will come next.

Odds are you're not shocking your brain any time soon, and you're not taking an MRI with you to the course, either. One problem with the MRI is that the machines are heavy and expensive (over three tons and a million dollars, on average), not to mention the fact that they are made of powerful magnets. Bring a golf club anywhere near an MRI, and you'll likely be decapitated. However, there are other tools for monitoring your brain activity, and they can get quite Zen. Meditation is one alternative because that's what it does—calm our brains. Seeing how this works requires a different machine, one that has been around for a lot longer than the MRI—the electroencephalogram (EEG).

The EEG is simple, measuring electrical activity produced by the brain and conducted through the skin to the top of the scalp. Because heads are poor conductors, the signal is weak, but it's still there. We can even look at brain activity as someone plays golf, and all it takes is a few electrodes and a bit of tape.

One benefit of the EEG is that it observes brain waves occurring over fractions of a second. This allows us to see how neural activity is coordinated in time, for example, in the form of alpha waves. These are the slow, rhythmic waves we get right before sleep, or when we meditate, and unlike with faster activity, they don't occur in isolated parts of the brain. Instead, they pass through wide regions of the cortex. This helps them coordinate different brain regions, and also quiet down background noise.

Alpha activity is the opposite of what we see using the MRI, because only coordinated neural firing shows up on the EEG. It even predicts who will make a putt, and who will come up short. When EEG electrodes were placed on expert and novice golfers before a series of putts, one thing differentiated the skilled players' brains.[6] For expert putters, their brains showed significantly more alpha wave activity, compared to the disorganized brains of novices.

The more alpha activity we have, the calmer our brains are and the more we focus on what really matters. Evidence of alpha activity being essential for a calm mind is seen in a study conducted by Claudio Babiloni from the University of Sapienza in Italy.[7] He and his research team had a dozen men and women attempt a hundred putts while having their brain activity monitored using an EEG. When successful and unsuccessful putts were compared, Babiloni found that only one thing predicted which went in the cup—alpha wave change. When players had more alpha activity before attempting the shot, they were more accurate and left the ball closer when they missed. Less alpha activity meant not even coming close to the hole.

Understanding alpha waves isn't just academic, because we have control over how our brains behave. We can actually increase our alpha activity by taking deep breaths and training our bodies to relax. Since alpha activity occurs any time we tune out our surroundings, we can enter this state simply by closing our eyes and emptying our mind. I told you we'd get Zen. Some call this meditation, others call it having a restful mind, but it helps no matter what name you give it.

Another option is to use biofeedback, which is slightly more complicated. This requires attaching electrodes to the head and monitoring brain waves in real time. Users are given updates on their alpha state by, for example, a tone letting them know when it gets low and they need to calm down. Though this option isn't available for everybody, it's a great tool and can increase putting performance by up to 25 percent. When a half dozen players were connected to biofeedback electrodes and warned any time their alpha activity fell too low,[8] their accuracy for medium-distance putt rates rose from 50 percent to 75 percent. The only difference was that they had immediate feedback about the state of their brain. Impressive, huh?

Before finishing this class on the brain, there's still one issue we haven't addressed, and it's a big one—so big, in fact, that it concerns the entire brain, which isn't really a single entity. Actually it's two, a left half and a right half, each working in different ways. The left side is our logical side, though it's also responsible for language. The right is more holistic and spatial, and consequently more artistic. Though these are broad generalizations (my dissertation was on right hemisphere language, for example), they are also quite accurate, and they mean a lot for our golf game.

Because golf isn't logical, the left side of the brain does very little for our game. By contrast, the right is very important because spatial awareness is key for sending dimpled balls into tiny cups. Perhaps that's why alpha activity in the right hemisphere predicts putting success, but not in the left. One study of alpha activity preceding 12-foot putts found that increases in alpha activity over right hemisphere motor areas predicted more accurate hits.[9] Changes in left hemisphere alpha activity predicted nothing at all.

Sadly, we can't look inside our brain when we go to the course, but we can recognize our own brain asymmetries and work with them. One trick is called the line bisection task, which you can even try at home. Start by taking a sheet of paper and drawing a straight horizontal line roughly six inches in length. Then, without the help of a ruler, mark the center of that line. This mark tells you something about how your brain is balanced, because now you can measure how close to center you actually came. Try it a few times with each hand and take the average deviation to find where you stand. An interesting thing about brain organization is that everything to the left side of our vision is processed in the right side of our brain, and vice versa. So if you look at the center of a line, the left half of that line will be "seen" by the right hemisphere, and the right side will be "seen" by the left. Now, let's assume you are right-hemisphere dominant—that means you'll naturally look a little to the right of center of that line. This leaves more of the line visible in your left visual field, to be processed by your preferred hemisphere. If someone asks you to mark the center of that line, you'll naturally "miss" a little to the left, because that's the side receiving unbalanced attention from your left visual field gaze. I know that sounds a little convoluted, and I suppose it is, but just be thankful we're discussing this in terms of your golf game, rather than with regard to being a stroke patient. That's the reason most people take the line bisection test, and in that case, it's also a lot less fun.

With regard to golf, though, people who miss more to the left in the line bisection task (which is far more common than missing to the right) are also more accurate while putting. The reason? Their right brains are more active. The effect is even greater when we perform the bisection task with our left hand, which is also controlled by the right hemisphere. Players who favor to the left land their balls just under an inch closer to the hole on seven-foot putts because their brains are asymmetrical in a good way. As a result, they sink significantly more putts.

So go try the experiment out yourself and see how your own brain works. Maybe even practice the bisection task on your own. There's no promise it will help, because brain organization is difficult to modify, but it can't hurt, and neither can knowing your own hemispheric orientation and learning to work with it.

The brain is often called the most complex machine in the universe, or at least the most complex one we know of. It certainly does more than make golf putts. That's great for living in a complex society, but terrible when you want to tune things out. It means we need to work hard to get the most from it. Sometimes that means meditation, sometimes mental rehearsal, and sometimes simply that we need to take some deep breaths.

It takes getting to know the equipment we're working with. And I don't mean our clubs.

READING LIST

Alpha waves

[8]Arns, M., Kleinnijenhuis, M., Fallahpour, K., and Breteler, R. (2007).

Golf Performance Enhancement and Real-Life Neurofeedback Training Using Personalized Event-Locked EEG Profiles. *Journal of Neurotherapy*, 11, 11–18.

[7]Babiloni, C., Del Percio, C., Iacoboni, M., Infarinato, F., Lizio, R., Marzano, N., Crespi, G., Dassu, F., Pirritano, M., Gallamini, M., and Eusebi, F. (2008). Golf Putt Outcomes are Predicted by Sensorimotor Cerebral EEG Rhythms. *Journal of Physiology*, 586, 131–139.

[6]Baumeister, J., Reinecke, K., Herbarth, B., Herwegen, H., Liesen, H., and Weiss, M. (2008). Brain Activity in a Golf Putting Task: The Effect of Skill Level. In D. Crews and R. Lutz (Eds.), *Science and Golf V: Proceedings of the World Scientific Congress of Golf* (pp. 208–215). Mesa, AZ: Energy in Motion, Inc.

[9]Crews, D. and Landers, D. (1993). Electroencephalographic Measures of Attentional Patterns Prior to the Golf Putt. *Medicine and Science in Sports and Exercise*, 25, 116–126.

Crews, D., Lutz, R., Nilsson, P., and Marriott, L. (1998). Psychophysiological Indicators of Confidence and Habituation During Golf Putting. In Farrally, M. and Cochran, A. (Ed.), *Science and Golf III: Proceedings of the World Scientific Congress of Golf* (pp. 158–165). Champaign, IL: Human Kinetics.

Brain Structure

[5]Bezzola, L., Merillat, S., Gaser, C., and Jancke, L. (2011). Training-Induced Neural Plasticity in Golf Novices. *The Journal of Neuroscience*, 31, 12444–12448.

[5]Bezzola, L., Merillat, S., and Jancke, L. (2012). The Effect of Leisure Activity Golf Practice on Motor Imagery: an fMRI Study in Middle Adulthood. *Frontiers in Human Neuroscience*, 6, 1–9.

[4]Jancke, L., Koeneke, S., Hoppe, A., Rominger, C., and Hanggi, J. (2009). The Architecture of the Golfer's Brain. *PLoS One*, 4, 1–8.

Milton, J., Solodkin, A., Hlustik, P., and Small, S. (2007). The Mind of Expert Motor Performance is Cool and Focused. *NeuroImage*, 35, 804–813.

Line Dissection and Brain Asymmetry

Roberts, R. and Turnbull, O. (2010). Putts That Get Missed on the

Right: Investigating Lateralized Attentional Biases and the Nature of Putting Errors in Golf. *Journal of Sports Sciences*, 28, 369–374.

Mental Rehearsal

Arora, S., Aggarwal, R., Sirimanna, P., Moran, A., Grantcharov, T., Kneebone, R., Sevdalis, N., and Darzi, A. (2011). Mental Practice Enhances Surgical Technical Skills: A Randomized Controlled Study. *Annals of Surgery*, 253, 265–270.

[1]Clark, V. (1960). Effect of Mental Practice on the Development of a Certain Motor Skill. *Research Quarterly for Exercise and Sport*, 31, 560–569.

[2]Driskell, J., Copper, C., and Moran, A. (1994). Does Mental Practice Enhance Performance? *Journal of Applied Psychology*, 79, 481–492.

Feltz, D., Landers, D., and Becker, B. (1988). A Revised Meta-Analysis of the Mental Practice Literature on Motor Skill Learning. In D. Druckman & J Swets (Eds.), *Enhancing Human Performance: Issues, Theories and Techniques* (pp. 19–88). Washington, DC: National Academy Press.

[3]Ross, J., Tkach, J., Ruggieri, P., Lieber, M., and Lapresto, E. (2003). The Mind's Eye: Functional MR Imaging Evaluation of Golf Motor Imagery. *American Journal of Neuroradiology*, 24, 1035–1044.

Sanders, C., Sadoski, M., van Walsum, K., Bramson, R., Wiprud, R., and Fossum, T. (2008). Learning Basic Surgical Skills with Mental Imagery: Using the Simulation Centre in the Mind. *Medical Education*, 42, 607–612.

Sociology Workshop on Gender and Race Studies

Prerequisites: Sociology 101: Crowd Behavior

Who is the best golfer of all time? It's a difficult question, because so many generations have played the game, all unique and accomplished in their own way. Ben Hogan? Jack Nicklaus? Tiger Woods? Any one of them could be an easy choice.

Yet, when this question is debated, the list seldom starts with Annika Sorenstam. That's a shame, because nobody has had a more dominant career than Sorenstam. Her 72 tour wins puts her one behind Nicklaus, ahead of such greats as Ben Hogan and Arnold Palmer. This is in spite of the fewer events during the women's professional circuit each year. She was LPGA Player of the Year eight times and had the lowest scoring average for six. Unlike Bobby Jones, Nicklaus, and Palmer, only Sorenstam has shot under 60 in a tournament, carding a 59 in the second round of the Standard Register Ping Tournament in 2001.

There's also Sorenstam's 2002 season, among the most impressive any golfer has ever seen. That year she won the first tournament of the season, the last, and nine in between.

Golf is often viewed as a man's game. That's why nearly everybody has heard of Tiger Woods, while players like Yani Tseng go relatively unknown. Tseng was the youngest player ever to win five major championships, male or female. By her fifth year on the LPGA Tour, she was only four points shy of qualifying for the World Golf Hall of Fame (points are based on number of victories). Yet, attention and endorsement deals have been sparse, despite leading the world golf rankings for 109 consecutive weeks from 2011 to 2013.

In this chapter, we'll explore growing diversity in the sport of golf, especially in terms of gender and race. Such changes may not affect your swing, but they certainly impact the sport and how it's perceived. Even subtle prejudices have no place on the course, and hopefully by recognizing them, we can spare future generations from suffering them, too.

Men and women play golf for the same reason—love of the game. When LPGA players were asked why they chose a career in golf, love of the sport was the top answer. That's the same as for men, indicating that golf has a universal draw, regardless of gender.

Yet, the sport has treated men and women very differently. For its first 80 years, women weren't allowed membership into the Augusta National Golf Club, a rule that lasted until 2012. That year, invitations were finally offered to Darla Moore and Condoleezza Rice, with Rice breaking more than one barrier. She is also one of the few African American members of Shoal Creek Golf Club in Birmingham, Alabama, a club notorious for historical exclusionary policies for both women and African Americans. Even as recently as 1990, the club only accepted white players for membership, which is shocking, almost as shocking as the fact that they still hosted several PGA events at the time of the policy.

If you think that recent progress has changed things, consider for a moment the Burning Tree Club in Bethesda, Maryland. It's still a male-only club that brags about not even having women's restrooms, despite routinely hosting presidents, members of Congress, and foreign dignitaries, including on one occasion the Australian prime minister. That last visit in 1986 was particularly interesting, because the prime minister was scheduled to be interviewed during his visit by a female U.S. Secret Service agent. However, the agent received the same treatment as Sandra Day O'Connor did when she became the first woman on the Supreme Court—no women allowed. It didn't matter that previous justices had routinely been offered membership. O'Connor was turned away, just as the secret service agent was forced to conduct the interview by radio from the parking lot.

Also problematic is the subtle bias within the golf world that often goes unnoticed. Even during Annika Sorenstam's amazing 2002 season, many people remarked that the press covered her differently from other players. Discussion of her game frequently focused on her looks, and her play was described using terms rarely applied to male players—words like "grace" and "finesse." This gave researchers an idea, so they decided to analyze the television coverage for themselves.[1] They specifically focused on the 2003 Colonial Golf Tournament in Fort Worth, Texas, because Sorenstam competed alongside the men for that event. Although she ultimately didn't make the cut and only played the first two days, press coverage was intense. It was a great opportunity to see how people would react to her play.

Each statement about Sorenstam and her male competitors was categorized based on topic, and the researchers found that announcers made 11 times more comments about her courage than the male players—presumably because a courageous woman is unusual enough to warrant noting. Commentators also made frequent comments about her attractiveness and emotional control, over six times more frequently than for all the male players combined. When one male player got lucky and saw his ball bounce toward the hole, one commentator called it an "Annika bounce," implying that he was stealing some of her good luck. How else could a female athlete make it so far?

We don't often think of the media being biased in how they describe athletes, but even mainstream outlets have a long history of favoring white, male competitors. A review of 30 years of *Sports Illustrated* coverage at the end of the century showed that males were the topic of 90 percent of all articles.[2] Whites also accounted for three-quarters of all athletes profiled, despite the rapid growth of African American athletes at the time. Articles that were written about females were also 16 percent shorter and included numerous sexist terms. These preferences don't always get noticed, but they definitely influence our thoughts and behaviors.

Some might say that prejudice is uncovered best by actions, not words. Even in that case, prejudice is frequently evident before leaving a tee box. Golf courses typically provide multiple starting locations for each hole, with white or blue tees for males and tournament play, and red tees for women. Not everybody can hit drives 300 yards or more, so designers provide alternate starting locations for those with lower strength. That's not sexist by itself, just a recognition that everybody is built differently. The standard benefit is 10 percent, though since tee boxes are chosen by course managers, there's lots of variation.

Here's where things get interesting—when Michelle Arthur, a professor at the Anderson School of Management in New Mexico, measured tee box ratios from hundreds of golf courses around the country, she found that some states give bigger advantages to women than others.[3] Specifically, states that are conservative by nature, as measured by Republican representation in Congress and voting in national elections, tend to start women more than four yards closer to the hole than do blue states. These differences also significantly predict women's salaries in marketing or managerial positions; in states where tee boxes most favor women, they also award women the lowest average salaries. In short, greater benefits on the course correlate with more conservative, less female-friendly perceptions in society.

This benefit reveals a lot about perceived differences between the genders. No doubt there are differences, because women do hit shorter off the tee than men. The top hitters on the PGA average over 300 yards for their opening drives, while women come closer to 270. This means women start off with a 7.5 percent disadvantage for most holes, which is why they have their own tee boxes. Yet, despite these physical differences, this still doesn't explain why the benefits are so inconsistent from one location to another. Courses in South Carolina give over twice the normal advantage, an average of 18 percent closer to the hole. Georgia and North Carolina are about the same. Compare that to courses in Washington, DC, which give almost no benefit at all.

This even led researchers to compare tee boxes in states from the Confederacy with everywhere else. Women's tee boxes in old confederate states were on average 2.3 percent closer to the hole compared to those in the north.[4] The more expensive the course and the more recently it was built, the greater the benefit.

Old views die slowly. Still, it would be wrong to ignore established anatomical differences between the sexes. Not only do women hit shorter drives on average compared to men, their body mechanics also differ. Women tend to make wider swings with larger hip and shoulder rotation, often leading to lower peak clubhead speeds. One cause is shorter average height, along with reduced body and muscle mass.

This raises interesting questions regarding the decreased attention to female athletes—do physical differences between males and females justify the reduced focus on women's sports? The average LPGA purse is under $2 million dollars, meaning the winners earn about $200,000 per tournament. Contrast that to the PGA Tour, where winnings are often four times that amount or more. One reason for this disparity is sponsorship involvement, as television audiences for male sports vastly exceed that for female competition. Another reason is differences in play, including shorter driving distances and higher average scores. What remains is gender bias, which begs the question—where does the difference in pay for women and men actually come from?

To find out, an economist from California State University, Stephen Shmanske, calculated exactly how much each swing was worth on both the PGA and LPGA Tours.[5] For example, he found that every yard off the tee earns an increase in pay of 2.3 percent. Improving greens in regulation leads to an 11 percent increase. With such detailed analysis, Shmanske was able to measure just how much each play is worth, and whether gender mattered in that result.

Now, finally for some good news—Shmanske found that females don't earn less because of their physical differences, they earn more. When controlling for average skill level (for example, putting, driving distance, sand saves), women earn $9,000 more per tournament than men for equivalent levels of play. If Annika Sorenstam had instead played on the PGA Tour, she would have earned almost half of her actual take. This isn't to say she didn't earn every dollar; it's just that prejudice alone doesn't explain the pay differences. The media may not always treat women fairly, and neither do conservative course owners, but the LPGA seems rather balanced. They just offer less money than their male counterparts because there are less advertising dollars to work with.

It's worth noting that such discussions are controversial, and in many professions women *are* paid less for the same work. All workers want to be paid a salary commensurate with their skill. However, skill isn't the only measure of a player's worth in professional sports. The average annual salary in professional basketball is $5.2 million, compared to half that in hockey and only $1.9 million in the NFL. Are basketball players really more than twice as skilled as football players? I doubt it. The point is that athlete salaries are based on many factors, one being how much fans are willing to shell out to see the big names play.

Let's hope that as golf evolves, so does our interest in seeing players of different races, genders, and backgrounds.

Of course, females aren't the only minority group that plays golf.

Though everybody has heard of Tiger Woods, few people can name another player of color on the PGA Tour. The Fiji-born professional golfer Vijay Singh has made a successful living from golf for over 30 years, and numerous Chinese players now compete in the United States, though the sport is still predominantly white. Even now, more than two decades after Tiger Woods entered the PGA Tour, only one other player self-identifies as being of African American heritage. By contrast, three out of four players in the NBA are black.

This lack of diversity surprises many people, especially those who predicted that the sport would change at the turn of the century. When Tiger Woods first emerged from Stanford as a serious competitor, many guessed that within a decade, a new generation of African American players would arise. But this hasn't happened, leaving many people to question why that is the case.

This lag leads to an important discussion about the concept of stereotype threat, which is an interesting phenomenon that unfortunately reinforces prejudice. It's based on the idea that we act as others around us expect us to act, and when those expectations follow stereotypes, so do our actions. For example, if women are reminded of the "fact" that females can't do math, they perform worse on quantitative tests because of the added pressure. This makes stereotypes even worse, because even if there's no truth behind the generalization, it happens anyway. It also helps explain the dearth of African Americans in golf, because of the common misconception that blacks can't play.

As a result, because of stereotype threat, many blacks and women avoid the sport because they're convinced they don't have the skill to compete. Take for example the study by psychologist Jeff Stone from the University of Arizona, who asked 80 subjects to make a series of putts.[6] Half the players were black and half were white, and all attempted putts on holes with inclines and obstructions to provide extra challenge. Players were told their goal was to sink the putts in as few hits as possible, with the experimenter recording their results.

But subjects weren't just sent off to play. Some were told that the test measured natural athleticism and complex hand-eye coordination. Others were told that it assessed strategic thinking, an ability to reason intelligently through problems. The rest were told nothing at all, other than to sink as many balls as possible.

The saddest aspect of stereotype threat is that it's so incredibly powerful that even these simple instructions were enough to affect performance. Though the average score was 23 strokes for ten holes, black subjects needed four additional hits when told that the experimenters were assessing their sports intelligence. When white subjects were told the experimenters were measuring athletic ability, they did just as badly.

Follow-up work by Stone has revealed that being exposed to stereotype threat causes golfers to practice less, which in turn makes them play worse. The effect is especially strong for players who associate performance with feelings of self-worth. There's a long way to go before racism is removed from the links, but at least occasionally we see positive stories coming from the discrimination. Take Bill Powell, for example, a World War II veteran and avid golfer. When he returned from England, having served in an early version of the Air Force, he found himself unable to play again. All the courses in his town of Canton, Ohio, were segregated, and despite his war record, the color of his skin prohibited his play. Some might have been discouraged, given his sacrifice. Others might have moved elsewhere. Powell had other plans.

When banks wouldn't loan him the money, Powell scraped up money from family and other supporters and built a course on his own. First with just nine holes, later with a full eighteen, the course was open to all races and was a huge success. This, despite the constant vandalism, including racist graffiti and broken flagsticks. The course thrived and eventually was included in the National Register of Historic Places. Powell's daughter even went on to become the second person of color to play on the LPGA Tour, and now he is a proud member of the National Black Golf Hall of Fame.

Prejudice and stereotypes on the course don't just affect the golf stroke. They influence perceptions of ourselves and our abilities. Every time blacks or women are blocked from play, we make it harder for future players to exceed expectations. Fortunately, a lot has changed in the past century, and now even conservative institutions like Augusta National include members of all genders and races.

It would be nice if that representation were larger, but it's a start. As golf grows, so will society, and apparently that growth will also have to include a large dose of patience.

READING LIST

Gender bias

Apostolis, N. and Giles, A. (2011). Portrayals of Women Golfers in the 2008 Issues of Golf Digest. *Sociology of Sport Journal*, 28, 225–238.

[3]Arthur, M., Del Campo, R., and Van Buren, H. (2011). The Impact of Gender-Differentiated Golf Course Features on Women's Networking. *Gender in Management: An International Journal*, 26, 37–56.

Arthur, M., Van Buren, H., and Del Campo, R. (2009). The Impact of American Politics on Perceptions of Women's Golfing Abilities. *The American Journal of Economics and Sociology*, 68, 517–539.

[1]Billings, A., Craig, C., Croce, R., Cross, K., Moore, K., Vigodsky, W., and Watson, V. (2006). Just One of the Guys: Network Descriptions of Annika Sorenstam in the 2003 PGA Colonial Tournament. *Journal of Sport and Social Issues*, 30, 107–114.

Daddario, G. and Wigley, B. (2006). Prejudice, Patriarchy, and the PGA: Defensive Discourse Surrounding the Shoal Creek and Augusta National Controversies. *Journal of Sport Management*, 20, 466–482.

[4]Limehouse, F. (2010). On Chivalry in Golf. *Public Choice*, 142, 335–337.

[2]Lumpkin, A. and Williams, L. (1991). An Analysis of *Sports Illustrated* Feature Articles, 1954–1987. *Sociology of Sport Journal*, 8, 16–32.

Maas, K. and Hasbrook, C. (2001). Media Promotion of the Paradigm Citizen / Golfer: An Analysis of *Golf Magazine*'s Representations of Disability, Gender, and Age. *Sociology of Sport Journal*, 18, 21–36.

Marple, D.(1983). Tournament Earnings and Performance Differentials Between the Sexes in Professional Golf and Tennis. *Journal of Sport and Social Issues*, 7, 1–14.

[4]McCormick, R. and Tollison, R. (2010). Chivalry in Golf? Significant Tee Ratios. *Public Choice*, 142, 323–334.

Moy, R. and Liaw, T. (1998). Determinants of Professional Golf Tournament Earnings. *The American Economist*, 42, 65–70.

[5]Shmanske, S. (2000). Gender, Skill, and Earnings in Professional Golf. *Journal of Sports Economics*, 1, 385–400.

Theberge, N. (1980). The System of Rewards in Women's Professional Golf. *International Review for the Sociology of Sport*, 15, 27–41.

Stereotype threat

Beilock, S., Jellison, W., Rydell, R., McConnell, A., and Carr, T. (2006). On the Causal Mechanisms of Stereotype Threat: Can Skills That Don't Rely Heavily on Working Memory Still Be Threatened? *Personality and Social Psychology Bulletin*, 32, 1059–1071.

Beilock, S. and McConnell, A. (2004). Stereotype threat and sport: Can athletic performance be threatened? *Journal of Sport and Exercise Psychology*, 26, 597–609.

[6]Stone, J. (2002). Battling Doubt by Avoiding Practice: The Effects of Stereotype Threat on Self-handicapping in White Athletes. *Personality and Social Psychology Bulletin*, 28, 1667–1678.

Stone, J., Sjomeling, M., Lynch, C., and Darley, J. (1999). Stereotype Threat Effects on Black and White Athletic Performance. *Journal of Personality and Social Psychology*, 77, 1213–1227.

Swing differences and gender

Egret, C., Nicolle, B., Dujardin, F., Weber, J., and Chollet, D. (2006). Kinematic Analysis of the Golf Swing in Men and Women Experienced Golfers. *International Journal of Sports Medicine*, 27, 463–467.

Horan, S., Evans, K., Morris, N., and Kavanagh, J. (2010). Thorax and Pelvis Kinematics During the Downswing of Male and Female Skilled Golfers. *Journal of Biomechanics*, 43, 1456–1462.

Zheng, N., Barrentine, S., Fleisig, G., and Andrews, J. (2008). Swing Kinematics for Male and Female Golfers. *International Journal of Sports Medicine*, 29, 965–970.

International Study Abroad (Elective)

Prerequisites: None

Before golf returned to the Olympics in 2016, the most recent gold medal winner was George Lyon of Canada. A former cricket player who took up golf at age thirty-eight, Lyon was already an accomplished rugby, soccer, and baseball player. He won the Canadian Golf Amateur Championship after only two years of play, with a swing motion once likened to a farmer harvesting wheat. Despite this lack of experience and being severely outnumbered by the Americans—Lyon was the only non-American to make the final round of 32—he still won. The year was 1904.

Golf's return to Olympic competition wasn't easy. Due to the fact that Brazil—a nation with barely a hundred courses—was the host, an entirely new one had to be built. Using the sand belt of Australia as inspiration, American designer Gil Hanse incorporated local mangrove trees and several ponds in the design. Three greens were located near the beach, and 79 bunkers were placed along the fairways. When asked if he would share any nuances about the course before the competition, Hanse's answer was clear: "Only [with] the Americans."

Yet, the Americans still didn't win. On the male side in the 2016 competition, Justin Rose of England took home the gold, followed two strokes behind by Henrik Stetson of Sweden. Matt Kuchar of Florida took home the bronze. For the women, gold went to Inbee Park of South Korea, followed by Lydia Ko of New Zealand and Shanshan Feng of China.

International competition in the world of golf is fierce, not just in the Olympics, but at the Ryder Cup and similar events, too. One could even argue that the PGA Tour is already an international event, with 30 countries and six continents represented. For nearly a century, America and Europe have swapped places as golfing epicenters, but a shift is on the horizon. Birdies are now being scored all over the globe, with one location growing particularly fast. In golf, as in the world economy, the sun rises in the East.

In this elective, we take a trip abroad, visiting a part of the world we seldom associate with the sport. Earlier, we learned that golf was outlawed in fifteenth-century Scotland because kings feared it was becoming a distraction for soldiers. The same prohibitions occurred in China only recently, and it's still supposedly illegal there to build new courses. Yet, a lot has changed lately. Competitive golf is now a part of Chinese culture, and the growth is sure to accelerate.

One reason international competitors should fear China is the Shichahai Sports School, located just north of Beijing. This campus of 13 training halls spanning ten acres is home to over 600 students, all with one goal—perfection. Students wake up at 6:30 every morning to study academics, discipline, and—above all—sport. Shichahai has produced Olympic medalists in too many events to count, from badminton to gymnastics, and now golf is also part of its curriculum. Young aspirants like Luo Junyi now spend their days thinking about nothing but chipps and putts, seeing her parents only on the occasional weekend. The next Tiger Woods has probably already been born, just not in California.

China has more than two hundred such state-run sports academies, Shichahai being one of the largest and most prestigious. They're part of the country's goal to establish a leading role in athletic competition, and it's working. China is now home to the PGA Tour China series, which includes eight events and counting. Though Americans and Brits still occasionally win, in recent years, local talent has begun to take over. Beijing native Yi Cao now stands atop the tour's "Order of Merit," and since he hasn't yet reached the age of thirty, more wins are surely in his future.

China is the perfect environment for breeding golf talent, as economic booms and a strong work ethic provide plenty of opportunity for growth. Already, we see outstanding players like Andy Zhang and Guan Tianlang competing in American major events and winning, too. In May 2013, Ye Wocheng became the youngest player ever to compete in a European Tour Event, and he wasn't even a teenager. He was twelve years old.

For China's golf program to continue growing, the country needs new courses, and that has been a problem. The first course wasn't built in China until 1984, and just two decades later, the country banned any new construction of courses. Not only does casual play encourage "extravagant eating and drinking," but according to the ruling Communist Party, the land is badly needed for other industry. Despite this prohibition, however, the number of courses has skyrocketed, usually under the guise of "public sports parks." Today, China is home to over six hundred courses, and that number is expected to exceed a thousand by the year 2020. At the moment, the only province on the mainland not home to a course is Tibet.

Which is a surprise, since I hear the young Dalai Lama used to be quite the golfer. Not a great tipper, but pretty good off the tee, at least (if that makes no sense, please Google it, because I'm only allowed one *Caddyshack* reference in this book, and it would be a shame to waste it).

China also holds the distinction of having the largest golf complex in the world, called Mission Hills and located in the Shenzhen Hills north of Hong Kong. It houses twelve courses, each designed by a world-respected professional (e.g., Jack Nicklaus, Greg Norman, and Annika Sorenstam). Five times larger than Central Park in New York, its features include two clubhouses, four spas, and even a 3,000-seat stadium. With facilities like that, it's hard not to grow local talent.

The complex is even expanding to nearby Hainan Island, with nearly double as many courses. When that happens, more space will be dedicated to golf in that one location than the amount of acreage you'll find in all of Manhattan.

If anybody doubts Asia's future role in the sport, just look at South Korea. At the moment, roughly a third of the top women golfers in the world come from South Korea, with Se Ri Pak winning four events and two majors in just her rookie year. This has led to the huge influx of Asian talent, particularly female, and even a clever nickname for female Korean golfers—the "Seoul Sisters." Males from Korea haven't fared as well, though players like Si Woo Kim and Byeong Hun An still compete near the top most weeks. One reason South Korean women outperform the men might be the compulsory military service for males, as well as the strong emphasis on academics. In South Korea, young boys grow up looking forward to being doctors and lawyers after serving their country. Athlete is more of a fallback.

This isn't to say that China is the only growing home for the sport in the East. Thailand, Vietnam, and India have all begun to see the sport grow within their borders. India recently received a big boost when Arjun Atwal became the first citizen to win on the PGA Tour, taking the closely contested Wyndham Championship in North Carolina. Though issues with money and available real estate still make the future of Indian golf uncertain, it doesn't hurt that the country has more potential middle-class players than the entire population of the United States. The 20-year waiting list to join the Delhi Golf Club isn't a bad sign, either. If ever the subcontinent starts getting bored with cricket, watch out, because as with China, numbers are on their side.

In fact, Japan seems to be the only location in Asia where golf isn't growing, and that's only because after its golf boom in the 1980s, there was nowhere left to go. But don't count out the land of the rising sun just yet, because the 2020 Summer Olympics are scheduled to be held in Tokyo, at the famous Kasumigaseki Country Club. Not only do officials hope the event will bring needed attention back to the sport, but Japan has seen other benefits. For example, the impending event has forced the country to address the problematic issue of female golfers being banned from many Japanese courses. Now, for the first time ever, the Kasumigaseki Country Club allows all players—not just males—to enjoy the links, meaning that the number of potential players has just doubled. More change is sure to come.

In a culture where business is paramount, young Asian entrepreneurs are learning that golf is more than a leisure activity. It's part of a growing economy. The United States and Britain might have St. Andrews and Augusta, but it won't be long before similar talk is made of Mission Hills. And when that happens, even more young Chinese golfers will start taking up the game.

READING LIST

Growth of golf in China

Larmer, B. (2013). Golf in China is Younger than Tiger Woods, but Growing Up Fast. *New York Times Magazine*, July 11.

Xu, G. (2008). *Olympic Dreams: China and Sports, 1895–2008*. Boston, MA: Harvard University Press.

Growth of golf in India

Kahn, J. (2010). India's Middle Class Waits for a Tee Time. *New York Times Magazine*, Sept 11.

Premedicine: Special Seminar on Aging

Prerequisites: Premedicine: Kinematics and Human Anatomy

Premedicine: Fitness and Conditioning

Before Gary Player, golfers weren't considered true athletes. No offense to John Daly or Jack Nicklaus, but let's face it—the sport doesn't require the same conditioning as marathoner or gymnast. It took Gary Player, otherwise known as Mr. Fitness, to break the mold.

When Player won his first major in 1959, wearing what would become his traditional slim-fitting black attire, his appearance received as much notice as his game. With broad shoulders and an open willingness to do one-armed pushups for the crowds, he showed that a fit body can take you far. It's no surprise that Player's career has been so long and influential; for over 20 years, he continued winning majors, and in 1998, he became the oldest player to make the cut at the Masters, at the age of sixty-three. In 2013, at the seasoned age of seventy-seven, Player posed nude for *ESPN*'s annual body issue.

Golf is unlike any other sport in that athletes can compete until a very late age. Lee Trevino, Sherri Steinhauer, and even old Tom Morris all won tournaments in their forties because golf is mental as much as physical. Yet, our bodies do change as we get older, and this alters our playing style. In this chapter, we'll review these changes, assessing what all players can expect from their mind and body as the years start to accumulate.

The great Kansas City native Tom Watson provides an excellent example of how our golf game changes over time. An elite player for over four decades, Watson couldn't have remained competitive without close attention to his fitness. Yet, decline was inevitable. During Watson's peak in the 1980s, he won five major championships, including several British Opens. Yet, even at this prolific time, his statistical performance showed signs of age. His greens in regulation slowly dropped from 77 percent to 51 percent. While his chipping and short game improved slightly, his birdie opportunities fell from 6.3 per round to 4. Although his scores remained impressive, these slight dips were enough to keep him from winning more championships, and his last major victory was behind him at age thirty-four.

Despite the fact that all golfers will eventually see a decline in their game, at least the sport is friendlier to older players than any other. Swimmers reach their peak performance around age nineteen. Tennis players reach theirs only five years later, and baseball players and long-distance runners have their best days behind them by twenty-seven. Yet, golfers play consistently well into their thirties, and even then, the drop is slight. Nobody is ever going to see a swimmer or sprinter achieve top performance in late middle age. However, golfers routinely play competitively even when their nonathlete peers are beginning to consider retirement.

One way to identify age-related peaks in golf performance is to look at the average age of PGA Tour winners—35 years old. That's not very old, but it's not young, either. On the European Tour, the age is slightly younger (30). The Champions Tour for seniors, with eligibility starting at 50, sees a steady dropoff with age.

Amazingly, women follow a different pattern. For them, the chance of winning is consistent well into the midthirties, but two ages are special. At 25 and 32, women have their greatest chances of winning a tournament, almost twice as likely as any other time. It's hard to guess what is special about these ages, or why female golfers have two times in their professional lives that stand out. One possible reason is the remarkable play of Annika Sorenstam, who was so dominant, she was inducted into the World Golf Hall of fame before even seeing her best play. She alone almost accounts for the increase in wins during the midthirties, the peak of her own career. Another possibility is that the bodies of female professional golfers age differently from those of males, though research on that topic is still relatively new.

While peak golfing age is useful to know, this still says nothing about how rapid the decline is. The good news is that the dropoff isn't sharp—though golfers usually experience their lowest scores in their thirties, significant decline doesn't begin until almost ten years later. Even then, the average loss is small, and it isn't until 50 that we start losing more than a stroke a year. This doesn't even take into account changes in lifestyle, since most players spend significant time on the course only after retirement. Odds are the increased leisure time to practice as we get older more than makes up for any breakdown due to age.

One trouble with recognizing changes in our play is that not all of us are as dedicated or athletic as Gary Player or Tom Watson. Most of us exercise when we can and wouldn't be able to do a one-armed pushup if our lives depended on it. That's why studies have also examined amateur players to see what happens to average bodies over time. The results are interesting.

It seems that players of all ability levels start adding strokes to their handicap by age 40. The decline is unavoidable, simply because bodies break down as they get older. However, handicap matters, too. For elite players, the dropoff begins the earliest, often in the thirties. For them, the skills have already been learned, so time becomes the enemy. By contrast, for high-handicappers, this is still a time for improvement, because increased practice outweighs any body-related decline. So decline depends more on your still level than the calendar. In fact, even if you're a skilled player in the middle of a falloff, you're still better off than your high-handicap partner. One study of more than a thousand male golfers found that the top 10 percent of golfers in their late seventies still averaged a handicap of about 12.[1] That's half as many free strokes as received by the worst 10 percent of golfers—in their prime.

So take comfort in knowing that age-related losses are still far weaker than the gains we get from practicing during our youth. Scores may rise, but the sport is generally forgiving, no matter what our bodies say.

Even past the age of fifty, Davis Love III continues to impress. When he won the 2015 Wyndham Open, he was already 51, which is pretty impressive. Yet, it wasn't a record. "Slammin' Sammy" Snead was over 52 when he won the Greensboro Open, which meant that Love still had another year before he could take that title for his own.

Sadly, a hip surgery has hampered his goal, and now he usually plays smaller tours or caddies for his son. Yup, you read that right—both Love and his son now compete professionally, and it's not hard to imagine one or both making a run sometime soon.

Changes in score are well linked to changes in the body, as older physiques bend and swing differently from their younger versions. One study found that average swing speed drops from 101 mph to 87 mph as we enter our fifties.[2] With this comes a decrease in weight shift during the swing, as older bodies experience a smaller and slower forward thrust. Much of this change is due to changes in flexibility and muscle density, and even in our sixties, half of our swing speed is determined by overall fitness, with golfers in the best shape showing the least loss.

Despite older players having reduced range of motion, slower rotation, and lower hip-spine coupling during the forward swing, they don't always swing slower. Oddly enough, most studies show that they swing just as fast, as measured by time from backswing to follow-through. Mind you, that's different from measuring the speed of the club itself. Club speeds do get slower as we age, and understanding how that happens requires exploring the link between golf and music, as revealed by a rather clever study conducted by scientists at The Ohio State University.

The golf swing is a complex process involving something called a 3:2 polyrhythmic movement. While the upper body goes through three distinct stages of movement—backswing, downswing, and follow-through—the lower body only goes through two. That involves shifting weight first to the back foot, and then returning it to the front. This 3:2 coordination of motions is incredibly difficult to time, as all musicians know, because the sequence can't be synchronized. Try this as a test—with your left hand on a flat surface, tap a beat twice every second. Then, with your right hand, tap three times in the same interval. Some professional pianists may succeed, but most of us fail right away.

An ideal golf swing has our lower and upper bodies timed independently, and that's a challenge for even the fittest of players. It can be especially hard for seniors struggling to maintain balance and flexibility, and so the psychologist Tae Hoon Kim and his peers at Ohio State put 40 young and senior golfers through a test.[3] First, the players were connected to sensors that timed their swings, and then they were sent to a tee box with a force plate under their feet to measure shifts in weight. They attempted over a hundred chip shots at two targets, one 40 yards away and another twice that distance. Last, they had their balance assessed by having them stand perfectly still, sometimes on one foot and sometimes in a standard "pre-swing" stance.

Tae Hoon Kim found that what separated older and younger players wasn't their swing speed or power applied to the shots. What differed was their coordinated movements. Older players were more than twice as likely to include what's called a "forward press" in their swing. That's when the lower body shifts too early, about the same time as our backswing. This eliminates the independence of the lower and upper body, and over 80 percent of all seniors adopted this rhythmic pattern to their swing. The result was screwed-up timing.

Perhaps seniors simplify the timing of their swing due to reduced balance. This is certainly supported by the balance tests—not only did older players "wobble" more while trying to stand upright, but this movement was closely related to variability of force during their swing. This suggests that older golfers are better off adopting a simpler, coordinated upper and lower body movement system, one that allows them to adapt to this lack of steadiness.

Not that all senior golfers are unsteady, or have inconsistent balance. When compared to those who don't play the sport, older swingers still have better balance and less sway than their peers. They also demonstrate better judgment. When young and old players are surveyed and observed on the course, seniors show a smarter, more conservative approach to their play, along with better cognitive and emotional control over their swing. With age comes experience, and that's worth quite a lot.

One last thing seniors should consider is that frequent play simply helps us live longer. One analysis of professional golfers showed that players have a life expectancy five years greater than their age-matched peers, simply due to their play.[4] This translates to cutting mortality rate by nearly half in older age, doubling the chances we'll each be around to see the next year. The benefit isn't limited to professionals either, as amateurs see similar benefits. Interestingly, the effect is still linked with handicap, with better players living the longest. Don't feel bad the next time you triple-bogey, though—even the worst duffers experienced significantly longer lives than nonplayers, so long as you hit the links frequently enough.

Aging is part of life, and it's part of golf, too. Many players don't even commit to the sport until after retirement, so it's no surprise that decline is inevitable. Unlike basketball or soccer, golf can be played for as long as we can walk and hold a club, and it does good things for our health, too. Not only does it improve mood and flexibility, but it helps us stay in tune with our body.

When Tom Watson led the British Open on its final day in 2009, he was 59 years old. Nobody thought anyone that old would win golf's most prestigious major, its long and unforgiving fairways too taxing for older bodies to master. Yet, it wasn't distance off the tee that ruined poor Watson. It was an eight-foot putt on the final hole, the kind of mental challenge that could rattle anybody, regardless of age.

Watson may have technically lost in a playoff to Stewart Cink, but in a way, he won, too. He showed that the game will always be as psychological as it is physical.

Older players have a lot to look forward to.

Reading List

General aging

Lindsay, D., Horton, J., and Vandervoort, A. (2000). A Review of Injury Characteristics, Aging Factors and Prevention Programmes for the Older Golfer. *Sport Medicine*, 30, 89–103.

Riccio, L. (1994). The Aging of a Great Player; Tom Watson's Play in the US Open from 1980–1993. In A.J. Cochran and M. Farrally (Eds.), *Science and Golf II: Proceedings of the World Scientific Congress of Golf* (pp. 210–215). Grass Valley, CA: The Booklegger.

Longevity

[4]Coate, D. and Schwenkenberg, J. (2012). Survival Function Estimates for Champions Tour Golfers. *Journal of Sport Economics*, 12, 1–8.

Farahmand, B., Broman, G., de Faire, U., Vagerim, D., and Ahlbom, A. (2009). Golf: A Game of Life and Death—Reduced Mortality in Swedish Golf Players. *Scandinavian Journal of Medicine, Science, and Sports*, 19, 419–424.

Peak age and golf skills

Baker, J., Deakin, J., Horton, S., and Pearce, G. (2007). Maintenance of Skilled Performance with Age: A Descriptive Examination of Professional Golfers. *Journal of Aging and Physical Activity*, 15, 299–316.

Baker, J., Horton, S., Pearce, W., and Deakin, J. (2005). A Longitudinal Examination of Performance Decline in Champion Golfers. *High Ability Studies*, 16, 179–185.

Berry, S. and Larkey, P. (1998). The Effects of Age on the Performance of Professional Golfers. In Farrally, M. and Cochran, A. (Ed.), *Science and Golf III: Proceedings of the World Scientific Congress of Golf* (pp. 127–137). Champaign, IL: Human Kinetics.

[2]Brown, D., Best, R., Ball, K., and Dowlan, S. (2002). Age, Centre of Pressure and Clubhead Speed in Golf. In Thain, E. (Ed.), *Science and Golf IV: Proceedings of the World Scientific Congress of Golf* (pp. 28–34). New York: Routledge.

Gao, K., Hui-Chan, C., and Tsang, W. (2011). Golfers Have Better Balance Control and Confidence than Healthy Controls. *European Journal of Applied Physiology*, 111, 2805–2812.

Jagacinski, R. and Greenberg, N. (1997). Tempo, Rhythm, and Aging in Golf. *Journal of Motor Behavior*, 29, 159–173.

[3]Kim, T., Jagacinski, R., and Lavender, S. (2011). Age-Related Differences in the Rhythmic Structure of the Golf Swing. *Journal of Motor Behavior*, 43, 433–444.

Lathey, C., Strike, S., and Lee, R. (2009). The Effects of Aging on the Hip and Spinal Motions in the Golf Swing. *Paper presented at the 27th Annual International Conference on Biomechanics in Sports, Limerick, Ireland.*

[1]Lockwood, J. (1998). A Small-Scale Local Survey of Age-Related Male Golfing Ability. In Farrally, M. and Cochran, A. (Ed.), *Science and Golf III: Proceedings of the World Scientific Congress of Golf* (pp. 112–119). Champaign, IL: Human Kinetics.

Mitchell, K., Banks, S., Morgan, D., and Sugaya, H. (2003). Shoulder Motions During the Golf Swing in Male Amateur Golfers. *Journal of Orthopedics, Sports, and Physical Therapy*, 33, 196–203.

Morgan, D., Banks, S., Sugaya, H., and Moriya, H. (1998). The Influence of Age on Lumbar Mechanics During the Golf Swing. In Farrally, M.

and Cochran, A. (Ed.), *Science and Golf III: Proceedings of the World Scientific Congress of Golf* (pp. 120–126). Champaign, IL: Human Kinetics.

Over, R. and Thomas, P. (1995). Age and Skilled Psychomotor Performance: A Comparison of Younger and Older Golfers. *The International Journal of Aging and Human Development*, 41, 1–12.

Schulz, R. and Curnow, C. (1988). Peak Performance and Age Among Superathletes: Track and Field, Swimming, Baseball, Tennis, and Golf. *Journal of Gerontology*, 43, 11–120.

Thompson, C. (2002). Effect of Muscle Strength and Flexibility on Club-Head Speed in Older Golfers. In Thain, E. (Ed.), *Science and Golf IV: Proceedings of the World Scientific Congress of Golf* (pp. 35–44). New York: Routledge.

Tiruneh, G. (2010). Age and Winning Professional Golf Tournaments. *Journal of Quantitative Analysis in Sports*, 6, 1–14.

Introduction to Prelaw

Prerequisites: None

Like the rest of Winged Foot Golf Club in Mamaroneck, New York, the par-three sixth hole is both beautiful and treacherous. The first things the player sees are the many sand traps hugging the green. Trees to the right penalize anything but a straight hit, and a steep incline behind the green punishes overhits. It's the kind of hole that requires deep attention, and few people even notice the three houses to the far right.

Unfortunately, this is a problem for Anthony Pecora, who owns one of those houses. When course managers cut down several trees separating his home from the green, he quickly found himself barraged by errant golf balls. Five windows were broken in less than a year, causing over $14,000 in damage. His dog even ate one and required emergency surgery. When he requested course owners erect a net, they declined. Winged Foot is a beautiful course, they claimed, consistently ranking among the top in the world. It simply isn't a place where golfers play next to unsightly nets.

The end result was a lawsuit, and the New York Supreme Court ordered the hole closed until the course's liability could be determined.

Pecora sued because he claimed the course was negligent in cutting down the trees and not replacing them with something else. His case is unusual, because he actually won and got what he asked for—Winged Foot eventually planted more trees and moved the tee boxes forward, enough to reduce frequency of mishits. The solution wasn't perfect, but at least now slices have to be both high and ridiculously off-target to cause significant damage.

In this class, your final at Golf University, we take an unusual turn.

We're about to explore a topic with little practical application to your swing, but which could mean a lot to your happiness and pocketbook. Lawsuits are a serious matter, and every golfer needs to know his or her legal responsibilities. Sometimes a slice can be costly, and not just to your score. In this chapter, you'll learn when to ease up on that swing. Winning side bets is great, but not when victory also brings a court date.

First, it's important to recognize that no player should rely on this book, or any other, to decide legal matters pertaining to golf. So if you have legal questions, you should always trust the experts. But I can share a few basic findings, with emphasis on the American court system, that serve as a starting point for understanding the concept of liability in golf, beginning with something called "an assumption of risk." That's the idea that risk is part of life, and sometimes we must accept when bad things happen. This is especially important for people who live next to courses, since houses are often hit by stray balls. Most owners install unbreakable windows just to be safe, but that's the point. It's a reasonable and manageable risk. Although etiquette may encourage golfers to pay for broken windows, the law seldom does. Some states even have laws specifically addressing the matter, and most side with the player.

This doesn't mean that homeowners are out of luck, however. If you hit one ball into a window, you're probably fine, but do it a dozen more times, and things start to change. This brings us to one legal case in particular, and it's a doozy. It's known as the *Roe v. Wade* of golfing lawsuits, and it changed the concept of liability in sport. The case was *Amaral v. Cuppels*, and again it involved golf balls, windows, and lots of damage.

Joyce Amaral's case is special, according to her lawyer, because it's not only based on risk. It's based on volume. When Amaral showed up for her 2003 trial, she brought six huge buckets, each filled with 300 stray balls collected from her property in Rehoboth, Massachusetts. That amounted to more than 1,800 in all, many having led to broken windows and dented cars after being struck from the neighboring Middlebrook Country Club. Her patio deck had become a war zone that made it impossible to spend time outside, and even yard workers had to wear hardhats. Although course managers relocated the tee and installed signs asking players to "aim left" along the narrow fairway, the balls kept coming.

The court initially ruled that Amaral and her neighbor were correct, and course owners owed them financial compensation for the damages. But upon appeal, judge Mark Green gave a different opinion—the real issue wasn't compensation. After all, homeowners had to expect collateral damage from living next to a course. Instead, it was a matter of trespassing. The sheer volume of golf balls meant that Amaral's yard was no longer her own, creating a situation called "continuing trespass." The course didn't owe her money, but they did owe her a course design allowing her use of her yard and property. Perhaps the manager of the course, Mr. Peter Cuppels, could change the hole to a par three?

The case meant that the course design was at fault, not individual golfers, which should be a relief for most of us. Just because you hit a bad tee shot doesn't mean you're subject to a lawsuit. But if everybody makes the same bad shot on a consistent basis, well, that's a different matter.

The same goes for accidentally hitting other players. This is problematic because it's both common and dangerous. Yet, courts have consistently ruled that being hit by an occasional golf ball is part of the game, too. So long as players aren't reckless or hit one another habitually, most courts will rule that you're safe, at least legally.

One dissertation by Kyongmin Lee of the University of New Mexico even examined the frequency of lawsuits submitted against golf courses for damage or liability. Less than a third of the lawsuits Lee reviewed between 1930 and 2013 ended with a plaintiff winning against a course, with the majority being outright losses. The primary reason for these dismissals was the difficulty proving negligence—golf courses must not only fail to keep their players safe, but that breach must cause unavoidable and substantial damage. So when Phyllis Davis decided to continue playing golf near her home in Tennessee despite impending storms, then take refuge from the rain in a shelter located next to the sixteenth green, there was no way for the course to know that she would be struck by lightning. They had built the shelters to protect their players, which is a good thing, and they had no control over how Mother Nature would treat their customers. While the lawyers argued that the shelter needed to be on lower ground, and that lightning rods should have been installed, there was no clear violation of duty. Thankfully, Davis survived, despite suffering significant injuries.

By contrast, when Gina Ryan sued the Mill Country Club in Connecticut for not maintaining its golf cart paths, which had led her cart to flip and Ryan to sustain serious injuries, she won because in that case duty to protect the player had been violated. Several other players had experienced similar problems before, yet no fixes were made. Even the path itself was bumpy and in serious need of repair. Too bad that duty to protect works in both directions, because Gina Ryan also found herself as a defendant in a parallel claim against her by the cart's passenger. He sustained serious injuries too, and since Ryan was driving too fast, she shared at least some of the responsibility for the accident. In the end, the courts found her 30 percent at fault, leaving her with only a fraction of the compensation she sought.

One of the most interesting cases to challenge the presumption of innocence was *Anand v. Kapoor*. Filed to the New York Court of Appeals, the case centered on an incident occurring at the first hole at Dix Hills Park Club in Suffolk County, New York. Anoop Kapoor had hit his ball into the rough to the left of the fairway, while his partner Azad Anand was about six yards ahead to the side. Both went to address their ball, neither aware that the other was about to hit. When Kapoor struck his ball and hit his partner in the left eye, the result was a detached retina and permanent blindness.

Anand alleged that Kapoor hadn't diligently checked for nearby players and also hadn't yelled "Fore!" to warn of the hit. The court ruled that no matter what Kapoor did, his partner must have known that an accident was possible. We all assume some risk by stepping onto the course, and unless a player intentionally hits a person, being struck by a golf ball is considered part of the game.

Just for the record, the same goes for hitting yourself with a ball. When Paul Sanchez blinded himself in the eye after bouncing his ball off a yardage marker, courts found that the course wasn't responsible. It's not as if the marker had appeared from nowhere.

Just be careful if you're an instructor, because then you're special. When Tom Stafford hit a steel pole after telling his instructor that he felt comfortable with the shot, the courts ruled that the instructor should have known better. It was his job, and by telling his student to take the shot, he took over responsibility for the consequences. This made the instructor responsible for the medical cost of Stafford's fifteen stitches.

Hitting other players with your golf club is a different matter. Just ask Mary Touhey, a Yonkers, New York, gym teacher. After Mary's opponent, Daniel Schapiro, erupted in frustration over a bad swing, he threw his club in the air. The club, in turn, flew 30 yards and hit Mary in the head, leaving her with constant headaches. After numerous visits to the neurologist, she still suffers from the blow more than a year later, and though she didn't press charges, she did apply for unspecified damages. According to the law, such damages were hers to ask for.

Just as several books have been written on the forward swing or putting, entire tomes have been written about golfing law. The number of lawsuits is overwhelming, which isn't surprising, since so many people play. Fortunately, we don't have to be lawyers to enjoy the game, but we should be responsible, and this includes using the cart properly. Countless players sue courses each year over crashes and collisions, and the results are always messy.

Courses can't control how players drive, and unless the cart is defective, they generally aren't responsible for its use. The burden must be on the player, because they have an obligation not to be reckless. The most famous lawsuit in golfing history involves a cart, though the defendant wasn't an individual or country club. It was the PGA, and the plaintiff was one of its own players. When Casey Martin became struck by a degenerative leg disease, leading to swelling and extreme pain, his golfing career suffered. The only way to play was by using a cart, yet PGA rules prohibited it on the professional tour. Next came a petition for exemption from the rule based on the disease, which was promptly rejected. The condition was terrible, everybody agreed, but professional sports can't make exceptions. If you can't walk, you can't play.

But the story isn't over. Martin sued the PGA based on the Americans with Disabilities Act, arguing that the cart provided no advantage, and the case went all the way to the Supreme Court. In a 7–2 ruling, the court agreed with Martin. Swinging the club and earning birdies is a fundamental part of the game. Walking between holes isn't.

Perhaps one of the most interesting cases argued against professional golf was that of Jane Blalock, who sued the LPGA for another issue entirely. Two in five golfers claim to never take mulligans, and 70 percent claim to take one only occasionally, which is of course ridiculous. Nearly everybody takes a free drop now and then, and unless money is on the line, these minor violations are harmless. Former president William Clinton was especially liberal in his attitude toward mulligans, sometimes playing three or more balls per hole, and he still won a second term. When researchers from Western Kentucky University secretly watched golfers play on a typical public course, they saw that half broke at least one rule—and that was just on the first hole![1] Although technically cheating, such minor violations are a frequent part of amateur play. Yet for those on the pro tour, not only will such behavior earn you penalties, it can get you disqualified. That's what makes Jane Blalock's story so fascinating, because it was so blatant. Not only did numerous people see her improperly mark her ball, the accusations became so widespread that the LPGA had to secretly start monitoring her play.

"She placed the heel of her hand on the marker and moved the ball by extending her finger toward the cup," claimed one official who saw her openly cheat during the Bluegrass Invitational in Louisville, Kentucky. "At no time did she deny the incident."

After accumulating significant proof that Blalock had been giving herself extra bonuses on the greens, and then hearing her admission, the LPGA suspended her for a year. Many peers argued that the suspension was too lenient, honesty being a cornerstone of the sport. But the LPGA thought the measure a reasonable punishment for a first offense and allowed her to eventually return. However, Blalock sued, arguing that the organization was violating antitrust laws. Cheating or not, the LPGA couldn't deny her the right to make a living.

Note that Blalock didn't immediately claim that she was innocent. Instead, her argument was that the LPGA had no right to keep her from playing without referring the violation to an outside agency. The court, which decided in Blalock's favor, awarded her the equivalent of her expected winnings during the suspension had she played, plus missed endorsement money and legal fees. And she didn't even have to swing a club.

I'm not recommending that you cheat, of course. And fortunately, most players don't have to worry about being hit by golf carts or being suspended from professional play. However, there is one matter that applies to everybody, because it can't be avoided. There isn't a player who hasn't lost a ball, or found somebody else's in the rough. Who owns all these lost balls? This question brings us to our final legal issue of this class—who wins the legendary case of *Finders v. Keepers*?

Recycled golf balls are a huge, multimillion-dollar industry because so many are lost each year. Most players don't care how many previous lives a ball has had, and some don't even bother walking in the tall grass if a drop looks reasonable. The legal position concerning these abandoned balls is murky, however. Who owns that Titleist you've just lost in the water hazard—you, the course, or whoever finds it?

Some people even make a living off digging through such hazards, though their legal ground isn't always clear. When Gary Thewlis and Philip Rzonca arrived in wet suits at the Branston Golf and Country Club just north of Birmingham, England, around midnight, they expected to find hundreds of abandoned balls. The club only dredged their water hazards twice a year, and surely plenty had accumulated. They hadn't expected, however, to be greeted by the police. The police claimed that the balls belonged to the course and that the trunk full of balls had to be returned.

When the case went to court, the defendants acknowledged that what they had been doing was cheeky. But they didn't think it illegal. The court agreed, saying that abandoned property belongs to whoever finds it, at least in Britain. In general, Yankee judges agree.

Still, this doesn't mean we're welcome to take any ball we find. Lost golf balls still reside on private property, and therefore there's still the issue of criminal trespass. That's what Daniel Curry and his three friends discovered when they snuck into the Aronimak Golf Club in suburban Philadelphia at three in the morning on April 18, 2012. After gathering hundreds (perhaps even thousands) of balls from the course's ponds, Curry and Co. were arrested, and police found even more golf balls stashed in their nearby van. The owner said club members were more than welcome to come look for their lost balls in the middle of the night, but Curry et al. were not welcome.

Curry and his friends were eventually charged, showing that taking used golf balls isn't a crime, but trespassing always is.

It's generally easy staying inside the law while on a golf course. It's not illegal to hit a house or playing partner with a ball, just as it's not necessarily illegal to speed in a cart, take the occasional mulligan, or pocket a lost ball. Yet, we must exercise good judgment. It's one thing to pull a Titleist from a water hazard, yet quite another to don scuba equipment and take several hundred. It's probably also not a good idea to swing when somebody is within your line of sight, either.

Those people behind you are probably making the same decisions as you, so think of them the next time you visit the course. Keep an eye over your shoulder too, and if you live on a course, you might want to consider installing some screens for those windows.

READING LIST

General

Lee, K. (2015). *Court Divisions Regarding Golf-related Injuries: A Quantitative Content Analysis and Binary Logistic Regression* (Doctoral dissertation).

Rule violating

[1]Erfemeyer, E. (1984). Rule-Violating Behavior on the Golf Course. *Perceptual and Motor Skills*, 59, 591–596.

Sample lawsuits

Joyce Amaral v. Peter Cuppels, case presented to the Appeals Court of Massachusetts, Bristol (2005).

Azad Anand v. Anoop Kapoor, case presented to the Supreme Court of the State of New York (2010).

Barbara J. Blalock v. Ladies Professional Golf Association; LPGA Tournament Players Cynthia Sullivan, Judy Rankin, Linda Craft, Penny Zavichas, and Sharon Miller LPGA Executive Director E.M. Ericson; and Tournament Director Gene McCauliff III, case presented to the Northern District Court of Georgia (1973).

Wilbur H. Coblentz v. Ronald N. Peters, case presented to the Eleventh Appellate District Court of Appeals in Trumbull Country, Ohio (2005).

Davis v. The Country Club Inc., case presented to the Court of Appeals of Tennessee, Eastern Section (1963).

Anthony Pecora et. al., v. Winged Foot Golf Club, Inc., case presented to the Supreme Court of the State of New York (2008).

Paul F. Sanchez v. Candia Woods Golf Links, case presented to the Supreme Court of New Hampshire (2010).

PGA Tour Inc. v. Casey Martin, case presented to the United States Supreme Court (2000).

Ryan v. Mill Country Club, Inc., case presented to the Appellate Court of Connecticut (1986).

Graduation

Well done, graduate of Golf University. Over these four semesters, you have explored the sport from perspectives few take. You've been the physicist and psychologist, environmental scientist and safety engineer. Hopefully, your game is stronger for it.

Graduation speeches typically share stories about school experiences, often with wise words from esteemed public figures. Sometimes the ceremony includes an honorary degree, for example, when St. Andrews University of Scotland recognized Charlie Sifford. He was granted an honorary doctorate of law in 2006 for being the first African American on the PGA Tour and for handling immense prejudice with dignity and grace. Routinely subjected to threats and abuse, Sifford still thrived, winning the National Negro Open six times. He also placed in the PGA Championship and won the Los Angeles Open. Changing opinions and social norms would take even more time, but we owe Sifford many thanks. If it hadn't been for Sifford's tenacity, players like Tiger Woods might not have been brave enough to try.

Identifying recipients for an honorary degree from Golf University isn't easy. Ben Hogan literally wrote the book on the modern swing. Old Tom Morris changed the way we look at course construction, and David Pelz tackled putting unlike any scientist before him. Yet, two names stand above all others because either could have been the university's founder.

One is credited with owning "The Perfect Swing," and he literally lived for golf. The sport wasn't just an obsession for this man, it was a science and a reason for living. The second wasn't just a player, but also a scholar of the game, rewriting gender roles and changing how we view athletic education. Those players were Murray "Moe" Norman and Patty Berg, respectively.

To say that Moe Norman loved golf is to say that the rest of us love breathing. In his life, he played 434 courses. One day, he hit over 2,200 balls, and over his lifetime he hit millions, though only once did one of those balls ever land out of bounds. And even then it only rolled out by a couple of feet, as he was quick to point out.

We know these things because Norman kept count. Though stories regarding Moe's background differ, we know that his unusual history began when at age five, he and a friend went sledding on an icy hill outside his home in Kitchner, Ontario. It was a gorgeous winter day in January, 1935, though everything changed when they crashed into a car driving by at the bottom of the hill. Both children were thrown clear of the sled, which was crushed by one of the tires. According to one version of the story, one of those rear tires also ran over Norman's head. In another, he was thrown free of the accident, but his face was badly bruised from being scraped by the vehicle's undercarriage.

Regardless of the accident itself, changes were soon to come. His parents were too poor to afford medical care, so we have no idea if the accident caused serious brain damage. All we know is that afterward, Norman developed some unusual habits.

Norman was already socially awkward before the accident, but afterward, that awkwardness entered full throttle. He started doing advanced math problems in his head and counting objects with frightening speed. Combined with an already healthy obsession for golf, he became a sports analysis machine, playing constantly and always finding ways to measure his progress. He avoided classes, skipped meals, and ignored chores, all so he could spend as much time on the course as possible. Golf became his school, and he studied it with a focus nobody has ever seen. Or ever will again.

This isn't to say players like Ben Hogan or Byron Nelson didn't take golf seriously. They also started playing at early ages and lived for the sport, but they didn't ignore everything else. Norman never married, didn't match his clothes, and seldom used a cart or caddy, preferring to carry his own bag. He lived at the edge of poverty by selling the prizes he won in tournaments, sometimes committing to the sale before the tournament began. At least five times, he intentionally finished second because that offered the prize his potential buyers wanted.

And he was good. One time, he played Sam Snead in an exhibition, and Snead laid up just before a stream 250 yards away. The hazard blocked the entire fairway, with only a narrow bridge allowing golfers to cross.

"You need to lay up, Moe," said Snead when Norman took out his driver. "You can't carry that creek."

Norman looked confused. "But I'm aiming for the bridge."

His straight shot was directly on target and easily rolled to the other side. Snead never offered advice again. Though Norman won more than 50 times on various tours, enough to earn him a place in the Canadian Sports Hall of Fame, those wins never translated to money or success in the United States. One reason was the crowds, which were too overwhelming for his sensitive nature. Another was the constant criticisms of his technique, his awkward and idiosyncratic swing often mocked despite its effectiveness. Physicists called it remarkably efficient, better even than the standard version, but that didn't matter—it was weird. He never aimed on target, always to the right, with a closed stance and a ball teed up so far ahead, he had to lunge forward just to make contact. Still, it worked, and he continued swinging well into his seventies.

Then there was putting, which he despised. He didn't even bother learning how until his playing days were largely over. Yet, when he did putt, he seldom missed.

Norman receives Golf University's honorary doctorate because he exemplifies the one characteristic that can't be taught—dedication. He approached golf like a science, and although he never excelled in school, he knew that school isn't about memorizing facts or abstract theories. It's about immersing yourself in a subject you love. For Moe Norman, golf was all the education he needed, and for that, he more than earned his PhD.

Our second honoree, Patty Berg, exemplifies another characteristic of true lovers of the sport—curiosity. Her most famous quote was "Always keep learning, it keeps you young," and she lived it better than any other. Not only did she win 57 professional championships, including 15 majors (still the record), in her career, she taught over 10,000 clinics during her lifetime. In an era when players were already dedicating themselves to either competition or instruction, Berg chose both, never abandoning her duty to grow the sport from the inside.

Berg was born in 1918, two years before women received the right to vote, but this never gave her the impression that she wasn't equal with her male peers. Before women routinely played competitive sports, she was a speed skater and quarterback of her neighborhood football team. She won her first amateur golf tournament at age sixteen, and when she turned professional, there were only a handful of matches on the women's "tour." Because she believed so strongly in golfing education, she taught a clinic at nearly every location she played, forming what became known as "Patty's Swing Parade." Knowing that frustration and lack of knowledge commonly held back new players, particularly women, she taught newcomers with patience and humor, showing that the sport is about more than just swinging a club. It involves self-confidence, love of the outdoors, and spending time with others. At the time, nobody thought of these things as the foundations of psychology, environmental awareness, or social science, but Berg surely deserved to be a professor of each. She ended up serving as the LPGA founding president and teacher of more new athletes than anybody at the time. Or ever since.

We can learn a lot from Norman and Berg, as well as greats like Hogan and Nelson, because they recognized that golf is more than just a game. It's a complex interaction of psychology and physics, business and law. We learn about these things through experience, not just our own, but also the experiences of those around us. That's what education is—the sharing of experiences. It's a means of communicating shared knowledge to others, and players like Berg and Norman have taught us a lot. They showed that practice is important, but it's only a start. We also need curiosity, dedication, and a desire to immerse ourselves in learning. Science and education are practical, nowhere more than with sport.

In these past four years, you have learned a lot, and although many of the findings came from universities, they were far from academic. They addressed the sport at its most fundamental level, not by giving advice, but by exploring what makes play so challenging. You've seen the sport as psychologists and sociologists see it, and also through the eyes of environmentalists and turf engineers. Thus, I bestow upon you a Bachelor of Science in golf, the most practical education a player can earn.

So go, esteemed graduates, and take what you have learned to the course. But more important, keep learning. Education isn't a one-time event. It's a process, one that applies to sport as well as life. Ignorance isn't bliss, it's giving up, and true golfers never put away their clubs when there's still a chance of halving the hole, or maybe even winning.

The day we stop learning is the day we stop breathing. Before that, there are a lot of great courses to play.

Acknowledgments

I'd like to dedicate this book to Dan Weems, my golf partner and father. Thanks for the many mornings spent on the front nine, sometimes on the fairways and sometimes not, but always with good humor. Thanks also to Mary Weems, the best caddy I've ever played with and also a remarkably patient mother. And Buddy, Johnny, Ola, and everybody else who has shared "Good shot!" on those scorching Mississippi days when we all knew it really wasn't.

Laura, thanks for teaching me the joys of sneaking onto closed golf courses to look for lost balls, a hobby that quickly developed into an obsession. Thanks also for teaching me that long walks are always time well spent, no matter what Mark Twain says, and that 25 years of marriage can go by pretty fast if spent with someone who inspires you.

Julie Ganz, thank you for your wise and professional guidance through the entire writing process. This isn't always the case, and I'm indebted to you for making the book the best it could be. Steve Schwartz, thank you for helping make *Golf University* happen, and for seeing the potential in what began only as an interesting idea. Thanks also to Bob Christina and Martin Toms for vetting the book, and for helping me avoid several possible embarrassments. Your feedback was immensely helpful. Also, much appreciation goes to David Gilden and Dan Mclaughlin, who were kind enough to speak with me about black holes, back injuries, and the joys of organic root beer.

To Cliff; you're the second person I see most mornings, always with a hearty "Have a great morning!" as we make our way to the greens. Thanks for reminding me that every day that starts outside, no matter what you're doing, is worth celebrating.